PSYCHEDELIC
MYSTERY
TRADITIONS

PSYCHEDELIC MYSTERY TRADITIONS

Spirit Plants,
Magical Practices,
and Ecstatic States

THOMAS HATSIS

Park Street Press
Rochester, Vermont

Park Street Press
One Park Street
Rochester, Vermont 05767
www.ParkStPress.com

Park Street Press is a division of Inner Traditions International

Library of Congress Cataloging-in-Publication Data

Names: Hatsis, Thomas, 1980- author.
Title: Psychedelic mystery traditions : spirit plants, magical practices, and
    ecstatic states / Thomas Hatsis.
Description: Rochester, Vermont : Park Street Press, 2018. | Includes
    bibliographical references and index.
Identifiers: LCCN 2018001374 (print) | LCCN 2018030786 (ebook) |
    ISBN 9781620558003 (pbk.) | ISBN 9781620558010 (ebook)
Subjects: LCSH: Hallucinogenic drugs and religious experience. | Magic. |
    Occultism—Religious aspects.
Classification: LCC BL65.D7 H38 2018 (print) | LCC BL65.D7 (ebook) |
    DDC 204/.2—dc23
LC record available at https://lccn.loc.gov/2018001374

Printed and bound in the United States by Versa Press, Inc.

10 9 8 7 6 5 4 3 2 1

Text design by Virginia Scott Bowman and layout by Priscilla Baker
This book was typeset in Garamond Premier Pro with Kommisar, Meridien, and
Avenir used as display typefaces

To send correspondence to the author of this book, mail a first-class letter to the
author c/o Inner Traditions • Bear & Company, One Park Street, Rochester, VT
05767, and we will forward the communication, or visit his website,
www.psychedelicwitch.com.

CONTENTS

Foreword by Stephen Gray   ix

Acknowledgments   xv

Onward   1

1   Generating Divinity   5

The Theogens

PART I

Psychedelic Mystery Traditions in Prehistory and Early History

2   The First Mystery   19

A Question of Shadows

3   Cosmic Graell   37

Mystery of the Sacred Feminine

4   Celebrations of the Living Fire   59

Psychedelics and the Sacred Marriage

5   Thessalian Roots   78

Psychedelic Magic in Ancient Greece and Rome

PART II

Psychedelic Mystery Traditions in Ancient Christianity

6   The Fire-Like Cup   109

*Psychedelics, Apocalyptic Mysticism, and the
Birth of Heaven*

7   Disciples of Their Own Minds   123

Gnosticism and Primitive Christian Psychedelia

8   Patrons of the Serpent   144

Psychedelics and the Holy Doctrine

PART III

Psychedelic Mystery Traditions in Renaissance Witchcraft and Magic

9   Wyld and Wyrd   174

Fairy Ointments and Goddesses Worship

10   One Constant Story   201

*Psychedelia in Medieval and Renaissance
Ceremonial Magic*

And Upward   **232**

The Psychedelic Renaissance

—◆•◆—

Notes   **237**

Bibliography   **252**

Index   **264**

FOREWORD

By Stephen Gray

What a long, strange trip it's been. Cave art of the proto-humans of pre-history; spirits and daemons of the ancients; legendary transformational ceremonies like the Eleusinian Mysteries (1600 BCE–392 CE); possibly our oldest existing trip reports from the oracles of Delphi; the potent "mixed wines" of ancient Greece; the "intoxicating grass" and the love potions of ancient Rome; the prominent role of mandrake in the experience of the proto-Christians; the psychedelic Eucharists of the gnostics in the early Christian era; the surprising acceptance of some "theogens" (even cannabis, hallelujah!) by orthodox church fathers of the time; the infused "mead of inspiration" that brought "ecstatic connection with each other and with the gods" during medieval Christmas festivities; the ecclesiastical demonization of medicine women in the late Middle Ages as satanic witches and the resultant suppression of the sacred feminine (from which we are still trying to recover); hashish-eating secret magical societies in nineteenth century England and France; and finally, "guarding the flame" in the early days of a new psychedelic renaissance "as though the future of the tribe hangs in the balance."

Let's skip any further preliminaries and get straight to the point. *Psychedelic Mystery Traditions* is a brilliant book that offers up a cornucopia of fascinating information and stunning insight. Its author, Tom Hatsis, is one of our most important and rigorous historical scholars in the field of psychedelics and their relatives. As just one telling piece of evidence I can offer to support this bold claim, I know that Tom taught himself Latin specifically so that he could investigate primary sources without having to rely on translations or interpretations filtered through the misunderstandings and biases of others. That is the kind of reliable veracity we can count on from him.

I used the word *important* to describe Tom in the above paragraph. But the most essential use of that word in this context is for the work itself. The subject of psychedelics, entheogens—or whichever one of Tom's inventive neologisms you fancy—is not an arcane study of interest primarily to academics and intellectually bent psychonauts (or psychenauts, as Tom prefers.) In fact, although the word *traditions* in the title clearly indicates a look backward, to my mind the greatest importance of *Psychedelic Mystery Traditions* is in honoring and building on that colorful history to look forward as we guard the ancient flame in the time of the psychedelic renaissance.

Tom Hatsis and other visionaries in this field have grasped a central fact of the human enterprise in the early decades of the twenty-first century. Humanity has for the most part been asleep at the wheel for too long now. There is a primordial, unconditioned reality underlying and encompassing life that almost all of us have been ignorant of. The great and universal "open secret" is that we are not born only to die and we are not separate—not separate from the living Earth, from each other, and from the eternal creative intelligence. Hints, clues, and reminders of the open secret are scattered liberally throughout the text, such as this brilliant quote from a Latin inscription. "I am ashes, ashes are earth, earth is the goddess, therefore I am not dead." Or this beautiful aphorism in Tom's words, "Surrender, child. *You're home.*"

Psychedelic Mystery Traditions confirms the suspicions of many of us who intuit that the life of the spirit, the soul, and the awakened heart has been in various places and times and could again be much richer (and wilder) than that which we see around us now. In realms spiritual and magical—or as mystics, shamans, and some young children might say, "in realms more real than this 'reality'"—there has been a lot more going on than is allowed to us in our received sanitized stories stripped bare of their original numinous power and possibility. And when you look deeply into what remains of the historical record, as Tom Hatsis has, you also see that *pharmaka* (Tom's more respectful term for "drugs") have played a far greater role in the spiritual life of humanity than we have been told.

There's a core metaphor for those of vision who see through the obscuring veils that hang heavy over a spiritually impoverished human landscape. The vision points its ecstatic finger toward the eternal truths and this largely untapped—and now more urgently needed than ever—spiritual potential of our species. The metaphor is this:

The "Temple" that was crushed and closed for
all this time is being reopened.

Don't be daunted by my description of Tom as a rigorous historian. This is a book for anyone interested in our incredibly rich history of plant-entangled religion and magic and, again, by implication, in where we're going and how we might open the gates of ecstasy and wisdom again. The writing is accessible, eloquent, at times poetic, and generously spiced with wit and humour. Take this gem for example. "Between the cracks and scraps of lonely ruins we find echoes of the ancient mysteries. Marble and iron, seemingly cold and lifeless, quietly exhale embedded wisdom passed down through time, even as their tears christen the memory of fallen empires."

While *Psychedelic Mystery Traditions* will appeal to and edify a wide range of readers, it's also aimed at researchers in related fields. The rigor that Tom brings to his investigations acts as a necessary corrective to the overzealous claims of less disciplined psychedelic social scientists who would like to see mind-manifesting plants around many a historical corner—Tom's irrefutable debunking of claims for a psychedelic Santa with his *Amanita muscaria* reds and whites and his symbolic shamanic-flight reindeer being just one of numerous examples.

So when I said earlier that we can count on Tom, I meant that unlike numerous other authors who have theorized about the long-dead past, he is cautious about conjecture, always making it clear that he's doing so ("We can only wonder . . ." or, "What we can do, however, is . . . observe the gems of possibility poking out from the subterranean bedrock . . ."), and only offering such speculative ruminations to inspire and intrigue in the larger context of verifiable evidence. You won't, for example, see Tom claiming that a visionary plant or fungus was the original inspiration for and central sacrament of any particular religion of antiquity without unimpeachable evidence to back him up. Put simply, you can trust what you read in this book.

We need to honor Tom Hatsis for the hard labor he has undertaken on behalf of the rest of us to uncover hidden treasures all but buried in the accumulated dust of many centuries and many historical revisions. The book is loaded to the rafters with wonderful stories unearthed from often obscure sources that only an obsessively committed investigator like Tom would trouble to look for. And there are surprises aplenty to be found in many of these stories. As just one of many examples, you may be surprised—as I was—to find out what was really going on with Jesus and the development of early Christianity. Again, minus the dubious speculation and hypothesizing.

Not only is *Psychedelic Mystery Traditions* generously sprinkled with great and instructive stories, the whole book is presented in story form as Tom brings us along with him from the mysterious symbolism of the cave art of ancient prehistory, to the beginnings of recorded history and the stories revealed in the archaeological and written record, through the millennia as he uncovers and shares with us secrets and treasures of the past, before finally leading us to the present day as we "stand tall against the winds of mystery."

This book reconnects us to the garden and embeds us in the ancient quest, as Alan Watts once playfully put it, "to eff the ineffable, and to unscrew the inscrutable." We humans of the twenty-first century of the Common Era are immersed in tumultuous times. The distinct possibility of either destruction or divinity is staring us squarely in the face. While no one knows how the great story of Earth and her inhabitants will play out in the decades and centuries to come, those of us who, like Tom Hatsis, have a deep abiding love for life and for this most beautiful sacred planet of the gods, are working diligently to nudge and nurture the reopening of the temple. In my respectful view, that is ultimately what this remarkable book is really about.

Note to readers: I highly recommend you make the effort to memorize Tom's short list of alternative names for psychedelics found in chapter 1 (pages 8–11). These are his own creations under the heading "theogens," and they appear frequently throughout the text.

ENJOY AND LEARN,
STEPHEN GRAY

STEPHEN GRAY is a teacher and writer on spiritual subjects and sacramental medicines. He has worked extensively with Tibetan Buddhism, the Native American Church, and with entheogenic medicines. The author of *Cannabis and Spirituality: An Explorer's Guide to an Ancient Plant Spirit Ally* and *Returning to Sacred World: A Spiritual Toolkit for the Emerging Reality,* he is also a conference and workshop organizer, leader, and speaker as well as a part-time photographer and music composer under the artist name Keary. He lives in Vancouver, British Columbia.

ACKNOWLEDGMENTS

I wish to recognize the following people and organizations for showing support for my research.

First to my parents, for giving me the gift of this gorgeously silly and absurd life. γιαγιά, you make my day every day. My immediate family for the support and encouragement you have shown as I make my way through the forest and into that soft, sunlit meadow.

My Rock; my Earth.

Magical people all over the world, especially my sisters and brothers of the Ordo Templi Orientis, for teaching me how to swim through shark-infested seas.

My Blood; my Water.

Psychenauts past and present as well as the organizers of numerous conferences dedicated to the psychedelic renaissance, notably Martin Ball of Exploring Psychedelics; Stephen Gray, Celina Archambault, and the Angels of Spirit Plant Medicine Conference; and the Breaking Convention team. Thank you for allowing this strange derbygypsy on your respective stages.

You are the wind gently pushing the fractal sails of the psychedelic renaissance.

My Ship; my Air.

Eden Woodruff, for stoking the inexpressible Fire far into the night.

ONWARD

It had been one of those perfect summer days in Southern California. The glories of wind, sun, and salty air moved through Los Angeles on a constant loop, kicked into the atmosphere by surfers drinking the elixir of life in Long Beach.

The San Diego Padres had taken the day off, or so Dock Ellis believed. Ensconced in the comforting serenity of his home, Ellis decided he needed to enhance his day—he desired *more*. Seizing the day and hoping to elevate it into the heavens, Ellis picked up a seemingly innocuous piece of paper, put it on his tongue, lay back, and closed his eyes.

An experimental new drug, LSD, had entered America with grand aplomb only thirty years earlier. In Switzerland, where Albert Hofmann first synthesized LSD in 1938, tests with that drug had indicated it had potential as a tool of psychiatry. Those scientists who first worked with LSD believed it a psychotomimetic, a mimicker of madness. The theory held that if psychologists and psychiatrists took LSD, it would better help them empathize (and perhaps even sympathize) with their more troubled patients. In fact, the original greeting that came with all orders of "Delysid" (LSD's first commercial name) sent out by its maker, Sandoz, stated specifically that the doctor should take the drug before giving it to anyone else! Throughout the 1950s and 1960s, tens of thousands of people would be introduced to LSD—not through shadowy street figures peddling a corrupt product but rather through the highest echelons of British and American academia.

By the late 1960s, however, street chemists across the globe were manufacturing LSD of varying purities, ushering in both the ecstasy and horror for which we remember that decade.

A rich and successful baseball player, Dock Ellis had access to the best of whatever he wanted, including good LSD. Desiring a dreamier day on June 12, 1970, he decided to take some acid. As the skies unfolded their mysteries to the talented pitcher, his assistant interrupted the streams of purple and orange to inform him that the Padres, indeed, had a game that day, and that Ellis, who played for the Pittsburgh Pirates, was their starting pitcher. Ellis hopped a plane to San Diego.

Ellis's teammates were immediately struck by his odd behavior as he stepped up to the pitcher's mound. Then Ellis did the unthinkable: he pitched an eight-walk, no-hitter victory while high on acid. He kept quiet about what had happened, eventually revealing his story to the public years later. Unable to quite remember the entirety of the game, Ellis did manage to squeeze out a few snippets from what he could recall from that magical, sunny late afternoon.

> The ball was small sometimes, the ball was large sometimes, sometimes I saw the catcher, sometimes I didn't. Sometimes I tried to stare the hitter down and throw while I was looking at him. I chewed my gum until it turned to powder. They say I had about three to four fielding chances. I remember diving out of the way of a ball I thought was a line drive. I jumped, but the ball wasn't hit hard and never reached me.[1]

Since then, however, the tale has fallen under scrutiny: many believe that Ellis made up the whole incident.

❦

The veracity of his claim, while an interesting academic exercise, is not the point of this brief introduction. I draw the reader to the story to illustrate a point that you will find throughout this book: namely, the role psychedelics have played in the spiritual, religious, and magical spheres since the days of the great ancient civilizations found in and around the Mediterranean.

Just like baseball, spirituality, religion, and magic have no absolute claim to the central use of psychedelics within their disciplines. All of these disciplines can be, have been, and will forever be practiced without the use of any psychedelic whatsoever. All of these systems (baseball, magic, etc.) exist perfectly unto themselves; take the psychedelic out of the equation, and the systems remain untouched.

And yet, that does not mean that spiritualists, theologians, magicians, and, yes, even baseball players did not include psychedelics in their performances every now and then. Although we do not see any psychedelic *built into* the dogma of many of the West's major religions, we do see accounts of individuals who subscribed to one belief or another and incorporated psychedelics into that discipline. This book aims to detail that history, specifically as it pertains to Western civilization. While an abundance of books dealing with the soma and *haoma* (intoxicating drinks used ritually) of Eastern traditions, and books about the peyote and mushrooms of Mesoamerican cultures grace bookstore shelves across America and Europe, very little has been written detailing the Western psychedelic tradition. Over the next few hundred pages, I would like to offer descriptions of the ways Western peoples have incorporated psychedelic plants in their lives before the psychedelic boom of the mid-twentieth century. From invoking spirits, to calling on fertility goddesses, to igniting the artistic imagination and finding wholeness with all creation, psychedelic florae have found a place in almost every Western spiritual or magical tradition since the beginning of the human story. The psychedelic state has been an anomaly, an inexpressible fire, the power of which no Western mind has yet to fully comprehend. Thus, we see not a single practice throughout Western history but a wide range of notions pertaining to the otherworldly state. There are, in fact, so many ways Western peoples have used psychedelics that I had to develop a series of neologisms in a perhaps fruitless attempt to transmit my interpretation of the annals of psychedelic history to you, the reader.

Let's take a look at these neologisms and then see how and why it is so difficult to fully uncover the psychedelic mysteries of history—the *inexpressible fire* that the Western mind has for centuries desperately sought to define.

1

GENERATING DIVINITY

The Theogens

If the word doesn't exist, invent it; but first be sure that it doesn't exist.
CHARLES BAUDELAIRE, *ARTIFICIAL PARADISE*

Certain terms will appear throughout this book that demand preliminary contextualization. Some, like psychedelic, are easily recognizable to most anyone; others, like entheogen, are recognizable to the initiated psychenaut.* Finally, some words are used that the initiated psychenaut hasn't heard yet—a family of terms I call the *theogens,* which are discussed below.

In March 1956, as various scholars wrestled over the nature of medicines like mescaline, mushrooms, and LSD, the new term *psychedelic* found its way to the pen tip of a most unexpected champion: Humphry Osmond. Conservative in dress, he looked nothing like the psychenaut who would one day change the discussion on this important topic. And yet, that's exactly who he was. Osmond had been working with

---

*To further distance these substances from the term *psychotomimetic* (discussed below), I prefer "psychenaut" to "psychonaut."

mescaline earlier in the decade and was the first to coin a term that, today, is considered taboo in psychedelic circles: *hallucinogen*. In those days, however, Osmond was trying to get away from *psychotomimetic,* the original term for these medicines, which means relating to or denot-ing drugs that are capable of producing an effect on the mind similar to a psychotic state.

For now, I'd like to focus on Osmond's foresight—what he did for later explorers of inner space. Namely, he allowed the conversation regarding these extraordinary substances to expand into new, more cre-ative, and advantageous directions. A word like *psychotomimetic* simply had a bad odor, as Osmond recognized. In the *Annals of the New York Academy of Sciences* (1957), Osmond laid out his case: "If mimicking mental illness were the main characteristic of these agents, 'psychotomi-metic' would indeed be a suitable and generic term," he wrote. "Why are we always preoccupied with the pathological, the negative? Is health only the lack of sickness?"[1] A fair question that may seem obvious to us today, but in the mid-twentieth century things were not so clear. The word *psychedelic,* on the other hand, meant nothing akin to causing lunacy in a person. Rather, it comes from two Greek words (*psyche* and *delein*) that together mean "mind-manifesting." Because of his efforts, negative words like *drug* and *psychotomimetic* went from the annals of spirit medicine to the dustbin of entheogenic history (so far as psychenauts concern them-selves). Perhaps I am biased, but I think Osmond was correct. People weren't experiencing insanity, as psychotomimetic implies; they were delving deep into the heart of their own mysterious consciousness, look-ing to gain insights that would lead to a better life. Osmond changed the trajectory of all future conversations about these sacred plants.

We owe him a debt of gratitude.

But the terminological journey that these medicines would travel didn't stop there. It would take another mind, equally brilliant, to coin another important word that would bring even a term as liberal as *psychedelic* into a whole new area of understanding. Carl A. P. Ruck, a classics professor at Boston University, did so when in 1979 he coined the word *entheogen. Entheogen* differed from *psychedelic* in that it specifically denoted the *spiritual* side of the psychedelic experience, meaning, as it does, to "generate divinity within." While *psychedelic* certainly serves a useful linguistic purpose, what were scholars to make of the revels of Dionysian ceremonies or the mysteries of the Rites of Eleusis, Ruck wondered. Clearly, some form of a psychoactive element was present at these and many other ancient pagan ceremonies (see chapter 3). To simply classify them as drugs or—perish the thought—psychotomimetics would only serve to perpetuate a historical folly. Even *psychedelic,* in all our modern understanding of the word,* would not suffice to couch these rituals in their proper historical context.

But *entheogen certainly* does.

Both these words (*psychedelic* and *entheogen*) are nouns and are used as such by the majority of psychenauts. However, as anyone familiar with my work already knows, I tend to complicate things. I have found that I more often use *entheogen* as an adjective. For me anyway, a psychedelic is the pharmakon† itself (i.e., mushrooms, cannabis, mandrake, etc.), but an entheogenic experience requires proper set and setting. A seeker might use a psychedelic entheogenically. *There is no entheogen without intention.*

At least, so goes my understanding.

---

*So this is weird. Technically, the classical Greek word *psuché* (from where we derive our modern word *psyche*) means "spirit." Now, *psuché* in ancient Greek also referred to what we today would call a person's psyche, her or his mental ability to navigate the world. Therefore, by an odd linguistic coincidence, *psychedelic* can also mean "spirit manifesting." So, while *entheogenic* only encapsulates a spiritual experience, *psychedelic* encapsulates both a spiritual experience and much more. However, to avoid dragging you into my linguistic lunacy, I will refer to both entheogens and psychedelics colloquially throughout this work.

†I use the word *pharmakon* (*pl.* pharmaka) in lieu of the more contentious word *drug.* Personally, I don't have a problem with the word *drug,* but I am aware that some readers do, and in deference to them, I use *pharmakon.*

And it is in this spirit that I gratefully and humbly present the following neologisms found throughout this book as my contribution to the psychedelic renaissance.

THE THEOGENS

I define the word *theogen* simply as "generating divinity" in one form or another. The prefix *en* in *entheogen* acknowledges such *divinity within the self*. And yet, what of generating divinity *outside the self*? Whether channeling, evoking, or calling out to spirits, tens of thousands of psychenauts the world over have used these sacred plants, at times, to generate divinity *outside* themselves. Is it still entheogenic at that point? I used to believe so. I no longer do. The following terms stem from that change in belief. The more psychedelics become integrated into modern society, the more conversations there will be in the future about them. And so while I offer nothing but praise to both Osmond and Ruck for changing the dynamics of the psychedelic conversation, I also believe that we need new terms to grow the dialogue. Indeed, the psychedelic renaissance can go only so far as the confines of the vocabulary that we set for it.

So let's expand that vocabulary!

The following words appear throughout this book. For ease I refer to them collectively as "the theogens." The suffix *gen*, as in to generate, will be found in all of them; *theo* ("divinity"), however, will not be. Briefly, my reason for this is that not all psychedelic experiences have a spiritual dimension to them. Material reductionists use psychedelics every bit as much as your weird, witchy, tree-hugging, Gaia-worshipping friend does. Thus, to couch *their* experience (the materialists' experience) in theological terms (as *theo* certainly does) strikes me as, in the very least, rude. Simply because I feel that the psychedelic experience has something to do with immaterial energies and intelligences waiting for us beyond the veil doesn't mean that a materialist shares such sentiments. However, most terms will include the *theo* aspect simply because the focus of this book is to highlight such spiritual and magical uses of psychedelics in history.

☙

Somnitheogen: As I will outline in the following chapter, I believe that the first theogen was *somnitheogenic* in nature. A somnitheogen is any psychedelic used to cast a person into a deep but lucid dream state so as to commune with otherworldly beings. The Victorian anthropologist Edward Tylor (1832–1917) first hypothesized that our sleeping progenitors met "ancestors" in their dreams. Working off his research, I posit that the first theogens would have most likely been soporific. Opium and those florae of the Solanaceae, or nightshade, family suit this purpose perfectly; the key to the doorway that first led proto-humans to other dimensions was found within the dreaming mind.

Poetigen: It is a near-universal truth that psychedelics unlock the creative spirit. To use psychedelics to fire the innovative imagination seems almost obligatory. And yet, what is the word for it? I offer up *poetigen* as a possibility. As you have no doubt noticed, *poetigen* lacks the *theo* syllable. Although I may find that art can express what can properly be called divinity, many fantastic psychenaut painters, writers, and musicians are materialists. To call their works divinely inspired does not pay respect to their creative process.

Entheogen: All right, you caught me. This isn't my term. However, since it is the foundational word from whence I have constructed all these others, I feel I should say something about what this word means to me in more detail than the brief description above. As mentioned, the term *entheogen* is a complicated one, as by my understanding it doesn't refer to any kind of pharmakon, per se, but rather to the use of a pharmakon in an experiential spiritual way. A person can use a pharmakon like cannabis as an entheogen (I certainly do!), but some troll sitting in his mom's basement smoking a bong while acting like an asshole on the internet isn't having an entheogenic experience by my logic. That aside, a person taking something stronger than cannabis, like mushrooms, shouldn't necessarily have the term *entheogenic* foisted on her or his experience either. What if this person is an atheist taking the mushrooms in a purely recreational way? While the term is useful, I don't consider a plant *entheogenic*; for me, a plant is *psychedelic*. Plants used to commune with (presumably) divine otherworldly entities for spiritual purposes are, for me, entheogenic. Additionally, I do not intend to use the term in the traditional Wassonian sense, meaning that I do not concede that the discovery of entheogens by proto-humans forged "the key . . . to religion."[2] We will probably never know what came first—religion or the entheogen. It really could go either way. While I do not deny that entheogens absolutely produced these kinds of heavenly appreciations in early humans, I think it is a mistake to attribute the genesis of religious experience to them. As stated above, I sit firmly in the Tylor school on this issue. Moreover, I use *entheogen* the way its coiner intended: the ingestion of a pharmakon that symbolizes a divinity (like those at the Rites of Dionysus), which causes the ingester to become enraptured by the god's powers.

Extheogen: The inverse of entheogen. *Extheogen* means "to generate divinity outside the self." With an entheogen, the participant knowingly ingests a pharmakon believing it to embody a deity. And yet, in later chapters, we will meet historical characters who were certainly using psychedelics (in the sense that these plants were "mind manifesting") to call on angels, demons, and even the dead. These psychenauts certainly were (and are) not generating these angels and demons inside themselves. This cannot properly be called entheogenic. It can certainly be called extheogenic—generating spiritual entities outside the self.

Mystheogen: As outlined above, sometimes a person would be welcomed into a mystery religion by ingesting the body of the god itself (like Dionysus). And yet, there are instances in ancient history whence a person would join a mystery religion by taking a psychedelic pharma-kon to induce a vision that was never considered the "body of a god." Since such an operation cannot properly be called entheogenic, I pro-pose mystheogenic: "generating visions in a holy setting." Although the spiritual experiences of mystheogens do overlap with those of entheo-gens, the relationship of the participants to the pharmaka differs.

Pythiagen: Pythiagen, like poetigen, also lacks the *theo* syllable—something about neologisms that begin with the letter *p,* I suppose. Pythiagens are psychedelics used for magical purposes. Now, a pythiagen *can* be used in an extheogenic or entheogenic setting, as we will see in a later chapter, but it also might not be. I know personally several deeply committed and practicing magicians who are materialists. For them, magic goes no further than psychology. And psychedelics certainly have a place in psychology. In my last book I spoke of *psyche-magic.* I would like to update that word with the new term *pythiagenic magic.*

OF MYSTERY AND MYTH

If you were to ask a friend or family member to define the word *mys-tery,* she or he would likely conjure mental images from a whodunit novel, replete with a gumshoe dressed in a plaid jacket and armed with a tobacco pipe and an oversized magnifying glass.* A mystery is some-thing to be solved.

We weirdo academics, as usual for the unusual, see things differently.

To the student of the ancient world, a mystery is a much bigger thing than a suspense thriller. A mystery is the recognition of seem-ingly irreconcilable opposites that plagued human existence. A mystery wasn't meant to be *solved;* it was meant to be *understood* and integrated into life. Mysteries give us insight into how early humans dealt with the sinister reality of having a bicameral mind all the while knowing

---

*Or, if you're me, Angela Lansbury as Jessica Fletcher in *Murder, She Wrote.*

nothing about bicameralism and mind.* Such proto-humans found themselves in quite a precarious situation. They could absorb the world around them, but they couldn't understand it. They could not yet reason, but still they sought reasons. They knew there was land; they could see it all around them. But how did it get here? What was it made of? Why do birds fly? Why do mosquitoes suck? Our ancestors could only wonder hopelessly about these irreconcilable questions. But they definitely understood antitheses: in and out, up and down, life and death, good and evil.

So they did their best.

☙

Which brings us to myth.

Ask a friend or family member to define *myth,* and chances are she or he will respond with words like *story* or *fabrication* or, on the more cynical side of the analog spectrum, *lie.* Examples might include Herakles, Santa Claus, and Jesus. In short, a myth to many modern people is nothing more than a made-up story.

But a myth to an ancient person was something radically different.

A myth explained mystery and reconciled opposites. It provided relief for ancient humans in a world that didn't make sense to them. Myth was not an escape from reality but a part of ultimate reality. Nearly every myth shares a common development: first the bicameral mind perceives some kind of problem, instigated by a rationalizing, fearful mind. Second, this problem is framed as a pair of opposites (up and down, inside and outside, light and dark); finally, the mind resolves the polarization in a way that assuages the fear.[3]

Myth is mental medicine.

---

*This human desire to make sense of the world has been called the "cognitive imperative." As proto-humans became more self-aware, their levels of anxiety about the world also skyrocketed. Andrew Newberg, M.D., sums: "[The cognitive imperative] . . . is the almost irresistible, biologically driven need to make sense of things through the cognitive analysis of reality." *Why God Won't Go Away*, 60.

To take a popular example: Eve and Adam in the Garden of Eden. The story of the Fall explained why humans (well, Hebraic humans anyway) could be both "made in the image of God" and still live lowly and not very splendiferous lives—certainly nothing like how a god probably lives. Even if the story of the Fall wasn't the *best* answer, it provided *an* answer, and any answer tends to satisfy human curiosity over no explanation. Especially intriguing would be a myth that so perfectly resolved the unyielding opposites that warred in the minds of these early Hebrews. The Eden myth—indeed, all myth—isn't the story of *how*, it's the elucidation of *why*. *Why* are humans supposed to revere a god that, by all Torah accounts, didn't seem to like them very much? The dualism for which the ancient Hebrews, Zoroastrians, and others were so famed first appeared in the proto-human struggle to come to terms with a world that both made sense *and didn't make any sense at all*.

Imagine that then, as today, there were proto-humans in a tribe who were naturally more curious than the rest. These people, these original shamans, somehow formed interesting and—most importantly—satisfactory answers to the questions assaulting the already beleaguered proto-human mind. This person might gather an audience over time—anyone who wanted to share in the alleviation of any burning question with a satisfying answer. This proto-human's myths and the people who listened to and accepted them could, perhaps, have formed a precursor to the later mystery religions. Tribal members would meet to eat and drink communally while watching (or participating) in a performance that acted out a story or myth, explaining an existential mystery. A mystery temple was the venue where the myth—the explanation—was acted out.

Mystery religions demonstrate an ancient awareness of intellectually intangible problems; myths provide the fulfillment. Everyone knew the mystery: anyone could question her- or himself about the fundamental frustration of irresoluble opposites. But only a few knew the *myth*; only a few knew *why*. Such knowledge was worth its weight in sacrificed livestock.

And ancient people paid plenty to have these answers revealed to them, to be allowed into the hallowed halls of those deepest answers lying somewhere between mystery and myth. This liminal space was filled with ritual. Ritual was the drama played out; the performance where mystery met myth. It should come as no surprise that the words *theology* and *theater* have similar word roots.[4]

RELIGION AND MAGIC

Now would be a good time for me to make things complex again. For just as I see differences in the varieties of psychedelic experiences, I also see differences in more common words like *religion* and *magic,* especially as they relate to the ancient world.

Our modern, popular notions of magic and religion tend to lump these two separate categories into one thing called spirituality. After all, it's all just mumbo jumbo anyway, right? And yet, this association is no truer today than it was in antiquity. Of course, it is easy to see similarities between them as both deal with *divine* realities. But that's like saying eating a cake and getting laid are the same thing because both deal with *ordinary* realities. And while the differences between magic and religion are few, they are crucial for understanding the ancient, though still-beating, heart of both disciplines.

It is impossible to determine which came first: magic or religion. Some scholars even think the two are inseparable. I disagree. I think we can see a very obvious difference between them. Religion—specifically pagan religion—involves giving the gods what they want (incense, sacrifices, adjurations, etc.) to win their favor. The gods, fully satisfied, would then bestow numerous numinous abundances, delivered from the Olympian realm to the mortal Earth. Even Hebraic religion was set up in such a way. The only thing Yahweh, the Jewish god, demanded was obedience to the Hebraic Law. Pagan religions were free from laws; Zeus didn't have a special list of commandments (ten or otherwise) that he ordered pagans to follow. Ethics and morals, which concerned your everyday pagan, were branches of philosophy, not religion. And religion can be further unpacked. As will be shown later, an entheogenic religious ceremony could have involved mass celebration (like the Rites of Eleusis) or a private ceremony (a lone worshiper and her goddess).

Magic is different; it circumvents the will of the gods and puts the will of the magician in the driver's seat. Think of it this way: while a priestess pours libations and calls on the goddesses to win their favor, a magician tries to manipulate those powers without such exchanges or requests. The magician does not submit herself to the gods' approval. Religion keeps divine power in the hands of the gods; magic puts divine power in the hands of the magician. And since this magician could be benevolent or nefarious, a skilled mystic or a base charlatan, Greek and Roman authorities did not tolerate magic any more than their later Christian rivals would.[5]

Magic can also be further broken down into two subcategories: daemonic and natural. A practitioner of natural magic uses spells, chants, and spirit plants to harness immaterial forces to serve herself or a client. Such natural magic included weather magic, love magic, mercenary magic, and many others. Daemonic magic involved calling on daemons (from whence we get *demons*) to perform a certain task. A daemon* in antiquity should not be viewed in our modern sense as an irredeemably evil entity. Instead, think of a daemon as a neutral spirit, neither good nor bad, but capable of either depending on the commands of the magician. A magician could call on a daemon to perform any task—from sinking a ship at sea to helping an elderly person carry groceries across the street safely. Of course, this depends on an individual's view of daemons. Even benevolent invocations, such as helping the elderly, could be viewed as evil simply because the act involves summoning a daemon.

---

*In recognition of the differences between our modern understandings of a "demon" and the daemonic entities of yore (*daemonia*), I retain the classical spelling throughout this book (unless otherwise addressed in a Christian context).

It should come as no surprise that an ancient people—the very kind of people who ascribed agency to thunderstorms and rainbows—would also ascribe agency to a powerful pharmakon. And such a natural force (especially one so readily felt), like all natural forces, would be revered as celestial or godly. Still, such obvious truisms continue to elude some wise owls perched in ivory towers. Only a few years ago historian David Hillman was forced to remove all references to the recreational use of pharmaka in ancient Greece and Rome from his doctorate dissertation. Despite the mountain of evidence Hillman provided for his claim, his dissertation advisers rather bluntly informed him that the ancient Romans "wouldn't do such a thing."[6]

Right.

Looking across the globe we see numerous examples of Mesoamerican, Siberian, Amazonian, and West African rites indicating that at some point in prehistory someone ingested a psychedelic pharmakon, interpreted the experience mystically, and built a religious system around it (or added the new revelations to a previously existing spiritual structure). Evidence also turns up in Eurasia, the Middle East, and Asia. There is scarcely a place on Earth untouched by these wondrous medicines.

On what grounds do conservative scholars explain how this *global* pattern skipped over Western civilization?

Magic?

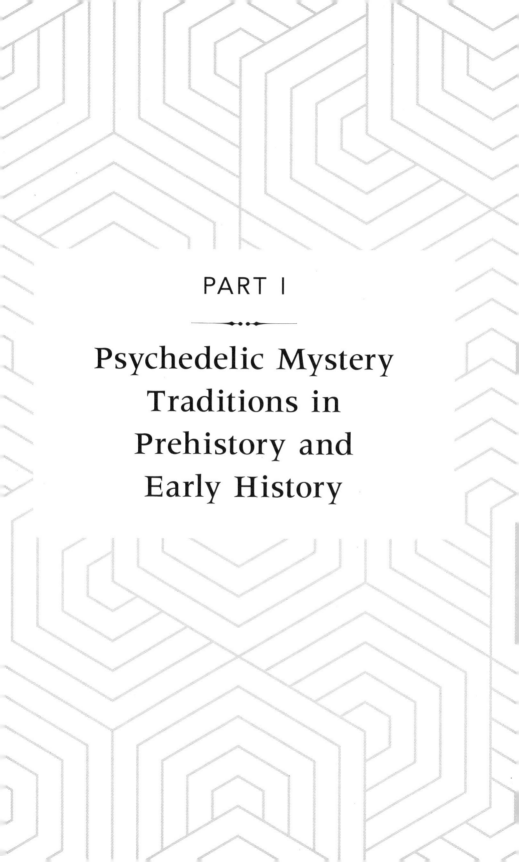

PART I

Psychedelic Mystery Traditions in Prehistory and Early History

B etween the cracks and scraps of lonely ruins, we find echoes of the ancient mysteries. Marble and iron, seemingly cold and lifeless, quietly exhale embedded wisdom passed down through time, even as their tears christen the memory of fallen empires. Blessings were the first gifts—dirty, elegant, bestial; apes pawing at the glory of the infinite.

And so they wondered if they could go deeper.

Our ancestors.

They wanted to go deeper . . .

No one remembered a time when we weren't human, but everyone knew we had once been beasts.

Our ancestors once walked as beasts.

Our ancestors.

Somehow, they started to go deeper . . .

2

THE FİRST MYSTERY

A Question of Shadows
c. 10,000–5000 BCE

*Those who in their lifetime have done nothing worthy of note,
everything which has pertained to them in life also perishes when
their bodies die, yet in the case of those who by their virtue have
achieved fame, their deeds are remembered for evermore.*
DIODORUS OF SICILY (C. 90–30 BCE), BOOK 1

ENERGIES

She ran—and that decision alone changed us forever.

If those in her clan made expressions, whether physical or verbal, that
she recognized as relating to her—*if she had a name*—we do not know.
Nor do we know other arbitrary details like her age, the color of her
skin or fur or eyes, and we can guess endlessly as to her height. We also
do not know more intriguing details like what she thought of the rising
sun; could she feel love?; how much of her was *human*? Most tragically,
we will never know her dreams, nor her waking thoughts of the world
around her, her emotional wounds, her cosmology—nothing.

All we know is that she ran.

And because she ran, we are here.

A startling rustle in the bushes could have meant anything. Usually it was that unknown, unseen *force** that moved the leaves, causing that brushing sound. Sometimes, however (the elders had taught), that stirring was not the wind but a predator. It was therefore best to assume that the crackles and crunches in the underbrush *always* indicate a predator. Should she or any of the females of the clan succumb to the realities of life on the food chain, procreation would come to a grinding halt; the clan would die. Any number of females could carry and nurse infants; however, they all only required *one* male. A single, reasonably healthy male could (without much encouragement) impregnate as many women as set before him. Thus, males were sent into the wilds to hunt (presumably joined by the infertile women of the clan), into environments where they were just as much prey as they were predators. As long as *one* male returned with a carcass dragging behind him, whether bestial or humanoid, the clan could persist and survive for the while.

And so she ran.

Better to assume the sound in the bushes implied a lurking predator instead of a stirring breeze. Better to assign *agency* to the world around than to suppose happenstance—causation *always* had a correlation. One mistake could be the difference between life and death. She put her hands over her bowed belly and ran. *Always assume agency.* If the rustling in the bushes were just the wind, running away in fear, while erroneous, only amounted to a harmless mistake. If, however, the rustling resulted from a large animal, and she erroneously assumed the sound was only the wind, her corpse would likely end up devoured by a den of hungry cubs.

---

*We have the luxury of recognizing this force as "wind."

And so our ancestors evolved "intuition" purely as a means to survive. But evolution, once it begins to unfold, rarely stays settled for long. Intuition evolved into intention, and intention evolved into magic. And magic opened our ancestors up to the occult forces of the natural world all around them. Such notions saw the birth of animism. Animism, the belief that all things (ambulatory, avian, and agricultural) harbor a spirit, probably developed shortly after proto-humans started to observe and calculate the natural wonders of Earth. These spirits acted in predictable ways sometimes—so much so that the careful observer could measure them. Such quasi-prehistoric calculations survive in relics left to us from the first *Homo erectus* astronomers clinging to life circa 350,000–250,000 BCE in the area we today call Germany. There, bones have been unearthed that show twenty-eight scores carved into the side. The cuts probably indicate the birth of astrology, those sky watchers having whittled the marks to measure the days between the moon's return to any fixed body of stars.[1] Several hundred thousand years later (c. 9000–8000 BCE), we see agriculture germinating.[2] We sought answers from the stars over one hundred thousand years before we planted the first gardens.

But how did the moon actually move—to say nothing of all those other tiny, twinkling objects in the sky? Why, some kind of invisible force must have been at work, of course! This force was not yet recognizable as god(s) to these proto-humans, nor did it exist in any kind of spirit realm yet. They were *energies*—part of the natural world, just as much as humans, animals, and florae. They existed in the wheat stalks and in the herd, in the rising sun and in the moon cycles. They were in the stars above, all billions of them, and in the blades of grass below, equally endless. Over the centuries, the individual animistic force of, say, a wheat stalk eventually grew into a collective spirit, a wheat field. The spirits that animated the individual bison ultimately developed into some kind of overall spirit of the herd, then into a spirit of the hunt.[3]

SPIRITS

What these spirits were like is anyone's guess. Through anthropological observation of contemporary, autochthonous societies, modern scholars have postulated at least five kinds of spiritual energies that may have been recognized in the remote past. We can imagine two of these spirits incarnating something like physical bodies: the first group comprises the ancestral spirits, those who had lived and died in the clan. They could communicate through dreams. The second group comprises the "puppeteers," those beings who oversaw the natural world (we would say, "the goddess of *this* river" or "the god of *that* mountain").

Another kind of spirit was more elemental—the innate power of regeneration itself to develop from seeds into small protuberances in the dirt, and then into long stalks, shoots, and trunks that brought forth food. Or even the power of a mammalian (or otherwise) baby to grow (hopefully) into an adult. We may call this the spirit of growth or development. This spirit exists within the stalk, within the human infant—no ancestral or puppeteer gods required.

The third type, known as organic spirits, are powers attributed to animate beings like animals. In modern terms, we would say that a black cat has the power to inflict bad luck on a person who dares to cross her path. A more humorous example can be seen on the show *It's Always Sunny in Philadelphia*. In one episode, the gang gets stranded in the woods. After one of the characters, Frank Reynolds, is led to believe that a rabbit he was hunting has stolen his soul, another character, Mac, vigorously declares, "Animals can see souls—that is a fact of nature!" Such is the power of the organic spirit.

Finally, there were the creator spirits (that I imagine need no further explanation). Each of these types of spirit, individually or in groups, could exist in one society and not another.[4]

None of these spirits were benevolent gods—or even creator Gods with a capital *G*, akin to the Abrahamic traditions. The spirits cared not about morality, sexual preferences, ethics, or political affiliations (the occasional, later war god notwithstanding). Even a creator spirit was not yet God. Humans did not yet know about gods.

Only spirits.

Only energies.

Such energies could be seen and felt, especially after ingesting a psychedelic pharmakon.

We do not know how, why, or when humans first discovered the awesome power of these plants, but at some undeterminable point, someone somewhere sought a remedy. A remedy for the ills of life, a remedy for loneliness, a remedy for pain or wakefulness, a remedy for sickness, a remedy for the constant anxieties manifested by the brutal realities of life on the food chain. Women and men alike searched for, dug up, and experimented with, presumably, most anything they found around them, learning through trial and error which plants healed, which plants killed, and which plants had rather extraordinary effects on the psyche.

Hypotheses regarding the accidental (as opposed to deliberate) discovery of pharmaka have likewise been advanced. Historian Chris Bennett theorizes that perhaps one eve, just as day sunk into twilight, a forager cut down some cannabis or opium stalks to throw onto a fire.[5] The buds (or pods) burned, a sweet aroma filled the air, and before they knew it, the clan was enjoying the physiological and psychological effects of either cannabis or opium.

There is nothing historically improbable about this.[6] Indeed, the ancient Assyrian word *qunubu,* from which we derive cannabis, comes from a verb meaning "to produce smoke."[7] Finally (but far from terminally), opium, cannabis, and ephedra remains turned up in a four-thousand-year-old Persian sanctuary where Vedic shamans prepared their entheogenic haoma.[8] Inarguably, evidence for the use of cannabis and opium can be found scattered across the ancient landscape.

❦

Likewise, Dan Attrell in his recent book *Shamanism and the Mysteries* (2017) asks us to consider that psychoactive mushrooms grow in and around caves, the first true telluric shelters of our ancestors.[9] Like Bennett's above hypothesis, there is nothing historically impossible about Attrell's idea. Indeed, who can't imagine a hunting party returning home empty-handed, with the consequence that hunters and tribal members desperately threw some mushrooms down their throats to avoid starvation?[10]

Those who survived the famine would have quite the tale to tell!

We do not have pipe residues or secret burial stashes to substantiate Attrell's theory, though. Unlike cannabis and opium, which Neolithic* peoples burned (leaving traces of their use caked in the bowls of smoking apparatuses), mushrooms (then as now) were eaten. But that is not to say that we have *zero* evidence for early psychedelic mushroom use. In fact, we just might have the best kind of evidence: cave art. In Algeria, in the eastern part of northern Africa, one will discover caverns that show some of the earliest expressions of human murals. These glorious renderings tell us the story of how Paleolithic human became Neolithic human, as archaeologists have determined at least five stages of cultural development embedded in the art.

The first naturalistic or Bubalus stage (c. 10,000–8000 BCE) deals mostly with engravings along the walls. These etchings depict only large animals like giraffes, lions, and giant buffalo (genus *Bubalus*). We can talk endlessly over a fine merlot about what the artists intended these animals to represent. In all likelihood, we are looking at the earliest religious expression known to us: sacred fertility. Perhaps a member of these early hunting parties, tired of coming home empty-handed, desperately ate one of the magic mushrooms that grew in and around the caves, which led her to a new idea: *magic used religiously*. Why not try to compel the natural spirits in the

---

*Thought to have "ended" roughly around 5000 BCE.

air to somehow increase the numbers of animals into larger herds? Spirits, after all, could be negotiated with; bargaining with animals is trickier.

We start to see evidence for mushroom use in the Tassili caves by the second period of artistic development, the Round Head Period (c. 8000–6000 BCE). One of the most famous carvings at Tassili dating to this stage shows what appears to be some kind of costumed (or supernatural) figure (figure 2.1), who clenches a bunch of mushrooms in both hands. Partnered with other paintings from this time that use beautiful expressions of color (figure 2.2), we might very well be looking at one of the earliest surviving appearances of poetigenism, and here we would even know the pharmakon used poetigenically: a magic mushroom. Perhaps these Neolithic psychenauts, after discovering the domestication of plants, also sought to domesticate animals. Perhaps their fertility magic carried over from animal hunting to animal husbandry.

The paintings from the Pastoral Period (c. 5000–2000) show us exactly this. Scores of cattle grace the jagged inner walls, indicating that the area once flourished with both livestock and shepherds. The

Fig. 2.1. Tassili cave shaman. One of our earliest surviving images of what appears to be a shaman associated with psychedelic mushrooms from the Round Head Period (c. 8000–6000 BCE) of cultural development in eastern Algeria.

Fig. 2.2. Tassili cave flourish. Embellished cave paintings from the Round Head Period of artistic development at Tassili.

fourth stage, (the Equidian or Horse Period), which saw invaders from the north conquering the lands and introducing the horse, lasted from about 1000 BCE to the Common Era. It eventually gave way to the fifth and final stage: the Cameline or Camel Period, when desert traders upgraded from horses to camels.

Let's return to the Round Head Period of Tassili cave art and the shamanic figure holding mushrooms. Here we see humanity's oldest religion, fertility ceremonies, preserved in stone for thousands of years. Clearly, by this time, humans understood full well the sacred nature of the female body. Ancient cities like Catal Huyuk along with the sixty Paleolithic cave dwellings that archaeologist André Leroi-Gourhan excavated have revealed a treasure of ancient figurines. The usually naked statuettes fit into two categories: pregnant goddess figures and models of women with animal features. Centuries later, a tapestry found in the grave of a Xiongnu woman of stature portrays soma as an incontrovertible mushroom.[11] When marked against the evidence of cannabis, opium, and ephedra scraped out of Vedic bowls, we are left with a single conclusion: the active psychedelic(s) in soma varied from place to place, depending on what was available.

In addition to the insightful theories of Bennett and Attrell regarding the origins of early humans' encounter with psychedelic pharmaka, there is yet another plausible, though totally meta, possibility.

THE FIRESIDE GODDESS

Like you and me, she dreamed.

Eons ago, when the ancestors still slept in the trees, dreaming, while possible, was often broken: rainstorms kept them skittish, arborous creatures like squirrels and birds defecated on them, insects stung and bit them, to say nothing of the general discomfort of using bark as a bed. Though safe from predators high up in the foliage, our ancestors likely had fitful sleep. Thousands of centuries ago, they climbed down from the trees and discovered that caves provided protection from predators comparable to trees, with a few advantages. Caves kept them safe from meteorological conditions, and significantly, there was less bird shit!

A large fire at the entrance of the cave, the first nightlight, would shine brightly throughout the night as long as enough wood had been gathered during the day. The fire would keep animals and insects away. She could rest comfortably with the others in the shelter, slumbering beside the awesome power of the harnessed sun, dreaming under the spell of smoldering cannabis flowers, left on the fire to burn throughout the night.

And so she dreamed with greater frequency. We can guess endlessly as to the content of her dreams, but it's safe to say topics were limited. We today dream under the impress of whole civilizations, histories, advanced cultural patterns, and infinitely more interpersonal relationships than early *Homo sapiens* could have ever imagined. All of this didn't exist for our hypothetical proto-human. Her dreams were much less complex and featured far fewer social relationships with those around her.

She didn't dream of gods yet.

The spirit world at this time did not yet contain four out of the five kinds of spirits outlined above. She didn't consider the mysteries of everlasting paradise any more than a mouse, secured in the beak of a hungry hawk, considers the principles of Taoism as it is chewed and swallowed. And yet, she *did* conceive of a spirit world. Unlike the spirit world of modern humans, hers was not populated by celestial entities harboring omnipotent powers. There were no angels. No demons or daemons. Rather, the spirit world housed only *one* kind of spirit mentioned above: the souls of the dead—the ancestral spirits.

It made total sense. She had been awake at times while others slept. They would lie motionless beside the glowing red embers, eyes tightly shut. Perhaps they didn't know what sleep was (do we?); however, they certainly recognized that there was a difference between a sleeping person and a roused one, and clearly the other world, the dream world, was *very* different from waking life. Likewise, the recently departed merely looked to be asleep. Such associations between sleep and death can be seen throughout the ancient world, turning up in both texts and inscriptions.* Presumably, the dead had gone to sleep forever, reachable only in the otherworld through the power of dreams. This spirit world began not *out there* in the heavens but rather deep within the darkest reaches of the human mind—the human *dreaming* mind, the original passage to the realm of the dead.

And so she dreamed of the ancestors. The ancestors were not yet those who lived centuries before her. They were the members of her clan—her mother or father, grandparent, sibling, or other close relative—people she knew who had gone to sleep but never woke up again. Or perhaps she never even saw the corpse. Sometimes a clan member would be eaten while on the hunt or injured in a way that resulted in sudden death far from home. In any event, these people never came back, though sometimes they would show up in dreams. We can only wonder how she interpreted such dreams. Maybe as help reaching out from the otherworld? Perhaps there, beyond the veil of waking consciousness, an ancestor appeared to her one night. Her heart filled with joy! For no one had known where the ancestor had gone, why she never woke up. In her ancestor's hand, a simple wheat stalk. Our slumbering progenitor had

---

*Such an association remains in evidence as late as the dawn of Christianity, an Egyptian inscription dating to the second or third century CE; see Torjesen, *When Women Were Priests,* 20. There is likewise the gnostic Gospel of Peter, line 10, which makes this analogy.

crossed wheat fields many times; wheat grew wild all over the known world. She usually ignored such flora in search of food. Indeed, wheat and vegetation existed to nourish fires, not humans. She looked on as her ancestor ground the grain in her hands and placed it in her mouth.

She couldn't believe the revelation!

The foliage all around need not be avoided. With her epiphany still flowing from the dream world to her conscious mind, she woke up excitedly and set about testing other shrubbery, discovering date palms, grapes, and apples. She had, in effect, transcended time and space, learning the secrets of the plants all around her. She set about teaching this revelation to all who would listen.

Her discovery would echo through time. Posterity remembered her as the discoverer of the medical—and through that, psychological—potential of those plants around her.[12] After she died, stories of her epiphany passed through the ages. Her medicines offered a spark of hope to those who lived a life nasty, brutish, and short. The adjurations she recited over the plants to redouble their efficacy proved so advantageous that her descendants remembered them and passed them down to their children. Generations later, tales of her revelation could be heard around small fires burning faithfully throughout the night. She would be the one called on in dreams, obtaining a stature high above all the other ancestors.

She became the first immortal.[13] She, the Fireside Goddess.

Her initial actions inspired many down through the ages to pluck, experiment with, and use (if beneficial in some way) any and all plants. Criminals and captives would also be used as guinea pigs. Many would die. But in this slow, generational process, proto-humans recognized that, nourishment aside, some of these plants had the power to relieve throbbing, illness, and even diseases caused by germs unknown to the healers. They began transporting these edible and medicinal plants and roots from the wilds into their settlements. A few of these plants held another remarkable property: they were soporific. They could cast someone deep into the dream state, to the realm of the ancestors, to the gods, where the seeker could query those divine beings over matters pertaining to the material world. These were the somnitheogens.

We start to see evidence of early cannabis and opium's somnitheogenic associations in the Neolithic Age. So-called pipe cups have been found scattered across Anatolia, Eurasia, and Asia. Resin scrapped off the sides of these pipe cups has tested positive for cannabis and opium. We, of course, do not know the cultural context for which these ancient peoples inhaled the fumes of burning cannabis and opium. We can say, however, that excavators unearthed these Neolithic bongs in graves and tombs, linking sleep with death and the somnitheogens that bridge the two worlds.[14] Such associations are seen elsewhere. Thousands of miles west, in a cave near the coast of Grenada, Spain, excavators unearthed tombs dated to circa 4200 BCE. Among other things, many bags of opium poppies were found with some of the corpses. Further evidence of a link with somnitheogens, sleep, and death can also be found just southeast of Spain, in Egypt. Juglets and other drinking and storage vessels dating to circa 1550–1300 BCE have been unearthed that still have opium residue crusted inside. Some of these containers even appear in the shape of an opium poppy, a trend we also see in the amphoras of ancient Greece.[15]

It is at this point in our story that two new characters appear in the historical embryo. First, spurred by the initial immortality of the Fireside Goddess, later peoples who lived exceptional lives could themselves become immortal one day. From there, it was one short step to becoming gods. These gods were not yet any kind of supreme creator; neither were they all good nor all bad. They were rather fallible and weak bunglers who could be seduced with gifts in order to ease the agonies of frail mortality; sacrificed humans and other animals would do nicely. These gods needed skilled practitioners with whom to communicate their advice, desires, and proper ritual techniques.

This brings us to the second emergent character of prehistory: that curious expert of the immaterial world, the shaman. Shamanism is a difficult term to nail down, coated in a variety of ideas on which scholars, in their infinite wisdom, cannot agree.[16] One renowned anthropologist referred to shamans as "specialists in ecstasy."[17] A shaman is someone with expertise in lucid dreaming; a person, woman or man, who has knowledge of the immortal realm. She or he brings messages from that world to ours for the benefit of the community, a bridge between regular reality and those lands found beyond the veil. Such a person used a variety of methods to enter these trance states: drums, chants, fasting, isolation, and, in some cases, somnitheogens. Using some or all of these tools, the shaman works herself into frenzy and then falls into a deep sleep, where her soul carries her across the vivid dreamscape. Eventually, this kind of person would be given authority over public rituals. These were the first priestesses and priests. They could commune with the ancestors through pharmaka and other techniques like drumming and dancing, all the while monitoring themselves. Most extraordinarily, they could guide others through the sacred byways of the otherworld.

One of these ancient spirit plants was undoubtedly opium. Opium had an ancient and widespread use in both magic and religion. But it had several dimensions. One person went mad; another person went numb. This dude took a little and fell asleep; that guy took too much and died. The spirits that possessed these particular plants were rather volatile. Adjurations might appease them; rituals could trigger them one way or the other. Most importantly, the pharmaka served as a way for shamans to enter the dream state to reach her, the Fireside Goddess, the first ancestor to attain immortality.[18]

And when they worked, they worked like magic.

She was given many names, sung in many songs, recited in many poems when remembered around firesides. Two of the most enduring designations for her survive to this day: the Egyptian Isis and the Mycenaean Gâ Mater (Earth Mother) later honored as Gaia by the Greeks. Isis appears under the moniker "the great sorceress" in the oldest medical manuscript extant, the Ebers Papyrus (1500 BCE).[19] The author of the text claimed to have been inspired by the gods themselves—whether in dreams or otherwise, the writer does not say. Isis apparently suggested to the author a "confection" of coriander and opium.[20] Patients would drink the potion, fall into a deep sleep, and dream of Isis, who "[stood] above the sick . . . giv[ing] them aid for their diseases and work[ing] remarkable cures upon such as submit themselves to her."[21] It appears that opium, in this case, wasn't strictly speaking a painkilling drug in the way we consider it today. Ancient patients didn't drink the elixir for its prized euphoric effects (although, those were certainly recognized as relieving) but rather to allow them to enter a somnitheogenic state where the infirm would meet Isis. Other medical gods, like Asclepius, following the womens' lead, also employed such methods; he treated his patients with "soothing potions."[22]

These are truly ancient traditions; evidence can be found tying this goddess with opium in Italy. Notably in a small Neolithic city (dating to c. 6000 BCE) called La Marmotta, twenty miles north of Rome. The city currently rests at the bottom of Lake Bracciano, though diver-excavators found preserved opium seeds in one particular structure. The room where these seeds were found appeared to be a religious room dedicated to a great mother. We cannot be sure, but perhaps healers used this chamber as a space to hold psyche-medical ceremonies. Such associations would suggest that the opium might have been used as a medicinal-somnitheogen—a way to meet that ancient ancestor in hopes of returning with a remedy.

Other residues of this ancestral woman can be seen in the remains of a small poppy goddess statuette found in Crete (c. 1500–1000 BCE). Six hundred miles away, over in Pompeii, an opium seed cake was also unearthed. Some scholars believe that the cake was used in votive offerings to Isis.[23] Perhaps the Pompeii cake served as a way to fall into the dream state, not to meet the ancestors but to meet the gods to receive healing in a ruthless world. Acknowledgment of opium's occult properties allowed these early Egyptians to induce sleep spontaneously to reach out to other worlds waiting in the dream state.

We even know of a particular myth about the Egyptian sun god Ra, which may well represent the earliest textual evidence (and accompanying festival) that recognized and celebrated the somnitheogenic state. It all started innocently enough: humankind had begun to ridicule the age of Ra, saying "Behold, the king has become old!" Ra's fiery skin was apparently fairly thin, so he assembled a council of other gods and complained to them. The council saw no other option than immediate liquidation of the human race. The eye of Ra descended to Earth in the form of Hathor, goddess of love, death, and motherhood (and, it would seem, humanicide should the opportunity arise). Hathor began her slaughter, later commenting that the human raze was "well pleasing to my heart" after walking among the fallen.[24] Spent from her busy schedule, she retired for the evening. The rest of us would have to wait until the following day to receive due penalty.

Thankfully, during Hathor's slumber, the sun god, *ahem,* saw the light. Acting quickly, Ra ordered "swift messengers who can outstrip the wind" to Elephantine, one of the many islands scattered throughout the currents of the Nile River. This particular island had achieved fame as a brewer of somnia-psychedelic mandrake beer. The beer was used in both medicine and magic and "figured prominently in Egyptian religion."[25] The messengers returned to Ra with the somnitheogenic beer; Ra collected the blood of our fallen comrades and mixed it into the brew. He then told the messengers to bring the potion vessels to the lands where the rest of humanity still lived and spill the contents onto the ground.

Hathor awoke, still thirsty for human blood. Becoming enamored with her reflection in the magic plasma potion flooding the streets, she began to drink. The mandrake, doing what mandrake does best, mellowed out Hathor to the point that she could no longer continue the massacre. An entire festival grew out of recognition of the somnitheogenic state. Egyptians saw the myth of Hathor as an explanation for the pestilences that tended to follow dry spells.[26] During the Feast of Hathor in the Egyptian month of Thoth,* congregations throughout Egypt drank the mandrake beer specifically to enter the somnitheogenic state.[27]

But then, such psyche-magical elixirs flowed throughout the land of the pharaohs. Aside from the somnitheogenic festival to Hathor, Egyptians found other spiritual uses for the wild plants all around them. As we saw, substances like opium could be found in Isis temples to help facilitate a patient's segue into the otherworld. But what of the priestesses and priests who worked daily in the temples? Indeed, that holy class was well known in the ancient world for having the ability to sit in their temples, silently, in "contemplation and adoration of the deity"—sometimes for days on end.[28] One way those in holy orders achieved such inner reflection came through ingesting spirit plants. St. Jerome remarked on the Egyptian priests' use of hemlock and water lily to achieve higher mental states.[29] St. Basil noted that, like the Egyptian priests, Grecian holy men of Athens also used hemlock.[30] Other times the preferred psychedelic cocktail consisted of opium and magic mushrooms.†

Such ideas quickly made their way to Greece. By the time Plato composed his *Symposium* (c. 375 BCE), somnitheogenically induced states were well understood. *Symposium* features the character Plenty drinking "nectar," which causes him to fall into a deep sleep. It is clear that this is some kind of pharmakon as, Plato assures us, wine hadn't been invented yet. Whatever this substance was (I would hypothesize an opiate or a plant from the Solanaceae family), Plenty ingested it in "the garden of Zeus," falling into a "heavy sleep."[31]

From Greece, the somnitheogenic use of psychedelics would make its way into Rome. Some Romans studied both rhetoric and magic—and became rather skilled in both disciplines. Lucian Apuleius (c. 130–170 CE), who once had to defend himself in court against charges of magic, gives us solid evidence that the somnitheogenic experience made it deeper into the heart of Western civilization. He writes:

---

*Roughly our autumn months. Hathor's Feast Day would fall on our September 17.
†Called "machomore," a wild mushroom that grew in Asai and northern Egypt. See Remondino in Wooster, *Pacific Medical Journal,* 527.

[I]t is my own personal opinion that the human soul, especially when it is young and unsophisticated, may by the allurement of music or the soothing influence of sweet smells be lulled into slumber and banished into oblivion of its surroundings so that, as all consciousness of the body fades from the memory, it returns and is reduced to its primal nature, which is in truth immortal and divine.[32]

Those "sweet smells" could have found their way into the human nose in either of two ways. First, burning incense made from cannabis, opium, or frankincense,* or a Solanaceae plant like mandrake or henbane, would surely do the trick. Indeed, so-called suffumigations† have been used for centuries for a variety of magical, medical, or other procedures.

Although it is also possible that Lucian refers here to the enchanting scents of the soporific sponge. Soporific sponges began in the medical realm; they were our earliest forms of anesthesia, used to induce a deep sleep (*soporatum*) in a patient before operating. This state was often accompanied with strange and lucid dreams due to the potency of the pharmaka added to the sponges: they were first dipped in the juices of opium, henbane, and mandrake. Then physicians either placed the sponge in the nostrils of a patient or draped a cloth, saturated in the pharmaka, over the nose. Apuleius's testimony makes clear that some people still knew an occult virtue of these pharmaka—to ease you comfortably into the otherworld.

Into the realm of the immortals.

Just as the ancestors had done.

To return to our progenitors clinging to life on the morning of history. The barren women and men sent out to hunt may or may not come

---

*The frankincense of the ancient and even early modern world was not the kind we are familiar with today. This frankincense seems to have had at least mild psychedelic properties. I will explore this further in a later chapter.

†From *sub fumo* to "fumigate from below."

back. But the fertile women faced equally tragic perils, for they, too, could find themselves on the business end of a hungry cat's dentures. And they certainly weren't safe from sharp projectiles lunged into their flesh by warriors from a competing clan.

But women also faced different hazards, the likes of which men would never have to experience—namely, childbirth. And how peculiar it was! Through some disastrous miracle, small, fragile people came out of robust, healthy people (pregnancy complications notwithstanding). Robust, healthy *female* people.

But *why?*, they must have wondered.

Consider for a moment the possibility that understanding female-male procreation is something we today take for granted. Though it may be difficult for us to imagine, there may have been a time in our progenitors' history when they did not know where newborns came from. Well, they *knew* where they came from—a woman's body, of course. But how did they get in there in the first place? The first signs of pregnancy, to say nothing of the nine months that ensued, are not immediately apparent after coitus. How and when humans properly linked the sexual act with procreation, we will likely never know; meanwhile, childbirth was considered a form of magic that only women possessed. Somehow the women grew other people in their bellies.

Fertile women, therefore, could not possibly be sent out to hunt; depletion of them spelled doom for the clan. Their magic was needed.

But it was a disordered magic. The very act of childbirth put both mother and baby at risk. Either of them might contract a host of diseases during the process, should one or both survive the process at all. Indeed, just like the men, a depletion of women would surely signal the end of the clan.

But perhaps the cruelest reality for these early people was that women died regularly while giving birth.

Death? While giving—*birth?*

Death? While bringing forth—*life?*

How very mysterious . . .

3

C⊙SMİC GRAELL

—◆·•◆·—

Mystery of the Sacred Feminine
c. 5000–500 BCE

I am ashes, ashes are earth, earth is the goddess, therefore I am not dead.

LATIN INSCRIPTION

Happy is one who has seen it!

HOMERIC HYMN TO DEMETER

OF GRAIN AND FLESH

Her lashes slowly released; every memory of the Grain Mother—stories heard in childhood, prayers she now recited over her own crops in adulthood—emanated from her mind into the sanctuary's air, smelting with the other parishioners' visionary reverberations into a collective, luminescent vision of the Goddess.

Blossoming beyond bicameral boundaries, every blink sent cool waves of inspiration through the souls of those gathered, the kind of cosmic honey we savor each time mystery gives way to epiphany; only then can we understand why the hierophants* sounded the gong; only then can we raise our glasses in honor of the dead.

---

*A priest of mystery religions.

Only then does the Cosmic Graell pour forth its mystery.

The divine howl of the ancestors echoed in the bones of the Eleusinian *mystai*.* They had drunk the *kykeon* potion, a mixture of barley, water, and mint. They had removed the sacred objects from a sacred chest called a *kistai,* placed them in a basket, and then put them back into the original chest.

Birth, life, death. It all made sense now. Gaia's harvest of wheat and flesh, an organic reaping of leaves and seeds, bones and breath. Likewise, cosmic sickles scything the heavens of stars and galaxy clusters. Now you are alive, now you are dead; now this universe is here, now it is gone. She recognized her part in this dance, this endless pouring forth of the Cosmic Graell into the vast seas of infinity. She was no mere spectator; she was the chalice itself, keeper of all the mysteries and miracles of conception. She was the contents as well, the waterfall of creative majesty. And in a moment her old life, which promised only fear of the ego's termination at death, dissipated in the radiance of this ecstatic baptism.

And so she danced with the other mystai.

Danced throughout the night.

Danced joyously in a waking dream . . .

THE LORD WHO RECEIVES MANY GUESTS

After plucking those brilliant roses, violets, and other pleasing florae of the plain of Nysa, Kore, daughter of Demeter, the Grain Mother, continued her stroll through the meadow with the daughters of Ocean, smiling back at the sunbursts that gently cooked the freckles on her nose. She came across the plant narcissus, an "object of awe for all to see." However, when Kore reached for the narcissus, she died rather painfully, screaming a "shrill cry," as Hades, lord of the underworld, received his next guest.[1] We do not know the species of the genus *Narcissus,* though some have advanced the daffodil, a member of the genus, as the

---

Mystai is the name for initiates in a mystery, as in Eleusinian Mysteries (singular *mystes*).

proper identity of the flora.[2] This presents a few problems, though, not least of which is that the word *narcissus* derives from the Greek word *narke*, meaning "numbness," an effect not caused by interacting with a daffodil. We will return to the identification of the narcissus later.

Hearing the cries of her daughter, Demeter searched the land trying to find Kore, only to discover that (with Zeus's consent*) she had been raped by Hades, and taken into his domain. Grief stricken, Demeter donned the disguise of an elderly woman, the symbol of a barren female, and wandered the countryside, mourning the loss of Kore. Her travels took her to the ancient city of Eleusis, where she sat beside a water well[†] and grieved; there, the daughters of the queen and king of Eleusis discovered Demeter and invited her back to the palace for consoling. Demeter agreed and followed them home. Once introduced to the royal family, Queen Metaneira and King Celeus, the party sat down for a meal. Metaneira poured a glass of wine for Demeter, but Demeter, still mourning Kore, could not accept the drink. Instead, she quenched her thirst with the kykeon potion. Although she was still upset, a house servant named Iambe relayed obscene jokes to the goddess, who eventually cracked a smirk. Metaneira also invited Demeter to stay on as nanny to her princely (and partially immortal) son Demophoön.[‡] Recognizing the semidivinity in Demophoön, Demeter agreed; she planned to secretly transform the young prince into a full immortal to make up for the loss of Kore. She fed Demophoön on ambrosia and nectar, the foods of the Olympians. She also secretly refortified his skin in fire every night after his parents had retired for the evening. Soon after, her plan was uncovered by Metaneira, who believed Demeter to be harming her son.

Now enraged and unable to keep up appearances, Demeter revealed her godliness to the royal household, ordering a temple built in her

---

*Mind you, not with Kore's consent.

†Later known as the Maiden's Well.

‡Metaneira appears unaware of Demophoön's divinity in the story. With regard to the larger myth, he likely represents all of humanity. Demeter tried to make us immortal but fell short.

honor. She withdrew into her temple to inhale incense, angry at the gods for allowing her misfortune. Her wrath stopped seeds from coming forth from the soil, as the anonymous author of the Homeric Hymn to Demeter wrote:

> *In vain the oxen pulled the curved ploughshare through the*
> *   fields.*
> *Many a white barley fell to the earth, where it was wasted.*[3]

Before passing any judgment on Demeter for ceasing the crops, let's take a moment to appraise the slights she endured: her pain over both her losses, first Kore and now Demophoön; Metaneira's knock to her godly pride, condescension, by a mortal, no less; the sense of betrayal perpetuated on her by the very forces she was supposed to control; and that Zeus's consent meant more than her daughter's consent.

No wonder she reacted with the piercing frost of a bitter winter!

No wonder her eyes saw only death for vulnerable mortals!

The Olympians tried to persuade Demeter to allow the fruits of Earth to grow again, but to no avail. Without human offerings of sacrifices, incense, and libations, the gods, too, would eventually wither and die. Fearing the end of Olympus, Zeus admonished Hades to release Kore to her yearning mother. Before leaving, Hades dubbed her Queen of the Underworld, granting her immortality and province over all plants and living creatures and assuring her that sacrifices and rituals in her honor would be "greatest . . . among all immortals."[4] The fields once again began to bring forth their nourishment. Humans would not revert to cannibalism, and civilization itself would be rescued.

Tragically, on her way back to Earth, Kore ate the fruit of a pomegranate. According to underworld protocol, any consumption of underworld food ties a person to that realm forever. Though Kore (now Persephone*)

---

*In the myth, Kore is the name of freshly planted grain; Persephone is the name she is given when she rises from the dead.

was released back to the loving arms of Demeter, she must return to the underworld for part of every year.

The myth of Demeter and Kore has long been seen by scholars as merely a mythological explanation for why the crops grow in the spring and die in the winter. It is a myth of seasonal change, nothing more. I agree with those like Walter Otto who think that deeper mysteries are lurking about and that the explanation of the harvest, while certainly a part of the myth, isn't the nucleus of it. Consider the following: The crops didn't immediately cease after Kore's descent. Demeter's agricultural wrath didn't begin until well later—after she lost Demophoön, representative of humanity. Thus, there are good reasons to believe that the myth has more to do with connecting human destiny with the cycles of nature, as opposed to seasonal change being the *only* explanation. And here, there is much to discover. Otto, limited by his time and place, missed certain clues about the Eleusinian mysteries: "What could it have been, the mere display of which . . . had the power to create so deep an impression?"[5] he asked.

And that answer can be found, perhaps, in the kykeon.

The kykeon was the potion drunk not only by Demeter in the palace at Eleusis but was also imbibed by those mystai joining the mystery on that cool autumn night. The kykeon brought them into relation with Demeter, and Demeter acted as a bridge to Kore, giving mortals access to the underworld. There is good reason for believing that the kykeon contained a psychedelic pharmakon, and it was this potion that aided the mystai into their first lucid contact with death.

It has been noted that the imbibing of this drink preceded the revelers' visionary trances during the Rites of Eleusis. Therefore, various academics have posited that the beverage contained some kind of psychedelic pharmakon. Indeed, the rites lasted for more than two thousand years uninterrupted and bestowed more or less the same experience on everyone. However, breaking with those contemporary scholars who see the ingredients in the kykeon remaining the same throughout the ages,[6]

I side with Amanda Noconi—that the potion contained a psychedelic, the identity of which probably changed over time, depending on what pharmakon was available.[7] We, today, care about the proper floral or fungal identification of the kykeon because we are psychenauts living at a time when concepts like botanical classification are encountered as early as primary school. So we just think in that way. The ancient Greeks, to say nothing of the Mycenaean culture that predated theirs, held no such models. At best, they classified medicinal and psychedelic florae in magical, not botanical, terms. As I hope to demonstrate in this chapter, while the psychedelic in the kykeon most likely changed over the eras, there exists enough evidence to take a snapshot of a time when a particular pharmakon remains frozen in Eleusinian history.

Now, it is totally possible to enter trance states without the use of a pharmakon, especially for a skilled shaman. For sure, such ancient techniques like fasting, isolation, and dancing have been used equally as long as any psychedelic to achieve higher states of awareness. However, ensuring that sometimes hundreds of celebrants at a time (who were ordinary people, not shamans) would see a vision of Persephone required some kind of prompt, something no one who drank the kykeon could have missed.

The ceremony for initiating the mystai into the Eleusinian Mysteries was conducted in the Telesterion, a great hall in Eleusis. And while the Greeks were well-known for their stage performances, the hall was not outfitted for theater. Instead of the familiar series of elevating semicircles found in a Grecian theater, which allows everyone in the audience to see, the Telesterion featured long benches lined against the walls for the mystai to park their keisters. In front of them, a "forest of pillars" blocked any possible view of a stage, should there have even been a stage at all.[8] This venue is hardly conducive to a theatrical act. Furthermore, surviving receipts for the temple say nothing of actors, props, drapes, or *anything* that would lead one to believe that the ceremony relied on a person enjoying a staged performance.[9]

There had to be a way for each mystes to generate a vision without fail.

Even without shamanic training.

Every time.

For more than two thousand years . . .

The theory of a psychedelic kykeon has gained acceptance by many modern ethnobotanists and scholars who no longer question *if* a pharmakon played a role at Eleusis but rather ask *what kind* of pharmakon the congregants imbibed. A recent debate between Ivan Valencic and Peter Webster outlines this deliberation. Valencic argues on the side of Terence McKenna and Robert Graves that the "astonishment and ecstasy" of the kykeon contained mushrooms; Webster, upholding the original view by Albert Hofmann, the father of LSD, believes that a form of ergot provided the necessary entheogenic additive.[10]

While I agree with both fellows (and their respective camps) that the kykeon was psychedelic in some way, I do not think the active ingredient was either ergot or a shroom. Or rather, I don't think the *only* possibilities are ergot or mushrooms. Or rather, I think that the entheogen pantheon was such that the kykeon, at one time or another, could have included ergot or a mushroom or a variety of other plants, depending on what was available.

By using critical historical methods, I believe it is possible to take a photograph of a certain time when the entheogen employed at Eleusis was, in fact, rather obvious and well known to those mystai drinking the kykeon. I'd like to first explain why I disagree in the details with the original hypothesis advanced in *The Road to Eleusis*. Indeed, while I agree with the broader premise outlined in that work (that a psychedelic played a role in the ceremonies), I do not believe that the pharmakon used was ergot—or, at least, not predominantly so.

Let's begin with the textual evidence. The Homeric Hymn to Demeter is clear that the kykeon contained only barley and mint mixed with water. Each of these three ingredients has its own significance outside of any psychedelic interpretation. Water, as everyone knew, was necessary for life. And mint, too, has a symbolic dimension, for it was widely thought in the ancient world to serve as a contraceptive or abortifacient; in other words, it symbolized termination of life, death.[11] The barley is obviously symbolic of the grain. As for this last ingredient, Hofmann pointed out that barley hosts the fungus ergot, from which he first synthesized LSD. Such a laced beverage before a vision seems obvious to us in our modern psychedelic culture where LSD is synthesized safely (for the most part) by chivalrous criminal professionals.

So case closed, right?

Not quite.

Raw ergot has some problems. Ergotism (also known as *Ignis sacer*, meaning the "holy fire") is a nasty illness, complete with gangrene, nausea, and ultimately death, which can develop from eating ergot. Could the ancient Greeks have developed a way to reduce the unsavory effects of ergot without compromising its visionary properties? Peter Webster says yes. Using "a technologically simple process," well within the ancient Greeks' knowledge of food preparation, the Eleusinian priestesses were likely able to negate the undesirable effects of ergot while provoking its psychedelic properties.[12] Even Hofmann claims "the separation of the hallucinogenic agents by simply water solution from the non-soluble ergotamine and ergotoxine alkaloids was well within the range of possibilities open to Early Man in Greece."[13] And yet, tempting as the words of these luminaries may sound, we cannot say for sure that the Greeks knew about this process. Indeed, it is easy to assume that what is obvious to us must have been obvious to the ancients. Still, I am not necessarily convinced that the kykeon included ergot, despite the reference to barley in the Homeric hymn. The barley may have simply been a symbolic ingredient, like the water and mint, and not the pharmakon. I believe another pharmakon, not ergot, was the active ingredient in the kykeon. Let's explore that possibility.

HOUSE OF THE GODDESS

The discovery of the somnitheogen in prehistory led to some interesting prospects. Might we one day meet the ancestors in waking life? But those proto-Mycenaean cultures had determined long ago that while one person was able to commune with the ancestors in dreams, it proved fruitless to try to do so as a congregation. Maybe there existed a way to lull several hundred people at a time, guaranteed, into a state where the borders of sleeping, dreaming, and waking consciousness begin to blur.

Maybe there existed a way to pull the dream realm into conscious experience.

Whoever founded these mysteries, we do not know. Either by prehistorical conquest or generational nepotism, two families retained control for the entirety of our knowledge of the rites. The Kerykes family supplied the herald and torch carrier, and the Eumolpidai family supplied the hierophants.[14] The ceremonies began on Boedromion* 13 when Athenian youths carried the sacred objects in the kistai from Eleusis and stored them in the Eleusinian temple at Athens. The Athenian lads then carried the sacred objects back to Eleusis in preparation for the ritual—perhaps a later addition to the ceremony commemorating the Athenian conquest of Eleusis circa 600 BCE.

Those who could afford the luxury of the experience (mostly wealthy Athenians) would first wash a pig in the harbor of Cantharus.[15] Offering the pigs as collateral for their own lives, the mystai would then sacrifice them in homage to Demeter, the Grain Mother. In order to see the underworld, *someone* had to surrender to death; it was the natural order. A pig could hardly protest, at least not until its eyes gazed on the dagger licking its throat and it bawled an anguished squeal—a cry that would remind the mystai of their place in the cosmos.

---

*Boedromion refers to the third month of the Attic calendar, roughly our September–October.

And by then it would be too late for the pig.

It need only surrender.

On Boedromion 16 the mystai purified themselves by collectively bathing in the Bay of Phaleron; a fast followed on the eighteenth, and the procession down the Sacred Road from Athens to Eleusis began the next day, on Boedromion 19. Priestesses carrying the kistai were surrounded by ecstatic dancers as they moved along the Sacred Road. Several narrow streams acted as ancient demarcation lines between Athens and Eleusis, and a chain of bridges had been constructed to allow trade and travel between those two city-states. On each bridge the mystai met the troupe of "obscene dwarves," masked performers who insulted and offended the congregants with foul language and lewd gestures. This was done in remembrance of Iambe, the jester who tried to cheer up Demeter when she first visited the Eleusinian palace. From there each mystes followed her or his personal escort (a *mystagogos*) through the gates of the underworld, a grotto reminiscent of Hades that fed into the Telesterion. It was at this point that the mystai encountered the sacred objects and performed the opaque ritual outlined above.[16] They were then led to a large courtyard within the sanctuary where they danced, as hierophants sacrificed a bull. At the climax of the ceremony, the hierophants filled two sacred jugs (*plemochoai*); one they poured in homage to the east, the other in tribute to the west. Those assembled turned their heads skyward and cried *hye,* and then faced the ground and cried *kye.**

The Rites of Eleusis offered the mystai both a lesser mystery (in March) and the greater mystery (roughly September), the former a preamble of what awaited them that autumn. The Lesser Mysteries served as a general purification ritual that in all likelihood held no place in the original rite and represents a later addition.[17] The Lesser Mysteries also served as a course in the nature and meaning of the rites. The Greater Mysteries gave initiates the chance to experience what they had learned

---

Hye means "rain" and *kye,* "conceive." See Hippolytus, *Refutation of All Heresies,* 5.2. We will revisit this concept (i.e., divine impregnation of the soil by the rain) later within the larger role of the Sacred Marriage.

during their education in the Lesser Mysteries. That autumn they would walk along the memory of Demeter's journey to find Kore. In doing so, the mystai realized their place in the infinite cycle of life; they would go from mystai to *epopts* ("those who have seen").

Deep in the sanctuary at Eleusis a priest would mix the kykeon. Because the rite revolved around specifically feminine creation, the Cosmic Graell, this man was no ordinary priest. Effeminate by nature, he had to renounce his masculine gender in reverence to Demeter; he was, in a sense, a priestess. This priestess mixed the kykeon and then passed it on to other priestesses along with the other sacred objects. Balancing the sacred objects on their heads, the priestesses danced around the halls and then poured the kykeon into smaller cups and passed them out to the mystai. While the majority of rites in the ancient world concerned appeasing the gods and goddesses, the ceremony at Eleusis promised a vision.[18] A vision of Persephone rising. A vision that resulted in contentment in the afterlife. A vision, it was said, that confronted that deepest fear: a fear so inaudible that it nonetheless booms in the beat of every human heart; a fear so nerve-racking that the gods stitched it shut with a constellation of veins in a futile attempt to prevent the despair from escaping; a fear that you, dear reader, share with these mystai; a fear that you and I share, even as perfect strangers—that first question we all asked ourselves that day we discovered self-awareness: namely, *Why are we born just to die?*

Nowhere in the West were those fears played out more than in the rites to the Grain Mother performed in ancient Mycenaean, and later Grecian, culture in their annual Rites of Eleusis. The Greater Eleusinian Mystery remains lost to scholars today, but certain clues found in the myth might help demystify even the most stubborn of shadows. For one thing, the fact that the two main characters are women (Demeter and Kore/Persephone) says something about the ancient origins of the myth in pre-Mycenaean Greece. It means that this particular myth (or at least its earliest form) recalls a time when divine mothers occupied the forefront of these tales of supernatural dominion. The going consensus in the academic world, both square and aware, places the depth of the mystery within agricultural rejuvenation.

Let's peruse the myth, at least in its earliest and most complete surviving form and supplement it with additional evidence found throughout the ancient world. While it is easy to merely rehash the ideas of others, I believe there is another way to dig.

Join me! Let's straddle our shovels and spades and sail across the sky into realms beyond the Maiden's Well, where the erudite dirt, hardened over the wise centuries, anticipates our questions. But I must caution you—impervious passwords and secret knocks will do us no good once we arrive; they are lost to us. This whodunit requires the critical detection of the stubborn sleuth, the calibrated reasoning of the drunken poet. So down the hatch and let the sands of ruin guide our brushes and spades to the artifacts patiently awaiting detection. Clues to the entheogenic nature of the mysterious kykeon lie ready for unearthing in those ancient soils from which other (and earlier) grain goddesses germinated and blossomed.

Saddle up, dear reader—let's see if we cannot successfully trawl those murky depths of a forgotten secret.

Our first stop takes us just across the Aegean Sea, where various Thracian kingdoms populated the area we today call Turkey. Some Thracians worshipped the Grain Goddess, Ceres,* as described in the late second century CE by Pseudo-Plutarch in the work *De fluviis* (*About Rivers*). After eating communally in honor of the dead, they would perform a rite to Ceres by throwing an unidentified pharmakon onto large fires. Then "they hold their heads over the smoke, and snuff it up into their nostrils . . . till at last they fall into a profound sleep." A sleep filled, no doubt, with revelations bestowed from the goddess herself. We can guess endlessly as to the pharmakon in question. However,

---

*This particular name has survived the centuries in our word *cereal.*

due to a tiny clue left by the author, we can narrow it down to two possible florae. The author writes that the Thracians inhaled "the tops" of this particular plant. Opium (whose active narcotic is found in its bulbous head) fits well with this detail.[19]*

However, my friend and colleague Chris Bennett would argue (forcefully) that cannabis is more likely the unnamed herb. And truly a good case can be made for his interpretation. After all, the tops of the plant to which our anonymous author refers may implicate the cannabis flower, the storehouse of tetrahydrocannabinol yummies. Additionally, the author tells us that the leaves of this plant look similar to origanum (*Origanum vulgare*)—a species whose leaves vaguely resemble a cannabis leaf. Indeed, cannabis use was widespread in ancient Anatolia, centuries before Pseudo-Plutarch wrote.[20]

Whatever this obviously psychedelic pharmakon was, these Thracians employed it in ways different from those worshipping the Eleusinian Demeter analogue. While the hierophants employed their kykeon in a mystheogenic way (i.e., drawing the otherworld into this one), these Thracians preferred a somnitheogenic finale to their rites: they would fall into a deep sleep, to the dream state, to the otherworld, where the immortals who had achieved godhood in life communicated prophesies in death to slumbering mortals.

Just as the ancestors had done.

Back on our shovels and brooms. Our next stop will take us east to what is perhaps the founding mystery of the Grain Goddess. Indeed, scholars have long known that the Eleusinian Mysteries had made their way West from the East, beginning in the enchanted sands of Sumer.†

---

*The author apparently got his information from Callionymus's *Third Book of Thracian Relations,* now lost. In a moment, we will see another reason opium plausibly fits the Pseudo-Plutarch description.

†Authors as early as Pausanias (c. 100–170) recognized the Eastern origins of Grecian understanding regarding the immortality of the soul. See Uvarov, *Essay on the Eleusinian Mysteries of Eleusis,* 25.

SILVER VULVA

One of the more extraordinary discoveries of the twenty-first century has been the famous Uruk Vase (figure 3.1). The Uruk period (c. 4000–3100 BCE) preceded the rise of the Sumerian Empire, the vase dating to roughly the end of the former era. Carved onto the vase we find three scenes that tell a story about the Sacred Marriage of Inanna, the Queen of Heaven, with (presumably) Dumuzi. The top scene shows Inanna, identifiable by the horn on her head, receiving baskets filled with the harvest from a naked servant who is noticeably shorter than she. Both her horn and stature are obvious indications of her queenship and divinity. Beneath, the second section shows several skyclad servants preparing the bounty. And finally below, we see rows of what the servants were harvesting—wheat and opium poppy (figure 3.2).

Fig. 3.1. Uruk Vase (c. 3100 BCE). The civilization of Uruk (the Sumerian precursors) left us this beautiful vase depicting the Sacred Marriage of Inanna and Dumuzi. The bottom row shows Inanna rising from the dead in the form of grain and poppies; the middle row shows her servants collecting the bounty; the top row shows the ceremony of the Sacred Marriage.

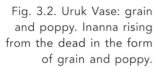

Fig. 3.2. Uruk Vase: grain and poppy. Inanna rising from the dead in the form of grain and poppy.

But what did the wheat and opium represent? Having only fragmentary materials to go on makes constructing the full symbolism of where and why the opium fits into Inanna's myth a fruitless, herculean task. But I have an interpretation that I would like to share with you that begins with Inanna's desire to enter the underworld; the story strikes me as both an ego-death experience and a death-rebirth experience, both of which are consistent with the entheogenic use of psychedelics. Before journeying to the underworld, Inanna tells her minister Nincubura to rescue her if she does not return in three days. She arrives at the palace Ganzer (the gates to the underworld), wherein she tricks Neti, the gate master, into allowing her entry. Inanna must pass through seven gates that force her to remove her "seven divine powers,"[21] symbolized in her royal accoutrements, including her crown, her necklace of lapis lazuli beads, and her *pala* ("garment of ladyship"), among other personal and symbolic affects.[22] I should note that, despite her travels to the underworld, Inanna is not "dead" in any sense of our meaning of the word; therefore, this is not yet a death-rebirth experience. But considering Inanna's renouncement of the garments of her identity—the objects of her powers—there seem to be some ego-death motifs present, the kind of which would have appealed to such modern psychenauts as the late Timothy Leary. During one of his LSD retreats, the defamed psychologist ordered trippers to remove their clothes and don white robes "to obliterate social distinctions."[23]

But to not leave Inanna alone in the underworld . . .

Upon venturing through the seventh gate, Inanna enters the throne room of her sister, Erec-ki-gala, Queen of the Underworld, where seven judges (the Anuna) sentence her to death. Inanna's flesh withers until she looks like a corpse; the Anuna then hangs her cadaver on a hook. After three days Inanna's servant Nincubura calls on the gods for help, but all decline except one, Enki, the god of wisdom. Enki creates two servants (*gala-tura* and *kur-jara*) and gives the "plant of life" to one and the "water of life" to another. They are to sprinkle these over Inanna's body. The gala-tura and kur-jara turn into flies so they can easily fit through the seven gates of the underworld. They meet Erec-ki-gala and negotiate for Inanna's body. The deal brokered, the gala-tura and kur-jara sprinkle Inanna with the plant of life and the water of life and she is rejuvenated. *Here* is the death-rebirth motif in the story: Inanna will rise from the dead. And yet, since no one is allowed to leave the realm of the dead unscathed, Inanna must choose someone to take her place, which ends up being her lover, Dumuzi.[24]* Thus, unlike the Eleusinian Mysteries, which feature a strictly feminine cycle of regeneration, those of Inanna recognized the male's role in this natural process. This coital union, the Sacred Marriage, will be further explored in the next chapter.

Let's bring it all back West and ask what this might mean for Eleusis. On the famed Uruk Vase, which began our investigation into the mysteries of Inanna, we see both the rising of wheat and opium along with that goddess's Sacred Marriage to Dumuzi. Oddly, there is no mention of wheat or any pharmakon in the surviving Inanna myths; by some miracle we just so happen to be fortunate enough to know about at least *one* person who considered opium vital to the tale—the unidentified

---

*Ergo, the pig sacrifices at Eleusis.

messenger from history who carved the Uruk Vase. Perhaps the opium was the plant of life sprinkled on Inanna in the underworld to facilitate her ascension back to Earth? After all, opium's use as a medicine, a plant of life, so to speak, probably predates the Uruk period. Might we be hearing an echo of its first discovery? When we consider that some people in the ancient world thought the water of life identical with the haoma of the Vedics, we are given a further clue that the gala-tura and kur-jara fed Inanna opium.[25]

Since wheat and opium are not found in the mystery of Inanna's descent in text, it is certainly possible that the Uruk Vase represents a version of the story that did not survive the passing of empires. On the other hand, the wheat and opium on the Uruk Vase may represent Inanna herself, rising from the underworld in the form of both the food that sustains life and the pharmakon that bridges people with the otherworld. She is harvested and prepared, as seen in the vase's middle panel, and bestows her bounty on humankind during the sacred nuptial to Dumuzi, as seen on the top panel. It is every bit possible that the rites of Inanna had *nothing* to do with actually taking any entheogen (in the form of opium) but rather trying to explain the mystery of how pharmaka of all kinds came to pass.

But maybe the same wasn't strictly speaking true at Eleusis.

While I think the pharmakon the Eleusinian hierophants added to the kykeon changed over time, enough evidence survives to at least offer us a photo of a time when said additive was probably opium. The variety of pharmaka points to a symbolic dimension with regard to the active ingredient. The stories, too, while displaying some commonalties (dying and rising, wheat, opium) are all very different as well.

So what does it all mean?

Into the darkroom now, where we can develop and examine that snapshot.

THE SERPENT, THE GRAIN, THE PHARMAKON

As shown earlier and reiterated throughout this chapter, opium had a widespread magical (and/or religious) use across the ancient Mediterranean. Archaeologists are in possession of a bas-relief that unambiguously shows Demeter-Kore (in her role as both mother and daughter) rising from the underworld. She holds in her hands three unambiguous items: serpents, grain stalks, and opium poppies (see figure 3.3).

Let's briefly unpack each of these symbols. The serpent represents the underworld, as it did in other parts of Greece, like Delphi.[26] It also could represent wisdom, as seen in the Garden of Eden story (Gen. 3:1). The grain represents the cycles of life—those of wheat and flesh. We are all coddled in the embracing arms of this bittersweet progression. The third item, the opium poppies, demands especial attention as it is possible for a cursory observer to conclude that Kore holds not opium stalks but pomegranate branches. This initially seems reasonable, as the

Fig. 3.3. Persephone rising from the dead (c. fifth century BCE). Here we see Persephone ascending from the underworld with wheat, opium poppies, and serpents. All three are ancient symbols of the cycles and questions of life and death, the first mystery.

story of Kore features her eating that fruit, thus ensuring her cyclical return to the underworld. Upon closer inspection, though, the carvings are clearly opium poppies and not pomegranates.

I conclude this for several reasons: First, Demeter-Kore's Sumerian analogue, Inanna, clearly shows some link with the poppy, wheat, death, and resurrection on the Uruk Vase (whatever such meaning may imply). Second, conceding that both florae in question (opium and pomegranate) look quite similar from a distance, we can nonetheless see floral features on the bas-relief that make subtle but crucial differentiations when viewed up close. The slits that run vertically across the bulbs that Demeter-Kore holds appear unmistakably on poppy capsules; the skin of a pomegranate runs smooth. Third, the tops of both the opium capsule and the pomegranate have what almost look like haircuts. The opium poppy has a flattop that sits on the bulb like a periwig on a head, while the pomegranate has more of a skinny Bart Simpson haircut that is a seamless extension of the fruit. The Uruk Vase shows this same noticeable rim that divides the opium between the "hairpiece" and the bulb.

The bas-relief in question shows this 'do sitting on top of the pod, again unmistakably depicting opium heads. Finally, the Uruk Vase and the bas-relief show the bulbs on stalks; pomegranates grow on tree branches. In another relief housed in the British Museum, these same features of the opium poppy (joined by wheat stalks) appear: vertical slits and a distinctive flattop (figure 3.4). We can therefore conclude that Demeter-Kore clearly holds serpents, grains, and opium stalks in her hands. We see in these three symbols enough meaning to unfold the mysteries of death, and how a person can ceremonially access them by walking the Sacred Road of Demeter.

A SECRET INGREDIENT?

But what of the Homeric Hymn to Demeter? Nowhere does it say that opium was added to the kykeon drunk by Demeter at the palace of Eleusis.

Or does it?

Now would be a good time to refresh (and ultimately reject) the daffodil as the narcissus that Persephone plucked. Indeed, there is a plethora of evidence to suggest that the fatal flora she procured was indeed opium. The motif of a maiden dying by picking a narcotic flower was common in the ancient world, as seen in the now lost work of Plato, wherein the woman abducted was named Pharmaceia (meaning "the use of drugs").[27] Additionally, both Plutarch and Dioscorides write of the "narcotic" torpor produced by the narcissus.[28] The detail that the narcissus is "one hundred headed" perhaps speaks to the variety of uses for opium in the ancient world.[29] Classicists have long known that Demeter's journey to Eleusis served as a *simulacrum,* a mirror that paralleled Persephone's descent into the underworld.[30] Even today, some secret societies share a similar rubric.[31] Should this be the case, then we can say that there was perhaps a *fourth*, unannounced ingredient in the kykeon: the narcissus itself. This cup of both life and death, waking and dreaming, connected the initiates to the experience of seeing the underworld while still alive in the hollowed-out caverns deep within the Telesterion.

Incidentally, there is anterior written evidence that confirms opium's role in the Eleusinian Mysteries, at least at one point in time. One late (relatively speaking) Christian author who either once participated in the rites or at least knew something about them records that the sacred objects found in the kistai included "cakes, pomegranates, a small statue of the vagina, and opium."[32] Additionally, poppies were also found, along with a host of other natural products (including wheat and barley, milk, honey, wool) within small cups that surround the *kerna*—a large bowl used in the ceremony.[33] Obviously, there were more ingredients in the actual rite to Demeter than in the Homeric Hymn to Demeter.

This mystery no doubt provided a fantastic fart in the ancient Mycenaean mind: how could pharmaka both heal and kill? Let's consider several important factors of the story so far: the gift of the Fireside Goddess (later remembered as Demeter, Isis, or Inanna)—that for which she was exalted to immortality—was the understanding that vegetation of all kinds could serve humankind. Isis's association with opium as a medicine and ancient depictions of Demeter with opium in her headdress (along with wheat and barley) also indicate that the medical and therefore spiritual-magical effects were known and that it was this narcissus (represented at least for a while as opium) that killed Persephone and allowed the congregants to witness her rise.

And it all came together at the height of the ritual, after the kykeon had started to take effect. A single stalk of wheat was presented to those gathered.[34] In seeing this stalk, the mystai become epopts. This perfect ancient meshing of substance, set, and setting resulted in a vision of the goddess rising; the anticipation kept the mystai awake, even as the opium tapped into the deeper metarealities of their subconscious minds. Symbols alone have the power to reach deep into the furthest corners of

Fig. 3.4. Funerary relief of the Decumius Vaarus. Roman woman holding both grains and poppies on a Roman gravestone. Again, we see our ancestors' association with sleep and death (the underworld) and the somnitheogens that bridged those realms.

our hopes, our fears, our passions, our loves—to even tickle the terrors of the unknown at the hour of our expiry. Whether in the form of opium, ergot, a mushroom, cannabis, or some other psychedelic pharmakon lost to us, both the medicines of life and the dreads of death could be seen, felt, and *experienced* at Eleusis. And yet, the hierophants also promised a vision that would lead to rebirth for the gathered mystai, for they already knew the secret: namely, it is Earth that births and heals, and ultimately, it is Earth to which we shall all return. In this divine madness the crypt of the Telesterion allowed the epopts to watch as the ancestor Grain Mother rose from the dead. They had become part of the myth.

And myth lasts for all time.

So dread not, delicate mortal, for like the grain of barley presented at the height of the ceremony, you are made of the same cosmic building blocks. You are the rain; you are the grain. You are hunter and hunted. You are the child born the moment you close your eyes for the last time. Rejoice, sweet one—you too shall rise again!

For you are the contents of the Cosmic Graell, the limitless elixir: existence.

Because you were born, by necessity you will spill forth forever.

Your eyes have opened, sweet epopts.

Now close them in capitulation.

For no pig's blood can substitute for your rendezvous with the inevitable.

Surrender, child.

You're home.

4

CELEBRATIONS OF THE LIVING FIRE

❖•❖•❖

Psychedelics and the Sacred Marriage
c. 5000 BCE–500 CE

The corn-giving earth brings forth many drugs in Egypt, many of them good when used in mixtures, but many of them baneful.

HOMER

PYTHIA PRIESTESSES

Huh . . .

Coretas squinted and then shook his head in disbelief.

Curious about the spectacle before him, he quickly summoned some other shepherds who tended their flocks nearby. As they approached Coretas, they could see past him the very oddity for which he had drawn their attention.

Ordinarily, goats behave rather tamely. Lazily nibbling along the fields, they appear unaware of the world around them (unless provoked by a predator). Thus, we can see the shepherd Coretas looking speechlessly at his goats as they began to bleat and kick about in turmoil while grazing along the side of Mount Parnassus. Coretas and the gathered herders walked toward the bewildered goats to investigate the matter, only to fall under a similar spell the closer they approached the flock. Before they knew it, the shepherds became entranced and likewise began bellowing madly into the mountains.

ᵛ

This event saw the founding of the ancient city of Delphi sometime around 1600 BCE, which the most famous oracle in the ancient world would call home. The area boasted no major cities or buildings, but rather a serene wonderland of sacred springs, gripping rock formations, groves, and woodland expanses. Therefore, it seems rather obvious that such a beatific landscape would inspire the locals to ascribe the majesty of their land to Gaia, the Earth Goddess. Like Demeter and Persephone, Gaia's roots ran deep into the ancient bedrock. And it is in that subterranean stratum, lost in the darkest corners of history, where we find another example of a truly entheogenic mystery, that of the Sacred Marriage of the sun god Apollo and the Delphic oracle, the pythia priestess.[1]

In this case, the entheogen took the form of naturally occurring vapors, as several ancient witnesses at Delphi attest. Oracles were certain kinds of priestesses, serving a different role than, say, the Eleusinian priestesses we have already met. While a priestess performed public ceremonies for the good of fertility and fortune, an oracle was expected to give prophecies to private (usually powerful) patrons. Each customer was allowed to ask one question. In answering, the oracle did not placate the goddesses and gods hoping to win their favor as did the priestesses and priests; she instead allowed Apollo, god of the sun, to penetrate her body. His divine touch, even the gentlest caresses of a god's fingers stroking her virgin skin, caused the woman to fall deeper into a rapturous trance. She would then relay messages found beyond the veil to her clients.

Like most psyche-magical practices of the time, a demanding prelude of ritual purification and fasting preceded the visions; the ceremony began properly on the seventh of every month, Apollo's holy day. A priest waited on the top of Mount Parnassus to welcome Apollo, the rising sun, with song and dance. The oracle was brought to a fountain (once a nymph named Castalia, whom Apollo transformed into running waters). From there, the oracle proceeded to another cleansing spring (that of Kassotis) where she would again wash, but also take a drink from the sacred waters. From there, she was ready to head back into the inner sanctum of the temple, where her handmaidens and priests awaited, wreathed in the smoke of burning laurel leaves.

Another attendee, though probably the least eager to participate in the rite, was the sacrificial animal, usually a goat, in homage to the initial discovery of Apollo's fumes. The priest would douse the animal with water and observe how it trembled, which would anticipate the oracle's own divine gyrations and frenzy once the fumes from the crevice overtook her.[2]

Now perched on her tripod deep in the inner sanctum of the Temple of Apollo, called the *adyton,* we find the oracle holding a laurel branch, ready to prophesy. Below the tripod, a crack in the earth spits "Apollo's gases" into the chamber "from which arises breath that inspired a divine frenzy" and filled her delicate nose, the god seeping into her consciousness.[3] She begins her divination—to war, to peace, to longevity, to doom. In the case of Delphi, an entire city was built around Apollo and the words the oracle foretold, as entheogenic gases escaped her lips.

In this case, the prophecies at Delphi can rightly be called entheogenically induced; the oracle was, after all, inhaling the essence of the god Apollo, ingesting him into her mind, body, and soul. *Generating divinity from within.* And yet, we can also make a strong case that these prophecies constitute pythiagenic prognostications. This was *magic,* plain and simple, although done through spiritual and entheogenic avenues, reconfirming an important principle in psychedelic historical studies: our modern paradigms do not always fit comfortably on the past, much as we would like to see more easily digestible traditions.

Let's also note that sometimes these visions caused by inhaling Apollo overwhelmed the oracle beyond her control. Plutarch, once a priest of Delphi himself, wrote of an incident when the oracle, instead of *holding space* (as we might say today), was "filled with a mighty and baleful spirit . . . she became hysterical and with a frightful shriek rushed towards the exit and threw herself down."[4] Even a mind as magically calibrated and socially conditioned to accept visionary states of awareness as that of a Delphic oracle could not always control the overwhelming power of an entheogenic experience.

Perhaps most intriguing about the oracles of Delphi was that their entranced prophecies were often recorded, some even coming down to us. We might even call those Delphic prophecies, instigated via an entheogenic vapor, the oldest trip reports known to humankind.

Ancient Grecians recognized four kinds of divine madness: those of prophecy, those of art, those of mystery initiations, and those of eroticism.* Any (or none at all) pharmakon could have been used in any number of ways to achieve any of those four states of sacred frenzy.

A symbolic motif underlies the oracle's prophecies. She had wed Apollo and could hold no relations with any other man, mortal or otherwise. This was a form of the Sacred Marriage, in this case one of a mortal with an immortal. The oracle wasn't merely "under the influence" of "hallucinogenic" gases; she was allowing Apollo inside her in the most sacred way. To reduce this solemn event to simple drugs and trickery misses the point completely.

For the Sacred Marriage was every bit part of the temple's allure as the prophecies gained through commercial exchange. The oracle only prophesied nine months out of the year. The rest of the time (roughly correlating to our November through February) the temple housed

---

*Or, if a pharmakon was included: pythiagenic (prophecy), poetigenic (creative arts), mystheogenic (initiatory), and pythiagenic (love magic). I will outline the latter magic more in the next chapter.

the crazed debaucheries of Apollo's alter ego, Dionysus. The origin stories of Dionysus are numerous, though most scholars agree that he hailed from the East: beginning in Sumer as Dumuzi, passing into Egypt as Osiris, and finally landing in Greece as Dionysus.

And yet, the Eleusinian Mysteries must have been functioning in some form before his arrival in Greece. How else can we explain the absence of his presence or any hint of the divine masculine in the myth of Demeter and Persephone? Dionysus initially played no role at Eleusis. He likely held no place in the earliest days at Delphi either. He would soon make a name for himself far beyond the confines of the sun god's shadow side. If Apollo represented enlightenment, reason, prophecy, and life, then Dionysus symbolized, well, let's call them more *Dionysian* appetites . . .

THE DIONYSIAN TRINITY

And then he stumbled on something extraordinary.

Crushing the grapes before storage had a magical effect on his yield, the process converting the sugar in the juice into ethanol. He knew nothing of this natural process, nor did he know of bacteria or yeast and its invisible transformation of ordinary grape juice into alcohol. It must have appeared nothing short of miraculous. Wanting more, he decided against crushing up the grapes in his hands as he had always done in the past. Instead, he built a small vat and placed large bunches of grapes inside; he then proceeded to stomp more grape juice to store and let whatever magical force was at work do its job. So inspired was he that he set about unlocking other mysteries of fruit cultivation, eventually understanding the proper pruning and storage necessary for a variety of produce, for its influence had inspired his need to care for, and properly store, other fruits like figs. Instead of carefully guarding this mystery, he spread it as far as he could, teaching anyone who would listen about the magic of the crushed grape. When he joined the ancestors, those who remembered him gave him "immortal honor" by calling him Lenaeus, "from the custom of treading the clusters of grapes in a wine-tub."[5]

Tales of Lenaeus's discovery would be told for ages to come, usually while sharing the very beverage he introduced to the world. Over time, Lenaeus become one of those regenerative spirits mentioned in the second chapter. He was the spark—the *force*—that allows grapes and other fruits to ferment into wine. And should a question arise about viti- or horticulture, Lenaeus could always be reached in dreams for answers.

There was another who lived years—perhaps centuries—before or after Lenaeus. Like Lenaeus, we do not know his name; the first people to call him anything at all called him Dionysus. Seeing the way country folk toiled in the fields, turning over the soil with their hands, Dionysus hooked oxen up to a strange assortment of sticks. To the amazement of everyone in his community, Dionysus's plough revolutionized how much land could be tilled at a time. He had transcended his humanity by working not with his neighbors to ready the fields for planting, but by doing the same job *faster* with animals. He eagerly showed this invention to anyone who would listen. When he died, he joined the ancestors in the dream realm. The living remembered him embellished with horns, a symbol of his unity with the oxen. "And in return for [his contributions of husbandry]," writes historian Diodorus of Sicily, "those whom he had benefited accorded to him honours and sacrifices like those offered to the gods, since all men were eager, because of the magnitude of his service to them, to accord to him immortality."[6] Dionysus was remembered as an ancestral spirit. He was human, but he also harbored superhuman powers. He once lived on Earth, but now resided in the otherworld, on the other side of dreams.

When Libyan king Ammon saw the virgin Amaltheia, he forgot all about his wife, the queen Rhea. Ammon and Amaltheia's affair resulted in a son. Fearing Rhea might discover the child-king, Ammon sequestered him in Nysa with his friend Aristaeus. One of Aristaeus's daughters acted as caretaker for the child, while he supplied the formal schooling; a certain Athena of "exceedingly ready . . . wit" took charge of keeping Rhea at a distance from Nysa. Athena also taught the boy many crafts, gifted as she was in the creative arts as well. This young man grew up to also be remembered as Dionysus.[7]

Surrounded in a veritable Atlantis-like Nysa, Dionysus cultivated his talents under the careful guidance of Athena. In manners unspecified, he used his learning to produce wine in a similar manner as Lenaeus: by squeezing out the juices from fruits and allowing that invisible force to magically transform the sugar into ethanol. He also developed a second drink called *zythos* out of barley, for those people who lived in climates unable to support the grapevine. This drink, once brought to Egypt by Osiris, offers a clue to be revealed now even if it may only be understood in its entirety later: an ancient reference to zythos from Zosimos of Panopolis, otherwise known as Zosimos the alchemist, who addresses those knowledgeable in the "false and wicked arts" (i.e., magic). He charges that they are using occult knowledge to brew a kind of Egyptian beer called *zythi*. Unlike the somnitheogenic mandrake beer used to calm the ravages of Hathor, zythi included, among other things, two other psychedelic pharmaka: "cannabis leaves and seeds, and . . . darnel."[8] Cannabis, I reckon, needs no introduction or exposé on its magical benefits. As for this latter plant, well, the Romans built recognition of its psychedelic nature right into its Latin name, *Lolium temulentum* ("the intoxicating grass").

Dionysus eventually developed whole rituals that acknowledged and celebrated the mystery of pharmaka and fermentation*; such rites included divine intercourse, the Sacred Marriage. For this, he would later be remembered as an ancestral spirit. His parents would also be

---

*In Nicander's *Alexipharmaca*, mushrooms are said to be *zumoma*, the ferments of the earth (see Ruck, *Dionysus in Thrace*, 191).

euhemerized: Ammon became Zeus; Rhea became Hera; and the erudite women of Nysa became the maenads—those votive followers of the Dionysian mysteries whose name means "to go insane." Over time he would make the upward climb from an ancestral spirit to eventually finding a seat among the Olympians.*

The three immortals had become gods: Lenaeus the natural force of fermentation, Dionysus of the plough, and Dionysus of ecstatic ritual. By the time this trinity reached Greece, the three had merged into a single entity: Dionysus. We tend to remember Dionysus solely as the god of wine, and this is certainly accurate. But at some point he ceased being solely the god of wine and became the god of *enthousiasmos* ("intoxicated revelry").

And let's consider an important point: ancient wines were hardly strong enough to cause the kinds of reactions that the accounts describe. Knowing nothing of advanced modern fermentation techniques, the wines would have only reached an alcohol content of 14 percent (under the best circumstances), nowhere near the level required to "induce madness" as the sources record.[9] The discovery of pharmakon-laced vino was precipitated by a desire to create that drink in places where grapes did not grow. Even the brewing of solely barley clearly wasn't strong enough, as evidenced by the creation of cannabis-infused zythos.

At the Theater of Dionysus, large crowds gathered in the cold of March to drink and celebrate the drama of that god. The wine drunk at the Dionysian theater was no ordinary wine, as one scholar has pointed out by noting its name, *trimma,* which specifically signifies "a special mix for the Theater . . . [with] additives ground into it."[10] The entire spectacle functioned as a communal transcendent possession, a "celebration of living fire."[11] We do not know the additives of those wines. We do know, however, that there was a readily available supply of them, as con-

---

*To clarify: some do not place Dionysus among the Olympians because he had a mortal mother.

temporary literature attests.[12] And within the joining of wine and phar-maka one can perhaps uncover an occult aspect of the Sacred Marriage in ancient history.

THE SACRED MARRIAGE

To again briefly return to our struggling ancestors. At some point along the story of humanity, proto-humans—starving, hysterical, naked—made a remarkable discovery. When our throats scratched we found relief by drinking water. We couldn't even recall a time when people didn't need water. We saw this same camaraderie in the herds as they drank from rivers. Over time, we even recognized a common sympa-thizer in those plants and grasses scorched by the sun. If humans and animals needed water, then plants needed water as well. Those florae that either grew near or had ample amounts of water always seemed to magically receive some kind of natural potion from Earth herself. Human, animal, and vegetable also received a natural potion from the sky, the rain, which had a noticeable effect on florae fertility. Maybe our progenitors saw the rain as impregnating the soil. How else does one explain the hye-kye cry ("rain, conceive!") of the Eleusinian mystai? I theorize that this symbolism—soil and rain, chalice and blade, Earth and sky, union of the feminine and masculine energies—can be seen in the wedding of Dionysus (or his non-Grecian equivalent) and the cross-culturally evident Poppy Goddess of the ancient Mediterranean. And just as Dumuzi wed Inanna and Apollo penetrated the oracle, so Dionysus ignited another kind of divine madness in his maenads, one found in the inexpressible fires of ecstasy.

IVY AND WINE

And what grand displays took place at the Temple of Apollo when the oracle was not in session. Some felt that the powers of alcohol held too much sway over the volatile emotions of the inebriated. Therefore, later writers would caution drinkers to mix wines with water to distill the intoxicating effects.

The historian Diodorus records the untoward outcomes:

> But when friends gathered together and enjoyed good cheer, the revellers, filling themselves to abundance with the unmixed wine, became like madmen and used their wooden staves to strike one another. Consequently, since some of them were wounded and some died of wounds inflicted in vital spots, Dionysus was offended at such happenings, and though he did not decide that they should refrain from drinking the unmixed wine in abundance, because the drink gave such pleasure, he ordered them hereafter to carry a narthex and not a wooden staff.[13]

The *narthex* was symbolic of gathering and storing plant pharmaka. Indeed, like the *thyrsos* of the maenads (discussed below), the narthex of the male worshipers was the symbolic counterpart of wild plant gathering.[14] Since not everyone took to diluting their wine with water, another way to calm the aggressive effects of drunkenness was to temper the drink with a soothing pharmakon, as we saw with the Egyptian Feast of Hathor. And some of these pharmaka, like cannabis, opium, mushrooms, or mandrake, can certainly fire the erotic passions as well. As noted earlier, wine in those days did not have a sufficient alcohol content to induce anything more than gossip at best and belligerence at worst—nothing like the ecstatic madness we read about wine inducing in the ancient sources. As shown over the previous chapters, early on psychedelic additives found their way into wines. For example, the maenads built themselves into enthousiasmos by eating a certain flora known to us only as ivy. As several have argued (myself included), there are a multitude of gaps in our understanding of ancient plant classifications.[15] Further complicating the matter is the unimpeachable way authors like Plutarch indicate that the maenad's ivy had some kind of entheogenic property.

For he assures:

Women possessed by Bacchic frenzies rush straightway for ivy and tear it to pieces, clutching it in their hands and biting it with their teeth; so that not altogether without plausibility are they who assert that ivy, possessing as it does an exciting and distracting breath of madness, deranges persons and agitates them, and in general brings on a wineless drunkenness and joyousness in those that are precariously disposed towards spiritual exaltation.[16]

Wineless drunkenness?

Plutarch clearly isn't referring to the kind of ivy you and I are familiar with—for there are no known species of ivy that would cause in a user such psychological and physiological reactions akin to a "wineless drunkenness." And yet, Dioscorides, Pliny, and Plutarch all note ivy's "deranging effect upon the mind." The root for the Greek word ivy, *kissos,* from which we derive *narcissus*, comes from some unknown non-Indo-European language, relating to some kind of prophetic or spiritual state of consciousness.[17] This ivy, whatever it was, had clear entheogenic properties: maenads ate it to induce enthousiasmos. They roamed the lands far and wide gathering pharmaka in their thyrsos (the feminine narthex counterpart). The name thyrsos is likely of Ugarit origin, stemming from a female goddess of wine, Tiršu, a name that means "intoxicating drink."[18] In fact, the ancient Hebrews' word for wine, *tirōš*, was derived from her name as well.[19] Her name would ultimately be used to describe the containers that maenads used to store their collected pharmaka. Even medical treatises adopted the metaphor of the thyrsos/narthex symbolizing root-cutting.[20] And that pharmaka, represented as "ivy," could have been *anything*.

Recent archaeological evidence has suggested the possibility of a mushroom as one representative for the enigmatic ivy of enthousiasmos. Those familiar with my work know that I hesitate when someone brings up the possibility of *hidden* mushrooms in artwork.* I'm often doubtful because when ancient peoples depicted a mushroom they did

---

*Those interested can see some of my thoughts on this topic on psychedelicwitch.com.

so without ambiguity,* such as we see on a hydria† found in an ancient Ainos‡ graveyard, which actually rivals the Uruk Vase in its entheogenic blatancy. The area, once controlled by a Thracian warrior people called the Satrae, had not been conquered by a foreign power even as late as Herodotus's living memory.[21] Instead, they established a vast and lucrative trade hub in the northern Aegean Sea, gaining them access to all the spices, foods, animals, and pharmaka available in the ancient world.[22]

The Satrae included in their ranks the Bessi, a priestly class who "possess[ed] the place of divination sacred to Dionysus." For up on the highest mountain in the whole of the Satrae territory lived a woman who oversaw the shrine of Dionysus, to whom the Bessi relied for their prophecies.[23] This suggests that she was some kind of maenad-oracle, a follower of Dionysus who prophesied through psychedelically altering her consciousness.

To return to Plutarch's opaque reference to the "wineless drunkenness"—the enthousiasmos—that drove the maenads into frenzy. According to the hydria found in those former Satrae areas, there is every chance that at some point the oracle of the Dionysian shrine drank a mushroom wine to enter a prophetic trance. Indeed, the hydria features two female and male couples placed alongside each other. In one scene, we see a woman presenting a man with what very much looks like a small mushroom; in the juxtaposed scene, we see the other woman presenting a grape vine to the man, who will no doubt add it to the mixing vat sitting below the couple. I hypothesize that the pharmakon (in this case, a mushroom) represented the feminine (the oracle) and the wine (as usual for any Dionysian sect) represented the masculine in the form of the Bessi.

In other parts of Thrace, diviners at the Temple of Bacchus received prophetic visions after drinking copious amounts of wine.[24] Considering

---

*Besides the Tassili cave paintings in Algeria and the mushroom-soma tapestry, other artifacts of ink and stone speak to psychedelic mushroom use. See Letcher, *Shroom*, 74, 113.
†A Grecian vessel for carrying water; the ashes from a cremated cadaver might also be housed in a hydria.
‡Modern-day Turkey.

the Thracian use of cannabis as outlined earlier, it is possible that the visionary wine found in these Thracian Bacchic temples was a form of zythos. However, it is equally possible they used mushrooms, or mandrake, or opium, or some other obscure psychedelic pharmakon. It is, of course, also possible that they used nothing at all. Though, when we consider the oracular nature (overlaid with Dionysian motifs) of these practices, this last option seems the least likely.

Another rendition of this solemn scene seen on a plate recovered from Pompeii depicts this familiar theme. Only the plate shows neither a mushroom nor opium that symbolized the sacred feminine pharmakon but rather a serpent (figure 4.1); the divine masculine clearly

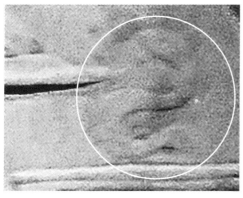

Fig. 4.1 Sacred Marriage: ivy and wine. Bacchus mixing pharmaka (symbolized as the serpent) into wine.

represented as Bacchus, the Roman analogue for Dionysus. The nuptial in this instance occurs between the python (representing pharmaka) and the vino. In still another instance, Dionysus wears the opium crown of the Poppy Goddess of the ancient Mediterranean on an ancient *krater* from Magnae Grecia while two women entertain him with music and dance.[25] Is it too far a stretch of the imagination to assume some kind of psychedelic Sacred Marriage symbolism in all of this?

THE HOUSE OF EVIL THOUGHTS

Not everyone was happy with Dionysus. His campaigns across the known world met with resistance among some leaders and warrior-kings who saw the constant intoxication of the people as antithetical to morals and virtue. Numerous prohibitions ensued. The Roman correspondent to the Dionysian cult, the Bacchic Mysteries, suffered a tremendous blow by the Senate when it ordered thousands of Bacchic celebrants arrested and executed.[26] Priests of Jupiter, likewise, were banned from wine consumption.[27] The Dacians (a Thracian tribe that united itself with the Getae), under direction of King Burebista's (82–44 BCE) high priest Deceneu, introduced a prohibition of wine.[28] Farther east, the Iranian religious reformer Zarathustra (Zoroaster, c. 600 BCE) lashed out against orgiastic rites that included bloody sacrifices of many oxen and drinking a psychedelic potion, haoma. Yasna, the Zoroastrian holy book, outlines the negative effects of haoma and how its use led drinkers past the gateways to the "House of Evil Thoughts":

> [The haoma drinkers] oppos[e] the message of Zoroaster. . . . This they do from an appetite that will not allow them to see right, an appetite that holds them fast, so that they, and even the Kavi* priests, constantly give in to it and surrender their reason to it, as they assist with the rites of the cow-sacrifice, presided over by the

---

*Seer priests.

impious master of ceremonies who pours into the fire the libation of the holy juice [haoma] pressed from a certain mountain plant.[29]

As shown in the second chapter of this book, resin samples from excavated haoma-mixing vats tested positive for cannabis, opium, and ephedra.

These Iranian psychedelic priests ousted by Zarathustra were not the only kind targeted for their religious convictions; ministers of an orgiastic cult to Sabazios,* a Thracian-Phrygian god, were expelled from their lands around 139 BCE. The rituals of these priests, who made their sacred potions *ex ordeo frumento* ("out of grain"),[30] might hint at another ritualistic imbibing of the psychedelic pharmaka darnel (*Lolium temulentum*).[31]

Sometimes Dionysus caused a commotion in a different way. Cleisthenes of Sicyon (c. 600–500 BCE), despite his tyrannical leanings, found so much value in the Dionysian Mysteries that he overthrew his own priesthood—those who up until that time had supervised the Adrastos Ceremonies.[32] Needless to say, while the Adrastos priests in all probability despised Dionysus, they likely squabbled with each other over who would enjoy continued employment at the new mysteries.

Political incentives might also turn someone away from the mysteries of Dionysus. We can all learn a lesson from the career- and life-ending act committed by the Scythian king Skyles. Skyles's fondness for Athenian culture often found him sneaking away from his troops, disguising himself in Grecian attire, and enjoying the civilized life for a while. But his proclivities went too far when he was initiated into the mysteries of Dionysos Bakcheios. Whatever pharmakon was in the wine that Skyles imbibed caused him to run around the city of Olbia with "the madness of a god." He even took up the title of Bacchant, leader of the mysteries. Perhaps he had been set up by a local Borysthenite, who wished to see the Scythian king embarrassed. This Borysthenite took the "leading men" of Skyles's army to a tower, where they observed their

---

*Another Thracian Dionysian analogue.

king leading a procession of ecstatics.[33] "You laugh at us, Scythians!" he said. "But now this deity has possessed your own king!" Skyles's troops, ashamed and embarrassed by such an unreserved display, mutinied. Skyles would feel the cold edge of a blade across his throat as a final reminder that Scythians did *not* condone Greek life, not even from their king.[34]

Others claimed that the Dionysian Mysteries had little to do with a Sacred Marriage and served as nothing more than an excuse to drink copious amounts of trimma-wine and bed women.[35] The snooty high priests of the Zalmoxis Mysteries, all men of stature, rejected the spiritual orgies of the lower classes, least of which any ritual that included women.[36] Such a reputation, despite the censorious intention of the priests, was destined to make the rites even more popular.

Outside the pagan world, Dionysus was all but stonewalled by the Hebrews as well. Hosea mentions a "strong drink," which was causing untoward effects in some of the rabbis: "These also reel with wine and stagger with strong drink; the priest and the prophet stagger with strong drink, they are confused with wine . . . they err in vision, they stumble in giving judgment" (Isa. 28:7).Whatever this trimma was, it was not well received by the Hebrews (at least some of them—others seem to have made a merry old time with it!).[37]

The problem really stemmed from a small dilemma: after Noah's ark finally settled on dry land after forty days and nights of flooding, his first action was to plant grapevines and start drinking (Gen. 9:20–24). This led to Noah passing out naked in a drunken stupor, which embarrassed his three sons, Shem, Ham, and Japheth.

Still, wine was not openly condemned in this story. It would take a commentary in the Midrash Tanhuma on the Genesis narrative to explain why wine wantonly wasted women and men. After Noah planted his vineyard, the devil (here named Shmadon) approached him and inquired about his winery. Noah replied that the grape was both sweet to the taste and could be made into wine, which "gladdens the heart." Shmadon offered to go into business with Noah, who accepted. But this devil was a trickster. He brought a lamb, a lion, a pig, and a monkey to Noah's vineyard, sacrificed them, and poured their blood over the soil where the grapes grew. He then informed Noah that eating the fruit of the vine would keep a person innocent, like a lamb, but if the grapes were fermented and drunk as wine, the drinker would become like a lion, at least in his own mind. The drunk is no real lion, however, and his belligerent behavior would only lead to trouble. Drinking wine habitually made a person a pig; drinking a lot of wine habitually made a person "jabber and jump about . . . silly and nasty like a monkey."[38]

I think there was more going on than Dionysus's detractors' accusations of sex romps. I believe we are witnessing one of the deepest traditions known to humankind, traditions that began in the Neolithic Age, as we see in the primordial poetigenic art of the Tassili caves. These traditions are the ultimate outcome of the human mind's struggle with bicameralism. They answered both how we got *here* and where we go when we go *there*. They explained why it rained. They explained what men had to do with the regenerative cycle. And most importantly for this work, they told the occult story of the chemical wedding between wine and pharmaka. Going back for a moment to the myth of Hathor and the mandrake beer that we met earlier, we can perhaps see an early cry of this particular aspect of the Sacred Marriage. What saved humanity was the joining of mandrake (representing the feminine in this case) with beer (representing the masculine). Ra couldn't simply give Hathor beer due to its well-attested ability to cause aggression in some drinkers. She might have redoubled her slaughter of humanity! But the mandrake pharmakon tempered the drink's less-desirable effects. When the revelers swigged their elephantine mandrake beer on Hathor's Feast Day, perhaps they too saw a symbol, an echo, of the Sacred Marriage in their cups.

DIVERGENT ROADS MEET

All this leads us back to our question of the kykeon at Eleusis. I believe the Eleusinian entheogen—whether ergot, opium, or otherwise—symbolized the pharmakon without the wine, perhaps in recognition of the Mycenaean people's own established pharmacopeia *before* the introduction of the male, Dionysus, into the Sacred Marriage. Demeter's rejection of wine from the royal family in favor of the kykeon thus reveals a clue about the developmental history of this particular myth; or more correctly, it shows how two mystery traditions grew out of a common (presumably) African ancestor—an ancestor that most probably began as a primarily female rite, as preserved at Eleusis. And we just might see the matrifocal residues in another story about Inanna's favorite possession: her vagina. In a fragmentary story titled *Inanna and the God of Wisdom,* we read, ". . .[H]er vulva was wonderous to behold. Rejoicing at her wonderous vulva, the young woman Inanna applauded herself." Other texts from Sumer speak of Inanna's "silver vulva" (*urû*),[39] perhaps a preservation of the original matrifocal narrative. Indeed, in *Inanna and the God of Wisdom,* Inanna receives the *me:* all those things necessary to birth civilization.[40] But somewhere along its journey eastward toward the Fertile Crescent, the male's role in impregnation was realized; a discovery that did not make it into the proto-Grecian areas, or at least, hadn't found its way into those early entheogenic ceremonies at Eleusis. Thus, when the rite circled back westward, through Egypt, it met with a version of the Grain Goddess mystery in Greece that was in all probability *closer* to the matrifocal African original. This bridge between Dumuzi in Sumer and Dionysus in Greece is most notable in the myths of Osiris, who was both "lord of wine preparation" but also a god of vegetation, having knowledge of psychedelic pharmaka.[41]

Once arriving in Greece, Dionysus entered the story of Demeter and Persephone as the divine masculine that had been lacking in the original matrifocal story. Some even began to call him Kissos, the "ivy" that his devotees ate to produce a wineless drunkenness.[42] The krater from

Magnae Grecia that shows him wearing the opium crown of the Poppy Goddess certainly points in that direction. In fact, the two women who entertain him on the krater may very well be Demeter and Kore.

And we literally get to watch these two ancient, diverging historical trends come face to face when Demeter rejects the wine in favor of the kykeon while at the palace of Eleusis.

Such is the labrynthine world of ancient psychedelic mystery traditions.

5

THESSALIAN ROOTS

Psychedelic Magic in Ancient
Greece and Rome

5000 BCE–500 CE

These phenomena are brought about by compulsion, through the agency of herbs and enchantments.

PLINY THE ELDER, *NATURAL HISTORY,* 25.5

At last, night had fallen.

The residual purples and oranges of twilight that moments ago had projected across the whole of the firmament slowly vanished, riding on the sun's tail, as it, too, drowned in the horizon. The vault of stars that guards the heavens unlocked, pouring tiny diamonds into the ether. Beaches along the jagged coastline of Thessaly looked especially beatific under the auspicious blessings of a full moon as it is charioted across the sky on a cool, midsummer breeze. A priestess positioned herself on the tallest rock overlooking the threshold where the fluid ocean gently caressed the sturdy shore. She disrobed, then pulled a small brazier, a simple iron dagger doused in sulphur, and a flint rock out of a sack. Striking dagger to flint, the priestess created a spark that ignited the coals in the brazier. For a moment, she stared intently at the growing flames, her pupils enchanted by this inexpressible fire. Returning to her task, she pulled a smaller satchel out of her pack, eagerly removing the string that secured its contents. Dipping her fingers into the cloth, the priestess pulled out a handful of dried foliage—conceivably cannabis, or opium, maybe mandrake, possibly henbane, or, most probably, some mixture of several. She dropped the florae onto the burning coal. Unfolding reality with ancient verse and sacred herb, she sent enchantments out to the stars, drawing down the moon so as to redouble the efficacy of her spirit plants.* As her visions grew more intense, she sang even louder, pulling her consciousness deeper into a prophetic state. In a moment, she would collapse onto the ground as her soul flew from her body, entering that anomalous space between the living and the dead.

Extensive trade routes and maritime systems meant fun and exotic psychoactives could be imported and exported from all across the ancient Mediterranean. Whether a person desired cannabis from Anatolia, trimma wine from Greece, opium from Egypt, hippomanes from Arcadia, or any number of exotic pharmaka imported from Persia, such demands could be met.

Despite those expansive trade ways, most everyone agreed that all the best psyche-magical plants came from one place: Thessaly, an area on the eastern coast of the Grecian mainland that touches the Aegean Sea. Thessalian roots and herbs contained such power that they could serve as a vector to carry incantations from the priestess's lips to the goddess's ears. The poet Marcus Lucanus (39–65 CE) wrestles with this ability of the Thessalian priestess to connect with the gods through pharmaka in his *Pharsalia* (c. 65 CE) when he complains in envy, "Why are the gods so anxious to obey [the priestess's] incantations and their herbs . . . why do they fear to ignore them?"[1]

---

*Called *virus lunare* ("moon juice") in the ancient sources. See Mirecki and Meyer, *Magic and Ritual,* 383.

By the time of classical Greece (fifth century BCE), the Fireside Goddess had become the psychedelic witch. And she hardly lived a monotone existence. We already explored the entheogens and mystheogens used in the cults of Demeter, Ceres, and Dionysus in the previous chapters. But invoking deities wasn't the only use of these phenomenal plants. Such pharmaka were used for a variety of magical reasons in the ancient world: to raise the dead from their tombs,[2] to shapeshift,[3] to stop someone from shapeshifting,[4] to call up ghosts,[5] to tell fortunes,[6] to heal (as we saw in an earlier chapter), and to gain the affections of a lover (discussed below). Skilled herbalists, witches, and priestesses produced many of these mixtures, which they sold to regular people for any one (or many more) of the uses mentioned above.

We even know some of the earliest names of psychedelic witches, or at least, we still have the designations that ancient authors ascribed to them: Hecate, Medea, and Circe. For certain, the tales we read about these witches in the epics are all fiction. But they *do* tell us something about how ancient people viewed the breadth of psyche-magical possibilities. Supplementing these archetypes with real, historical personages from antiquity allows us to discover the polygonal pythiagenic practices of the psychedelic witch in ancient Greece and Rome.

Considered by many in the ancient world the homeland of witches, Thessaly first gained recognition as the birthplace of the mother of the occult, Hecate. Hecate was said to be insatiable, surpassing her infamously cruel father, Perses, "in her boldness and lawlessness."[7] She would eventually find credit among mortals as the overseer of crossroads, magic, and occult knowledge. Her esoteric inclinations included being a "keen contriver of many drugs." She also points to an ancient entheogenic priestess role: it was her duty to find and test all available spirit plants. Such excursions turned up many interesting florae, indeed. One of her discoveries, the powerful narcotic aconite, would later turn up in some early modern flying ointments.[8] The ancients associated

Fig. 5.1. The triform Hecate (dog, woman, horse) holds the laurels, which "manifests the fiery power of the sun," (*ramum quidem Laureum, quoniam a Sole ignea fit*) and opium, symbolic of the underworld.

Hecate with the moon and forged relics of her flanked by torches. Sometimes artists depicted her holding keys. Other times, she appears as a dog spirit from the underworld, which later gave rise to the practice of using dogs to pull mandrake from the ground.* In a sixteenth century manuscript, *Hieroglyphica, sive, de sacris Aegyptiorvm aliarvmqve gentivm literis commentari* (1575), the woodcutter portrays Hecate holding burning laurel leaf-wrap in one hand and an opium stalk in the other.[9] All of these attributes—moon, torch, psychedelic pharmaka (like aconite, opium, and mandrake), dog, and keys—point to her connection with the underworld and the mystheogens that unlock its secrets.

Hecate, of course, passed such psyche-magical horticulture onto her daughters, Medea and Circe, the latter later lauded by Pliny as another expert in "plants endowed with potent effects."[10] Circe's potions were the original *pocula amatoria* (or "love philters")—essentially recreational pharmaka in the ancient world, which included any number of psyche-delic and symbolic ingredients, usually with wine or wash water serving as a base.[11] And yet, Circe is most known for using her pharmaka to transform a person into an animal. Transformations of humans into

*For example, Cerberus, the original three-headed "hell hound," guarded the gates of the underworld.

things like animals, rocks, and trees appear all over the Greco-Roman literary landscape. Such transformations were often used as revenge, say when Galanthis successfully deceived Lucina, Goddess of Childbirth, to allow Alcmene (mother of Herakles) to bear another infant. Galanthis celebrated her ruse by mocking Lucina, which was always a bad move. Enraged, Lucina "caught [Galanthis] by the hair," and dragged her down to the floor. As Galanthis tried to get back up again, she felt herself arching over, unable to stand. Worse still, Galanthis started growing tiny furs out of her skin. By the time she realized what was happening it was too late; Lucina had transformed her into a weasel.[12]

But Circe didn't have the natural magical transforming powers of Lucina, and so relied on pharmaka to achieve her ends. However, I do not think her potions originally caused the legendary transformations found in Homer's *Odyssey*. They came to represent the dark side (and eventual consequences) of perpetual indulgence. The nature of Circe's recreational love potions would be remembered quite differently by authors who exaggerated their effects in order to make a broader warning about recreational love potion mixtures; they were not recreational and there was nothing loving about them. They dulled the mind so much that the imbibers forgot all about their lives and responsibilities, rendering them no better than beasts. With a stroke of Homer's pen, Circe's psyche-magical love philters metamorphosed into a metamorphosis metaphor; drinking them, it was said, transformed a person into a base animal. One is reminded of the story of Noah's vineyard in the Midrash Tanhuma, which perhaps borrowed from these earlier pagan traditions.

This, I believe, is how the ancients explained addiction to both pharmaka and sex.

And the culprit that tied the two together was love magic.

MAGICA EROTICA

One of the most complicated forms of psychedelic magic in the ancient world to adjudicate must surely have been love magic. In no other magical law arbitration did intent matter more. Additionally, even a malicious intention could be pardoned by that all-powerful legal exoneration mechanism: social status.[13] The ancient annuls detail several accounts regarding the occult nature of pharmaka that caused a person to lose her or his senses and any semblance of self-control. Such magic usually included ingesting a love philter. Both Theophrastus and Dioscorides name the highly psychoactive mandrake as the most sought after ingredient in those potions. Mandrake, when found in love philters anyway, was even called "Circe's plant" and used to excite love."[14] Helen's famous scene in Homer's *Odyssey,* wherein she mixes nepenthes (an unspecified pharmakon) into wine in order to fall into a blissful stupor for a day, is not tied to any religious or spiritual practice but is more closely related to what can be called recreational use. Rumors circulated that Homer himself had tried nepenthes (perhaps *poetigenically?*).[15] Nepenthes supposedly came from Thebes, where women used it medicinally to cure "anger and sorrow."[16] Nepenthes seems to have skirted a line between recreational and medicinal use. But maybe this shouldn't surprise us. Is not a brief reprieve, even something as simple as a coffee or cigarette break, somewhat mentally healthy? To say nothing of the delightful health benefits of magic mushrooms and ecstatic dancing.

Two kinds of love magic appear in our ancient Greco-Roman records, each having the potential (or not) of involving psychedelic pharmaka. The first was *philia,* a kind of magic usually reserved for women who wished to keep their husbands faithful.[17] Philia spells worked somewhat like this: the wife would feed her husband a stimulating or pleasurable pharmakon, which would both intoxicate him and set afire his carnal instincts. He would, in effect, become "addicted" to both the pharmakon and (as was hoped) the supplier. This would keep him from seeking extramarital affairs.

The other major kind of love magic was called *erôs* and had more to do with gaining a lover. Like all magic in the ancient world, both philia and erôs magical procedures may or may not employ psychedelic phar-maka. Let's briefly peruse some of the times that they did.

Since using love potions was mostly a private affair, we only tend to hear general warnings about their use. Early Common Era authors often referred to the "daughters of Deianeira," those women who "devise love potions against their husbands and control them through pleasure." But the practice was a double-edged sword, wrote Plutarch, for the potions so deteriorated the spouses that they became "dull-witted, degenerate fools."[18] This might have been the result of opium found in the pocula amatoria. Indeed, it is highly addicting (guar-anteeing the men stay loyal) and can damage the body through pro-longed and regular use.

Christian authors in the third century followed their pagan prede-cessors when it came to love philters. The frustrations from holy celi-bacy scream off the page of one of St. Basil's letters when he writes, "If anyone has concocted some magic philtre for some other reason, and then causes death, I count this as intentional. Women frequently endeavor to draw men to love them by incantation and magic knots, and give them drugs which dull their intelligence."[19] A homily written by John Chrysostom, archbishop of Constantinople (c. 350–400 CE), blames a love philter for the Fall in Eden. Accordingly, Satan gave Eve a love philter to drink to deceive her senses. In that altered state, Eve foolishly ate the fruit from the Tree of Knowledge of Good and Evil.[20] It is interesting that Chrysostom specifically blames the pharmakon for Eve's actions: "Listen to the account Scripture gives so as to learn that she was bent on this course *after* receiving that deadly poison through the serpent's advice. . . . Why was it, after all, that before that wicked demon's advice she entertained no such idea, had no eyes for the tree, nor noticed its attractiveness?"[21]

Many descriptions of philia love magic read much like this. They are usually misogynistic attacks, which place the blame on the woman (*surprise, surprise*) despite there being little evidence that sharing these potions was anything but consensual.

❦

Let's get a little closer to these spells by looking at the ways erôs magic might be used. Here we meet a few interesting procedures for gaining the affection of another by ingesting some kind of pharmakon. These spells focus on the selfish desires of an interested party taking the potion in a private, ritual ceremony. The *Greek Magical Papyri* features a complex love spell called Sword of Dardanos that incorporates both ancient Grecian and Jewish magic and a long prayer to Aphrodite and was designed specifically for a male magician. The formula instructs the magician to find a magnetic stone and carve a scene of Aphrodite sitting on top of Psyche. Above her head the magician should write "ACHMAGE RARPEPESI"; below Aphrodite, he should scrawl an image of Eros "standing on the vault of heaven, holding a burning torch and burning Psyche." On the other side of the stone the lovelorn individual must draw a scene of Psyche and Eros embracing each other with the letters "sssssss" under Eros's feet and "ĒĒĒĒĒĒĒ" under Psyche's feet. The stone should be placed in the mouth of the magician as he says a long spell: "I call upon you, author of creation. . . . Turn the 'soul' of her NN to me NN, so that she may love me, so she may feel passion for me, so that she may give me what's in her power. Let her say to me what is in her soul because I have called upon your great name." A gold leaf should then be inscribed with angelic names of the Hebrew mystery traditions: Thouriel, Michael, Gabriel, Ouriel, Misael, Irrael, Istrael. The leaves are then fed to a partridge, which should be killed and worn around the neck.

The magician is now ready to ingest the pythiagenic potion both through burning the pharmakon as incense and then drinking a magical concoction composed of the same ingredients: manna (whatever that is), four drams* each of storax, opium, and frankincense, and a half dram of dried fig. The magician has now transformed (at least, psychologically)

---

*A dram in ancient Greece equated roughly to 3.30 grams. That's a lot of opium!

into the "likeness of the god or daimon whom [the object of affection] worships." He is to go to her house and say a prayer, then return home, burn more pharmaka incense, and set the dinner table for his expected guest.[22]

Another instance of this kind of psyche-magical love potion also turns up in another ancient book of spells, *The Demotic Magical Papyrus*. The operation is less involved than the aforementioned, skipping the long preambles and going right for the psyche-magical potion.

> One mingles various ingredients in a cup of wine [thus making a trimma] and says over it "I am he of Abydos . . . I am this figure of one drowned that testifieth by writing . . . as to which the blood of Osiris bore witness . . . when it was poured into this cup, this wine. Give it, blood of Osiris [that he?] gave to Isis to make her feel love in her heart . . . give it, the blood of [the magician] . . . to the daughter of so and so in this cup, this bowl of wine, today, to cause her to feel a love for him in her heart, the love that Isis felt for Osiris when she was seeking after him everywhere."[23]

But what about women? They certainly engaged in this kind of magic as well. In Theocritus's classic poems about rustic life, called the *Idylls,* we read the lyrics of "The Spell" (from his second idyll, *Pharmakeutria,* c. third century BCE). Not a magician himself, instead a poet and scribe, Theocritus was an outsider. As such his passage detailing the enchantments remains a medley of unrelated magical musings.[24] In the very least, "The Spell" shows us how Theocritus understood philia magic in his own day.

One of the characters, Simaetha, is a young woman desperate to keep the affections of her lover, Delphis. To do so, she uses philia magic. First, Simaetha calls out to Hecate to render her love potions "no less powerful than those of Circe, Medea, or blonde Perimede." She charms herself with fumigations, throwing symbolic ingredients like barley and bay leaf and the classic (though obscure) sex magic pharmakon *hippomanes* onto a blaze, which she calls a "fire-philter." Only she intends to direct the oncoming madness brought about by the burning hippomanes not to herself (as the Sword of Dardanos directs) but rather onto her lover, Delphis. She calls out, "[Hippomanes] makes every filly, every flying mare run a-raving in the hills. In like case Delphis may I see, aye, coming to my door . . . like one that is raving mad!"[25] Maybe the idea was to build herself into an ecstatic frenzy via psychedelic incense in hopes of sending those very feelings to Delphis via her incantation?

If this doesn't work, Simaetha has a contingency plan, one she learned from "an Assyrian stranger mistress."[26] She will powder a newt and make an "ill drink" to give to Delphis.[27]* It's clear that if Simaetha can't have Delphis, she will make certain no one can.

And so the legacy of Circe's potions saw condemnation by authorities and poets. They too often stirred a person's lesser instincts, so best to keep them safe in the temples, where they could be used properly. As for Circe's sister Medea, a wealth of information regarding her magic survives.

ENTHEOGENS AND MYSTHEOGENS

Medea was a priestess of the cult of Artemis-Hecate, and so picked her plants in the wildest and weirdest ways! Deep in the recesses of the House of Aeetes, where legend holds Medea grew up, one would find a sacred grove filled with laurels, trees, and cornels parading the interior sanctuary. Mortals were forbidden to enter this sacred space, for it was reserved only for Medea to gather her magical plants. A floral plethora of psychedelia awaited her: mandrake, opium, aconite, and "many other noxious plants grew" in that sacred grove.[28]

And it is here where we may find the famous witch. Standing naked, Medea dipped her loosened hair three times in a river that ran through

---

*Virgil seems to have lifted this story from Theocritus to create his own scene of philia magic performed by a Thessalian girl. He literally titles his eighth eclogue *Pharmaceutria* (such were copyright laws in those days).

the grove. Falling into a divine frenzy, reaching for the stars, howling at the moon, invoking Mother Gaia and Hecate under the influence of the "piles of incense" heaped onto an altar, she called out:

> *O faithful Night, regard my mysteries!*
> *O golden-lighted Stars! O softly-moving Moon—*
> *genial, your fire succeeds the heated day!*
> *O Hecate! grave three-faced queen of these*
> *charms of enchanters and enchanters, arts!*
> *O fruitful Earth, giver of potent herbs!*
> *O gentle Breezes and destructive Winds!*
> *You Mountains, Rivers, Lakes and sacred Groves,*
> *and every dreaded god of silent Night, attend*
> *upon me!*[29]

But such use of psychedelics to invoke or otherwise communicate a desire to the goddesses and gods turns up outside fiction. During his travels throughout the Grecian lands, the geographer Pausanias (c. 110–180 CE) stumbled on a cadre of priestesses in ceremony to the goddess Hera. These holy women shaped into garlands and burned as offerings an herb that Pausanias called asterion. Earlier textual evidence from Dioscorides (living two generations before Pausanias) confirms asterion as cannabis.[30] Incidentally, Hecate's mother, Asteria, suggests another association with cannabis. Asteria did after all engage in some of the earliest forms of dream divination, perhaps spurred on by moderate use of cannabis.

One scholar has observed that the consonants *s, t, r* appear in the names of a variety of psychoactive plants. For example, another potent plant medicine called satyrion was used by the ancients as a recreational pharmakon, an aphrodisiac.[31] Unfortunately, Pausanias does not record in what way these Hera priestesses used their cannabis pharmakon. Entheogenically? Mystheogenically? Some other way that is simply lost to us?

If we cannot know how cannabis was used by the priestesses Pausanias describes, we can at least have an idea of how it was used mystheogenically in other temples to Hera. In an obscure account, *De dea Syria* (*On the Syrian Goddess*), written by Lucian of Samosata sometime in the mid-second century, we get some insight. Lucian had traveled through Syria to Hieropolis, a city "architecturally and spiritually" based on earlier Egyptian designs. Hieropolis was dedicated to the great Mother Goddess known in Greece at the time as Hera;[32] although people in Syria referred to her as Astarte, a name with our familiar consonants of *s, t, r*.[33] The Temple of Astarte in Hieropolis was among "the richest in the world," where "the gods speak" to their devotees. Lucian takes a cautious stance. He had heard many tales from many mouths, many of which he didn't believe rang true. A careful chronicler, he decided to make a personal visit to the temple at Hieropolis to investigate and record what occurred beyond the hallowed walls. His account survives as one of the few to describe temple rites to Hera, making it invaluable to us today.

Entering through the northern entryway, Lucian first stumbled on a couple of dicks: two phalli erected in stone had greeted every initiate since the days of Dionysus. A puppet sat at the top of one of the heads. A priest would climb to the top of the penis, remove the puppet, and pray to Dionysus. Then he would receive gifts from pilgrims and return in kind with blessings. Promptly passing the penis priest, Lucian walked up a wooden ramp, where he came before two golden doors that opened to a large, golden room. It is here where the fragrance of a "heavenly perfume" enveloped Lucian. The scent "lifts you to the shrine's inner hallway," toward the large chamber where golden statues of Hera (flanked by two lions) and Zeus (flanked by bulls) greet their new disciples.[34] Can it be any surprise that those who attended the rites were dosed with the sweet perfumes *before* meeting the divinities?

Just outside the temple sat a beautiful lake, which housed sacred fish used in the daily ritual. As the congregants gathered around the water, an altar covered in colorful ribbons rose out of the center of the lake. Lucian theorized that the altar sat on a column that was somehow raised and lowered, perhaps through a pulley system of sorts. As the flock took their places around the lake, priestesses and priests swam out to the altar to burn incense on it, which wafted over to the people gathered around the rim of the water.

The devotees watched as the priestesses and priests acted out the holy drama. A priestess taking on the role of Hera was brought down to the water. She must see the sacred fish before the priest (Zeus) who follows behind her, for should Zeus see the sacred fish first, all the congregants would die. These were Hera's people, so she could not allow it. She blocked and pleaded with and eventually fought off Zeus. After Hera's triumph (which probably staved off more than a few panic attacks from the stoned congregants), she dove into the lake, "to herself a goddess born like Atargatis/Aphrodite in the sea."[35]

The reason I believe Lucian was talking about cannabis here is threefold: First, he is in a Temple of Hera, whose worshippers, as we saw, were no strangers to that magnificent, medicinal, safe, heavenly, fun, philosophically motivating, universally useful herb. Second, Lucian says the incense came from "sweet Arabia," which may implicate cannabis, known since time immemorial as the "sweet cane" (*kaneh bosm*) of the East. Third, Lucian mentions an undeniable feature of cannabis known all too well to every teenager who has ever tried to avoid her parents as she sneaks home after a party: the smell "stays in the folds of your garments [and] on your body."[36]

Admittedly, this is not as confirming as Pausanias's direct textual reference of asterion use in Grecian Hera worship. But placing Lucian's account within the context of both Pausanias's travelogue and the *s, t, r* consonants, cannabis may very well have been the strong redolent odor that stuck onto Lucian's clothes and supplemented the drama of Hera and Zeus. Should this be the case, it would offer a fine example of the ancient mystheogenic experience.

Returning to literary sources, we see that a priestess may not have always used her knowledge of entheogenic and mystheogenic operations for strictly spiritual purposes. Medea, as expected, provides a fictional—though I would argue still archetypal—demonstration of such instances. Let's examine her role in the story of Jason and the Argonauts.

After joining Jason and the Argonauts on their quest to recover the Golden Fleece, Medea brings them to the home of her father, Aeetes. Deep in the House of Aeetes, past the gates of Artemis and into the sacred grove, the fleece swung gently on the branch of an oak tree. Guarding it was a gigantic snake sporting golden scales, its body coiled around the trunk. The snake never slept, vigilantly surveying the area to quickly detect any intruders. The party faced a dilemma: to get to the snake overseeing the fleece they would first have to pass into the sacred grove itself, but they couldn't. Mortals (in this case, noninitiates) enjoyed no such privileges, forbidden as they were from entry into this garden of psychedelic mysteries.

Only Medea could help. As a priestess of the cult of Artemis-Hecate, she could appease Artemis by initiating Jason into the mystery, allowing him entry into the sacred grove.

Here, we get to see the psychedelic priestess at work!

Tucked away in the crypts of the manor, Medea's father, Aeetes, kept a storehouse of exotic incense for use in his religious observations. These mixes were no doubt created from the flora Medea ritualistically reaped from the sacred grove. As such, she knew where to find this storeroom to smuggle some truly psychedelic mixtures from the coffers. Most likely taking the aconite, mandrake, or opium (or all three and more) that reportedly grew in the grove, Medea brought the pharmaka to Jason and the Argonauts, who waited for her outside the Gates of Artemis. Medea built a large fire and threw the pharmaka onto the blaze. She then instructed Jason in the proper rites: He must don the dark robes of an Artemis-Hecate pledge. Then, fashioning two small figurines out of barley meal, he followed up by sacrificing three black puppies in homage to the dead. The puppy blood didn't just honor the dead but also revered Artemis, to whom the black dogs were sacred. Wringing out the puppies like wet rags, Jason mixed their sacrificial blood with copper sulphate, bronze-plant, and other herbs and stuffed the concoction back into the slit tummies of the forfeited canines. The carcasses were then thrown onto the fire along with Medea's pharmaka. Jason sounded cymbals and made his prayer to the goddess.

As the "unclean flame sent high its smoke," the mystheogenic visions faithfully seeped into the minds of the participants (despite the profanation of the rites). Manifesting in the fire, figures began to take shape: Pandora, with her body of iron, along with the mother of herbal occultism, Hecate, and the Furies. The holy herbs Medea had thrown onto the fire must have been particularly strong psychedelically, for Jason watched a horse head draw forth from Hecate's left shoulder, forming from her right shoulder, a canine cranium. The goddesses, Pandora, Hecate, and Poinai danced around the fire pit. Artemis had been pleased; her statue that guarded the gates turned its eyes to heaven, and the large bolts that had secured the door leading into the sacred grove loosened. Jason invoked sleep on the snake, and Medea used her pharmaka to kill it. The Golden Fleece was retrieved.[37]

The obvious fictional nature of the story aside, we are offered a window into how these different kinds of pharmaka found employment. The psychedelic witch in her role as priestess had access to all kinds of supernatural privileges that regular people simply did not. Such privileges could be used, sometimes, even to profane the sacred. In this particular example, I would say that Medea used a mystheogen pythiagenically; she used a sacred rite for magical purposes.

The message from the ancient world is clear: intent changes the nature of every psychedelic spell.

PROPHECY AND DIVINATION

As shown in the last chapter, some forms of divination included Dionysian orgiastic entheogenic revelry. Not all divination methods were so involved (or fun) though. Some did not include any kind of pharmakon at all.* Other times, the choice to use pharmaka to induce visions was up to the individual prophet, as we see with fire divination. Two kinds of fire divination existed in the ancient world. The first, pyromancy, involved looking at the inexpressible flames of a roaring fire. A pythiagenic pharmakon may or may not have been included, depending on the operator. However, another kind of fire divination, libanomany, involved burning incense and prophesying based on how the smoke lifted into the air. Such divination operations may have included the psychedelic thesagle mentioned by Pliny (with no further description of what it is), who notes how magi use it to enter a divine trance.[38] The second-century Syrian Christian Tatian, in his *Address to the Greeks,* admonished women who "lose [their] senses by the fumes of frankincense." Now, frankincense in those days ought not be confused with the more innocuous forms we encounter today. Ancient frankincense might hold any level of potency when burned and inhaled. Modern clinical trials investigating some forms of frankincense found them to contain tetrahydrocannabinol, the active compound in cannabis.[39] Even Virgil differentiates between regular frankincense and "the strongest frankincense."[40] The physician Dioscorides, no stranger to an assortment of pharmaka, recognizes the potency of Syrian frankincense.[41]

Sometimes pharmaka were used somnitheogenically to trigger prophetic visions. Aristophanes (c. 440–390 BCE) wastes no time creating such a scene in his play *Wasps.* As the opening curtains reveal the first act, two of Philocleon's slaves discuss visions they had in dreams after drinking a laced wine.[42] In other cases, sacred waters may have emitted similar vapors as those in the adyton at Delphi, as we see with the oracle of Colophon, who would drink from a spring to induce visions. Pliny even noted that the oracle who drank from the sacred spring of Colophon would soon see deleterious effects from the water. Indeed,

---

*Aeromancy was the practice of throwing sand into the air and studying how the wind separated the grains.

his life would be "shortened."[43] What charged this particular water, Iamblichus (c. 245 – 325) records, was not "for everyone to know." But according to his description, the water had been possessed like no other kind: "For the divine . . . illuminates the spring, filling it with its own prophetic power."[44] Whether through some naturally intoxicating property of the water or through the addition of pharmaka, the oracle of Colophon "begins to prophesy." There is still another possibility, one not triggered by any pharmakon but rather through a biological prompt. Before drinking the water, the oracle fasts for a day and night.[45] Such a sharp change in the body's metabolism can produce an altered state of consciousness, no pharmakon required.[46]

These prophetic capabilities would one day be sold to the public at large.

And you had choices.

You could either visit a wise woman who would use her psychedelics and enchantments to deliver messages to you from beyond the realm of the living. Or, should you fancy yourself a more intrepid seeker, any number of visionary prophecies could be experienced by taking part in a rite yourself. We even have a sourced picture of what this looked like by the first century of the Common Era. Pausanias, the same traveler who encountered the cannabis-using priestesses of Hera, detailed a complicated ritual that he personally endured for his initiation into the mysteries of the oracles of Trophonius. First, he had to lodge in a special building for a few days while feasting on the meat of sacrifices made to Trophonius, Hera, Demeter (called Europa), Apollo, Zeus, and Cronus. A diviner was present during all these sacrificial meals to interpret the viscera of the slaughtered animal so that Pausanias may know beforehand how Trophonius will receive him. On the final night of preparation, a ram was slaughtered under incantations to Agamedes; for whatever the earlier sacrificial intestines may have foretold, only the ram could confirm their prognosis.

Pausanias was then led to the river Hercyna by two adolescent boys who first washed and then anointed him. The anointing oil could have been psychedelic[47] but equally may have been a nonpsychoactive, pleasant fragrant used in the ritual. I say this because I think the actual mystheogen was not the oil but rather the drink, called the Water of Forgetfulness, that the priests gave Pausanias to imbibe so that he may "forget all he has been thinking of hitherto"*; he then drank from another cup, this one containing the Water of Memory, so that he may recall his visions. We can all only hypothesize, but perhaps the cups contained two kinds of plant ingredients that worked synergistically with each other. Or maybe the drinks contained different psychoactives: an opiate in the Water of Forgetfulness to relax the initiate into the experience; the Water of Memory may have contained something stronger and stimulating (like a mushroom) enough to keep the initiate awake and focused on the visions.

As the elixir took effect, Pausanias prayed to an image and was then ready to see the oracle. He descended into a lower cave, cut with "the most accurate masonry," to a shrine that would send him visions. He finally emerged and was seated in a special chair (also called Memory), wherein he shared his vision with the others. The experience must have been quite the ordeal. Pausanias gives us another clue as to the possibility of psychedelic pharmaka involved in the rite. He tells us that after the visions fade and the person is brought back up to the light of day, she or he may be "paralyzed with terror and unconscious both of himself and of his surroundings."[48] In other words, despite the termination of the rite, an inductee may still feel the effects from the pharmaka.†

With Pausanias, we see the range of cult rites in ancient Greece: some involved cannabis for obscure (possibly fertility) ceremonies, like those

---

*One is reminded of the nepenthes of Helen.

†Pausanias records other instances of cult initiation that don't require an entheogen, such as the Isis-worshipping Greeks in Tithorea. But then, he also doesn't give a full description of those ceremonies, warning of two others who "described what [they] had seen, and immediately died." Macmullen, *Paganism and Christianity,* 46.

to the goddess Hera; others involved opaque though nonetheless sacred substances to enter a dream-like trance so as to receive prophecies from gods like Trophonius; and still others, like those mysteries of Isis (at least a Greek form of them), may not have used pharmaka at all.

Still, there are more pythiagenic spells to peruse.

MALEFICIA

A skilled professional gained the most power and wealth by selling her services to warlords and general kings. An early example of purely mercenary pythiagenic magic can be seen in an act of warfare from around 1000 BCE. The Athenian king Cnopus had waged war against the Ionian state. His target? The city of Erythrae, an area in western Asia Minor (modern Turkey) across the Aegean Sea from the Grecian mainland. An attentive king, Cnopus first sought counsel with an oracle before attacking. The oracle advised Cnopus to locate a certain Thessalian priestess of Hecate named Chrysame and make her the general of his armies. Chrysame's profession as a priestess of Hecate assured Cnopus of success.

She did not disappoint. Of the Hecate school, Chrysame knew all about psychedelic pharmaka and how they worked. She devised an elaborate sacrificial ritual that was really a ruse meant to fool Cnopus's enemies in Erythrae. First, she ordered a bull be brought before her; she then decorated it in a way that was perhaps usual for priestesses of Hecate: ribbons of purple and gold covered the animal's back, garlands hung from its neck, and even gold shielded the creature's horns. Chrysame also mixed a "medicinal herb that would excite madness" into the bull's fodder and held him in the stall while the pharmakon took effect.

Whatever the pharmakon was, it was apparently powerful enough to transfer its active properties from the bull to a person, should the person eat the bull's meat. A likely pharmakon in this instance might be a psychedelic mushroom, as such transferences (at least through the urinary tract) have been observed in reindeer.[49] In any event, Chrysame walked bravely toward the enemy lines and set up an altar. She ordered the mystified bull brought to the altar for sacrifice in honor of the Athenian gods. The bull, deranged from whatever Chrysame put in his food, broke free and ran toward the enemy camp. The Erythrae army saw this as a sign of the futility of the Athenian gods and the superiority of the Ionian gods. We can imagine them laughing at this cheap "priestess," all the while Chrysame suppressed a shrewd smile from her lips lest she give away the plot.

Excitedly, the soldiers captured the bull and sacrificially slaughtered it to their gods—exactly what Chrysame wanted them to do, for sacrificed animals were then feasted on as a way to share a meal with the goddesses and gods. Chrysame kept close watch; once the soldiers, well fed from their sacrificial dinner, began to run around the camp in a frenzy, she ordered the Athenian troops into the camp. The Erythrae soldiers' bad trips ended with sharp blades through their chests.

Chrysame finally released that smile.[50]

Another instance of a holy woman using her knowledge of pharmaka in ways less entheogenic or mystheogenic and more pythiagenic rests with Camma (birth and death unknown) from Galatia (central Turkey). Camma was not only "virtuous and fair" but also, as a priestess of Artemis, seated in "the office of highest rank" possible by a Galatian woman.[51] As such, she was always adorned in the most magnificent regalia when overseeing all the public sacrifices and ceremonial processions. On a personal level, she is remembered as kind to her subordinates, modest, and humble.[52] Her marriage to the Galatian tetrarch Sinatus made for quite the power couple. Another Galatian tetrarch, Sinorix, was jealous of their betrothal and murdered Sinatus. He then forced himself on Camma. Eventually, Camma, pressured by her friends and relations, caved and promised to marry Sinorix.

She retired to the Temple of Artemis and sent for Sinorix, as well as others who were to attend the wedding ceremony. She prepared "poisoned mead," which she first poured in libation on her altar. She then drank and gave it to Sinorix to drink. The chalice empty, Camma fell to her knees before the altar and cried out, "I thank you, venerable Artemis, for granting me in this your temple a glorious revenge for my murdered husband!"

With that, both bride and groom dropped dead.[53]

NONLETHAL PYTHIAGENIC MALEFICIA

Not all mercenary magic involved killing an enemy. Sometimes an operator simply wanted to drive a person crazy or torment her or his sleep with pharmaka that caused turbulent dreams. One spell for putting someone in a cataleptic state included pounding scammony root and a dram of opium with milk and secretly slipping the pharmaka into someone's food. If a magician wished to rid herself of this person for a longer period of time, she should add an ounce of both mandrake and henbane. The magician should carefully administer the potion secretly over time "four portions . . . from morning to evening." Considering the lethal nature of the pharmaka involved, an overdose would be difficult to avoid if given that amount in one shot.[54] Instead, this would slowly lull the target into a deep sleep, so that one could go about one's business uninterrupted for a while. We have not but a few references of ancient peoples using pharmaka (usually involving *philia magica*) in such ways. Unfortunately, in the records that dealt with such psychemagical infractions, words like *bewitched* or *dazzled* and ideas like "drove . . . mad with drugs"[55] or "ruined his mind [with drugs]"[56] are often all we have.

But what did this actually entail? Let's finish this section of our journey through the history of ancient psychedelic magic with two final examples, the first from history, the second featuring our archetypal wise woman, Medea.

Unlike Camma, whom we met above, Aretaphila had no intention of killing her husband, Nicocrates, the "tyrant of Cyrene." But she did want to make his life a living Hades. She endeavored to slip him a pharmaka, not strong enough to kill him but certainly strong enough to cause alterations in his psychological and physiological makeup. Her plan worked. Despite Aretaphila's arrest and subsequent torture, the courts found her innocent on the behest of Nicocrates himself. Unrecorded is exactly why Nicocrates had a change of heart. He even began to treat her with respect and appreciation—lest she unleash her magic against him again. He would later be killed by his own brother, Leander, due to the smooth talking of Aretaphila.[57]

Let's close this chapter with my favorite example of pythiagenic magic from antiquity. Our resident witch Medea takes center stage as she heads with Jason and the Argonauts to Iolcus, a city in Thessaly. When she first met the Argonauts on a beach in a precinct of Helios, the Golden Fleece remained under the control of Pelias, king of Iolcus. Medea promised to kill Pelias, but first she had to ingratiate herself into his home. Secretly administering her pharmaka to the family (say, in dinner), Medea pythiagenically created "phantom snakes" that slithered across the air. These visions convinced those in Pelias's household to "believe the goddess herself was present and bestowing good fortune upon the king's house."[58] Pelias, eager to have the ear of a goddess for any future inquires, appointed Medea top council-woman of his affairs.

It's very difficult to nail down this kind of magic. Medea used psychedelic pharmaka to cause visions that convinced a family that she was a goddess. Such magic would normally fall under the rubric of a mystheogen. I am more inclined to dub the episode an example of pythiagenic magic, as the spell wasn't meant to initiate Pelias's family into the cult of Artemis-Hecate but rather to deceive them.

Despite the fictional nature of this story, we are seeing an underlying truth with regard to ancient pharmaka. That is, the ancients recognized their ability to cause visions—of phantom snakes or otherwise.

TEARING DOWN THE MOON

The prophet Jeremiah (c. 600 BCE) threw up his hands in exasperated disbelief. He clearly knew religious truth, knew the real God.

What exactly did his neighbors not understand?!

Far removed from the Italian peninsula where excavators disinterred opium cakes used by the ancients in reverence to the Great Mother,* we find Jeremiah railing against these same pastries in the Holy Land. The locals baked these devotional cakes to honor the Queen of Heaven (Inanna or an obscure Hebraic equivalent). Jeremiah lamented these rites infiltrating the Jerusalem community. His prophecy revolved around explaining the disasters sent by Yahweh. He placed blame on the families living in Yehudah and Yerushalayim who still performed matrilineal goddess rites instead of the patriarchal traditions of Jeremiah's forefathers. The youths headed into the wilderness to gather firewood, the fathers built the fire in homage to the Goddess, and the women "knead the dough and make cakes of bread for the Queen of Heaven" (Jer. 7:17–18). These cakes, however, are said to contain the rather innocuous "fine flour and honey." That certainly doesn't rule out any other ingredients (like opium) any more than the opium cake found in Pompeii rules out any nonpharmaka ingredients like flour and honey.

The very best we can say is that some ancient quasi- or non-Semitic peoples living in proximity to Hebraic communities performed some of their rites in homage to the Great Mother, of which two (probably incomplete) recipes of a sacred cake exist today. One of those recipes pays no mind to the possibility of a psychedelic pharmakon; the other certainly does.

Like most ancient Hebrews, Hosea despised the pagan world and all of its practices. It would seem that some of the followers of Yahweh didn't heed Hosea's haranguing. As late as the first century CE, Justin Martyr addressed Jewish magicians who exorcized daemons in the name

---

*See chapter 2 of this book.

of mortal kings and people of legend. In his *Dialogue with Trypho,* Justin says their efforts won't work, for only invoking the name of the God of Abraham would ensure the daemons would listen. Adding incense to injury, Justin compares the magic of these first-century Jewish mystics to that "of the Gentiles," who rely not on the power of God but rather on "magical techniques . . . [like] fumigations and incantations."[59]

Pagans, too, participated in the rebranding of the matrifocal religious artistry of the priestess into the destructive magic of the "witch," which would prove to be the downfall of some of these women. As news of their occult powers spread, priestesses were called on more and more by wealthy customers to perform special deeds. Depending on their success, their credibility rose or fell—as did their ability to make money. The devolution from devotional, mystheogenic, and entheogenic rites to services performed for a fee moved proper religious techniques into the realm of the magical arts. Indeed, it seems some priestesses and even Christian monks had off-the-books side work to supplement their income.

For example, we know about the priestess Theôris, who also tended to private clients on the side. In a careless move, she sold her pharmaka to an unnamed trickster. We learn that this man used Theôris's pharmaka for a variety of pythiagenic intentions: "Now he [using her pharmaka] plays magic tricks, and cheats and claims that he cures epileptics." This man did, however, come to Theôris's defense when she was arrested (though having a criminal in your corner doesn't always bode well for a verdict of innocence). Perhaps most telling about this case is that while Theôris was executed, the charlatan was simply "shunned on sight as an evil omen."[60]

Men were not necessarily immune from these charges, though. Across the Mediterranean in Egypt, Shenoute (c. 350–450 CE), the abbot of the White Monastery, complained about clergy using their *ars magica pharmaka* to heal the quotidian woes of regular people: "Those fallen into poverty or in sickness or indeed some other trial abandon God and run for enchanters or diviners . . . [m]oreover, this is the manner that they anoint themselves with oil [concocted by] enchanters and drug-makers, with every deceptive kind of relief."[61] The problem, as Shenoute saw it, was that monks were employing the famed Egyptian pharmacy in ways that he determined wholly unorthodox. Also, he was fighting against deeply rooted pagan medical magical beliefs. The church in the fourth century (when Shenoute lived) hadn't grown into the monolith it would become in the following centuries. As shown in the next chapters, despite his frustrations, Shenoute failed in his campaign to stop the flow of pagan pharmaka into Christianity.

With our examples of Theôris and the monks of the White Monastery, we can recognize transference of spiritual pharmaka into magical drugs as bastardized by both Grecian and Roman and even later Christian authorities. Archbishop John Chrysostom would ridicule the medicines of wise women in his work "Eighth Homily on Colossians." Here, he warns his congregations about the true nature of these women's medicines.

> [It is] that wiliness of the devil to cloak over the deceit, and to give the deleterious drug in honey. After he found that he could not prevail with you in the other way, he has gone this way about, to stitched charms, and old wives' fables; and the Cross indeed is dishonored, and these charms preferred before it. Christ is cast out, and a drunken and silly old woman is brought in. That mystery of ours is trodden under foot, and the imposture of the devil dances.[62]

We have only scraped the froth off the top of a much deeper cauldron. What we see in the ancient world was not so much a scheduling of pharmaka (like we schedule drugs today) but rather a classification of magical acts. The psychedelic pharmaka, whatever it might be in any given case, points to a curiosity of the ancient world: the kind of substance didn't matter (at least, not in a narrow sense). Broadly speaking, of course, soporifics were still sought after due to their ability to induce a somnitheogenic or dream divination state and their use as magical medicine.

These pharmaka offered not only medicinal healing but also served as entheogenic keys that allowed both priestess and congregant to share in communion with the gods. But as wise women and magi alike more and more discovered the occult properties of these spirit plants, they fell more and more out of the world of religion and into the world of magic. We see both historical and literary evidence of this transference from the priestess's entheogens to the witch's pythiagens. Medea's initiatory rite into the cult of Hecate-Artemis so that Jason may enter the sacred grove to fetch the Golden Fleece demonstrates this, I think, if even from a work of literature. Moreover, records like those of Theôris show that priestesses didn't hesitate to vend their pharmaka to other wonder-workers, regardless of the buyer's reputation. And even regular, nonmagical people sometimes sought a wise woman for love philters—certainly a lucrative business in the ancient West. A distinction between magic and religion still existed, but it was becoming ever harder to find the line that separated the two.

Let's turn now to a group of religious devotees on the other side of the pagan spectrum: that cadre of domestic terrorists who appeared in the mid-first century called Christians. Indeed, early Christians (especially those who converted from an array of pagan religions) were not immune to the draw of the awesome powers available in psychedelic pharmaka.

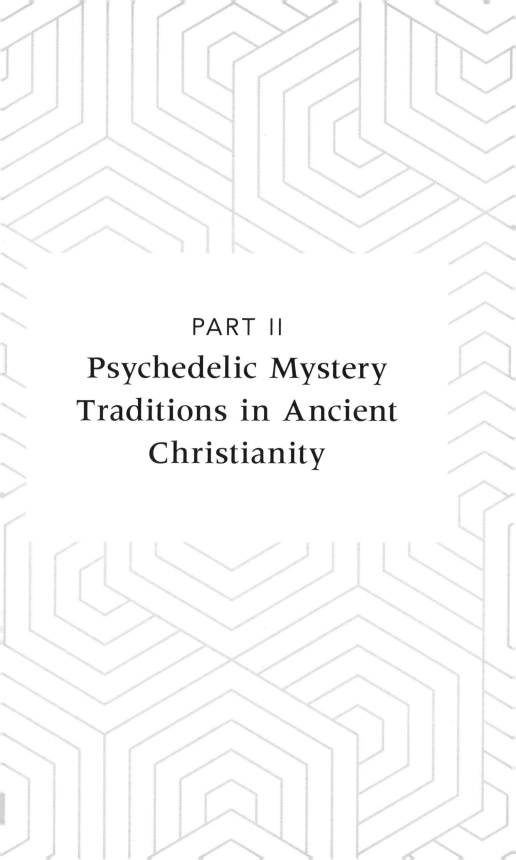

PART II
Psychedelic Mystery Traditions in Ancient Christianity

As the previous chapters have shown, the act (and art) of employing theogens for a spectrum of reasons, while not absolute, was nonetheless common in the pagan Roman world—the very world into which Mary birthed Jesus.

Available evidence discussed earlier points toward two broad kinds of mystery rites in the ancient Greco-Roman world: those for people who enjoyed a theogenic boost to their spiritual experiences (Rites of Eleusis and Feast of Hathor) and those who did not (any number of ancient rites for which no entheogen was required or expected). Both kinds of mystery (theogenic and nontheogenic) existed side by side in the ancient world. And we must not allow modern conceptions of psychedelia to cloud our judgment of ancient psychedelic mystery traditions—even as we must use the tools of modern historical dissection to reclaim them. Psychedelia was, in many ways, legal in the ancient world (even if magic was not), and it is simpy historically inaccurate to imagine otherwise.

As the next three chapters aim to demonstrate, we must not think of early Christians as an exception to this rule. Like the pagan and mystical Hebraic traditions that surrounded them, primitive Christians sects were no more or less susceptible than their pagan neighbors to the allure of local and exotic pharmaka, easily obtainable through traders, seafaring merchants, and itinerant wonder-workers eager to make a living.

Within the Christian psychedelic mysteries, I feel I have stumbled upon at least three (broadly speaking) traditions. The first two traditions (apocalyptic mysticism and gnosticism) seem to directly tie to who Jesus, the actual guy, was in history. The third represents a terrible lost history of theogenic spiritual intolerance.

Further, all three can be placed on a rough time line.

First were those psychedelic traditions found in mystical apocalypticism, perhaps originating with the earliest followers of Jesus: such believers held a very different view of who Jesus was in those days—so different that we cannot really call it Christianity yet. Instead, this group I will refer to as the Nazarenes,* those earliest followers of Jesus's message who believed him not to be the Son of God of later Christologies (like that found in the Gospel of John), but instead a healer-prophet or divine messenger who would usher in the Kingdom of God. In those days, Jesus and the Son of God were two different people. Jesus was still the Nazarene. He was not yet the anointed one.

Second, we have the pagan Neoplatonists who converted to Christanity but found their pagan religious excesses too difficult to give up. These early Christians mixed cosmic notions about who Jesus was with (at times) pharmaka-induced visions complete with Neoplatonic hierarchies of celestial beings called aeons. This group would come to be known (again, broadly) as gnostic-Christians. The term *gnostic* does not respect the breadth of alternative Christianities in the ancient world, but it is useful here as a counterbalance to those Christian beliefs that ran contrary to those of the proto-apostolic (which survived as orthodoxy).† Various gnostic groups used pharmaka for three historically

---

*The term *Nazarenes* is typically used by scholars to refer to Jesus's original group; they were not exactly Jews, but they weren't yet Christian either.

†Although many scholars use the term *proto-orthodox,* I find it a misnomer because *all* of these various groups viewed their particular school as the correct form of Christianity. I use *proto-apostolic* because the major tenants of this group (i.e., the group that won the battles and later defined proper orthodoxy) had to do with apostolic succession. This group believed Jesus was a human and hoped to trace their beliefs back to what they thought was his original message. Hence, they saw themselves as *succeeding* the original group. As for gnosticism, Tertullian (ca. 155–240 CE) was equally resolved. This kind of Christian cared not for apostolic succession championed by those like Irenaeus, but instead "modifies the traditions he has received . . . according to his own will." See Tertullian, *The Remedy for Heresy,* 42, and Pagels, *The Gnostic Gospels,* 23. Additionally, Irenaeus denounced gnostic leaders for publishing sacred books "totally unlike what has been handed down to us from the apostles"; see Irenaeus, *Against Heresies,* 3.11.9.

detectable reasons: as mystheogens, as pythiagens, and as entheogens. It was, in fact, these widely practiced gnostic spiritualities that led the proto-apostolic-cum-orthodox to develop their own psychedelic mystery traditions.

Third, we have (what I call) the orthodox tradition. The orthodox tradition can also be broken down into three subcategories: first, using soporifics as somnitheogens to meet the Christian godhead; second, using these same psychedelic pharmaka to wipe the various pagan beliefs from the minds of the masses; and third, as the recreational "ecstasy drinks" popular during the many winter festivals celebrated by people all over the Western world.

Despite the claims made by the *discipuli Allegrae** that psychedelic spirituality was "covered up" by Christian theologians, nothing could be further from the truth. There exists a body of evidence that offers a different historical interpretation of the matter. Psychedelics, at least those used somnitheogenically to meet a "Christian" godhead, appear to have been tolerated by the emerging church, as long they were ingested in a Christian manner.

For the while, I ask you, oh-most-appreciated reader, to suspend what modern popular culture has portrayed as historical Christianity. We are dealing with a span of roughly two thousand years, through the triumphs and tribulations of humanity.

Needless to say, it gets a little weird.

But I believe in us! I believe that, but for the sake of the psychedelic renaissance, we can put our biases aside and consider nothing more than the actual truth pertaining to the Western history of these spirit plants.

No matter where that road takes us.

---

*A general term I use to refer to those who agree with the theories of John Marco Allegro, whose book *The Sacred Mushroom and the Cross* (1970) argued that Christianity evolved out of a magic mushroom–eating sex cult.

6

THE FİRE-LİKE CUP

Psychedelics, Apocalyptic Mysticism,
and the Birth of Heaven

c. 30 CE–100 CE

Truly I tell you, today you will be with me in Paradise.
JESUS OF NAZARETH, GOSPEL OF LUKE (23:43)

A new spirituality was needed to explain the failures.

Jesus had not returned. The Kingdom of Heaven, expected to descend from the clouds in glorious triumph, had not manifested (2 Thess. 1:6–10). The pagan oppressors still ruled. The righteous still suffered. The temple lay in ruins. The apocalypse did not unfold. The Nazarenes desperately clung to their Hebraic heritage, even as proper Jews avoided any association with them. Here in their deepest hour of despair, instead of uniting, the Nazarenes continued to splinter.

Far from reigning in God's Kingdom as the Savior of all human-kind, Jesus was remembered quite differently in those first few decades after his gratuitous execution by the Roman guard. Indeed, most pagans and Jews regarded him as a kind of religious fanatic who dabbled in sorcery.[1] He deserved to die an outlaw's death—a *terrorist's* death.

And such a finale he received.

This presented an uncomfortable truth for the Nazarenes. They could not escape the unrelenting ridicule generously offered by their pagan and Jewish neighbors, business partners, and even family members. Were they really worshipping nothing more than a state-executed religious extremist? Someone whose prophecies had not been fulfilled?

A new spirituality was needed to explain the failures.

As Roman war chariots tilled the landscape, the blood of the fallen necessarily fertilized the seeds of rebellion. Insurgent groups aimed at dismantling the expansion of Roman conquest sprang up across the expanse of the empire. One of those subjugated groups was a headstrong and reverent assortment of monotheists called Hebrews. The Hebrews had been fighting off Roman occupation for centuries, always on the losing end of the battles. Despite the readiness of the Hebrews to die for their faith, they lived on for generations under Roman rule. The various Hebraic clans were far from the only peoples subjugated by Rome: many lands and peoples fell under caesar's dominion. But for the various Hebrew bands, the conquest was especially insulting as a key part of their faith was the belief that their God had given them the land they occupied. Their efforts to reconcile this contradiction—their status as a chosen people with their lowly existence—gave rise to a branch of Jewish mysticism commonly called prophetic apocalypticism.

Prophetic apocalypticism literally taught "the end is nigh": those who supported the pagan oppressors would soon be cut down by the mighty swords of angels, and the righteous would be rewarded with paradise. Since the Hebrew faith prophesied a savior—a messiah—who would topple the Roman guard, there was no shortage of gallant (but silly) men who adopted the appellation. Judas of Galilee,[2] Simon the

Zealot,* and one known to us only as "the Egyptian" took up arms against their Roman oppressors (Acts 21:38–39). One by one these messianic hopefuls and their meager forces felt the eager swords of Rome cut them down, and with them any hope of emancipation come judgment day.

Sometime in the first century of the Common Era, an apocalyptic prophet from Galilee began to preach the end-times. This Galilean man encouraged families to fight among themselves. He took the Law of Moses into his own hands and rebelled against both the pagan authorities and their Jewish surrogates. The scribes and Pharisees despised him; his neighbors thought him a sorcerer with a drinking problem.

A GODLESS AND LIBERTINE HERESY

"My son is crazy," said the man's disappointed mother.
"His disciples are drunkards!" piped up his Jewish detractors.
"He keeps a demon," his catty neighbors gossiped.
"He is a terrorist," his powerful enemies maligned.

Nonetheless, this accursed man continued his mission to usher in the apocalypse.

His name was Jesus.

He came from a small, impoverished town called Nazareth. He and his secret posse of twelve disciples were just another one of these Hebraic mutineer groups. This brought obvious problems to those disciples who survived Jesus's arrest and passion.

"The time is fulfilled and the Kingdom of God has come near; repent, and believe the good news" (Mark 1:15). These words, the first recorded of Jesus, make an apocalyptic proclamation. The time of the pagan world would soon come to an end, and the heavenly Kingdom would

---

*This particular radical was counted among Jesus's twelve disciples (see Luke 6:15).

reign supreme. In those days, the Kingdom was considered a physical realm (odd, I know, as we tend to think of it as originating as a spiritual sanctuary). But Jesus spoke of the Kingdom in physical, not spiritual, terms.[3] True, a person had to be spiritually ready to enter the Kingdom, but the Kingdom was not yet meant to infer an immaterial existence. The Kingdom, in fact, was quite material. In a sense, a person needed to be *spiritually* ready to enter the *physical* Kingdom. But none of this had anything to do with our modern notion of heaven. Heaven, as we know it today, did not yet exist in history.

There was only the Kingdom.

The spiritual preparation for entry into the Kingdom meant abandoning worldly goods (an absurd notion to the Roman gentry) and reversing the social order (a treasonous notion to the Roman guard).

For this, Jesus (and many more like him) was crucified.

Still the visionary apocalyptic seeds Jesus had sown flourished in eschatological literature. As time went on and Rome still dominated, the physical nature of the Kingdom slowly gave way to *something else*. You see, Jesus had promised that he would return with the physical Kingdom in clouds of glory in the lifetime of those who followed him (Matt. 16:28). But as more of those earliest Christians passed away, their survivors started to wonder what would happen when (and now, *if*) Jesus ever returned. Could the dead be saved? What if they were really nice people? Such were the concerns of the Christians from Thessalonica. Some of the Thessalonian flock had passed on; their surviving sisters and brothers eagerly wrote Paul the Apostle asking what such a fate entailed. Indeed, they had abandoned their old gods for new hope in Christ. They demanded answers! Paul told them to "not grieve as others do who have no hope." Since God had raised Jesus from the dead, those who still lived would "by no means precede those who have died." Indeed, the dead would be the first to rise in Christ's name. "Then we who are alive . . . will be caught up in the clouds together with [the souls of the dead] to meet the Lord in the air" (1 Thess. 4:13–17).

This is a rare treat!

For in the face of Jesus's unfulfilled prophecy, we see the earliest developments of the physical Kingdom giving way to the spiritual heaven. It also tells us something quite interesting about some of those first non-Nazarene Christian communities: while we tend to think that most Christians are such because of the promise of salvation in heaven, these Thessalonians converted to the new faith having no such concept. For this fact, the Kingdom slowly drifted from a physical place to an abode that could be accessed through the temporary suspension of the senses—sometimes via pharmaka.

In recent decades, scholars and conspiracy theorists alike (taking note of the psychedelic mystery traditions ubiquitous in paganism) have wondered about the possibility of such practices in the emerging Christianity of the first few centuries CE. Working off the theories of the now discredited John Marco Allegro (1923–1988), these researchers have argued that the main Christian entheogenic sacrament was the *Amanita muscaria* mushroom.[4] Personally, I find the lack of evidence for this claim disappointing. The supposed mushrooms that appear in Christian art are easily explained away through a series of sound, tried-and-true historical criteria, which those who still support the theory (in one variety or another) have simply not considered.*

Now, some of these scholars are correct to a certain degree; Christians *did* experiment with theogens. They are also correct in thinking that these Christian mystery traditions are glosses of ancient Hebraic literature like the story of the Fall in Genesis.[5] But the occult lessons of the Fall have nothing to do with the Tree of Knowledge. There is, in fact, no evidence that any Christian *ever* interpreted the forbidden fruit in such a way.

Here is where the discipuli Allegrae and I part company. While they

---

*My thoughts on the problems of the hypothesis can be found on my website, psychedelicwitch.com. See specifically "Mushroom's in Mommy Fortuna's Midnight Carnival" and "The Secret Christian Radish Cult."

believe that the key Christian psychedelic mystery traditions rest in the forbidden fruit that Eve and Adam ate in the Garden, I hold a different opinion. There isn't a shred of evidence to suggest that medieval artists secretly signified entheogens as the fruit by depicting the *Amanita muscaria* mushroom into art.[6] There *does* exist, however, evidence for such psychedelic mystery traditions, buried in obscure literature long forgotten. The proto-orthodox seem to have developed a somnitheogenic cleansing of the soul into the messianic godhead. If you'll indulge me, I'd like to unpack the occult history of psychedelia in Nazarene apocalyptic mysticism and unravel how it got there in the first place.

THE CURSE OF ADAM'S SEED

Jesus himself may have spoken about the Tree of Knowledge of Good and Evil. He was, after all, well-versed in the Law and the books of the patriarchs. Even still, we have no record of Jesus mentioning Eden. The earliest interpretation of the Fall from a follower of Christ presents itself in Paul's letters. In several instances, Paul speaks of the fall of humanity stemming from the transgression of Adam (not Eve).* Such a letter like the one Paul wrote to the Christian community in Rome makes this clear: "If, because of [Adam's] trespass, death exercised dominion through that one, much more surely will those who receive the abundance of grace and the gift of righteousness exercise dominion in life through Jesus Christ our Lord" (Rom. 5:17). He repeats such contrasts when he addresses the Corinthian church, albeit with refreshing brevity: "For as in Adam all die, so also in Christ all will be made alive" (1 Cor. 15:21–22). Paul's Christology is obvious: Adam initiated death by disobeying Yahweh when he ate from the tree. The fruit and accompanying Fall provided metaphors for temptation itself. Christians carried Adam's original trespass while ordered to forgive those who trespass against them.

---

*Although in two places, both Pauline (2 Cor. 11:3) and Pseudo-Pauline (1 Tim. 2:14), he places the blame on Eve.

Other early Christian authors picked up this mantle; Luke's original opening of his gospel has John the Baptist touring "all the region around the Jordan," bringing a gift, a "baptism of repentance for the forgiveness of sins" (Luke 3:3). In the story, John the Baptist even likens the unbaptized masses to "vipers" (Luke 3:7), no doubt referencing the serpent in Eden.

Luke desires to contrast Adam with Jesus. He accomplishes this with a genealogy and introduction of Jesus to the reader. He speaks of Jesus's baptism by John, after which Luke demonstrates why this is most important: Jesus is different from the vipers that John hopes to baptize. His bloodline extends all the way back to God.

Another point seems to have been that Jesus's obedience to God replaced Adam's offense against him, for after running off a genealogical battery of ancient names (beginning with Jesus), Luke designates Adam as the penultimate figure, the list then terminating with God, creator of all. The very next story we read is titled the Temptation of Jesus. It's obvious that Luke desires to further contrast Adam with Jesus here. In his story Luke invokes an ancient Hebraic understanding of the devil as Satan or "the adversary"—the same cosmic flunky who tormented Job (Job 1:6–12). The story goes that Jesus has been fasting in the desert for forty days. During his sojourn, the devil entices him to perform a series of miracles. Jesus's reply directly refutes Adam's offense: "It is said, 'Do not put the Lord your God to the test'" (Luke 4:12). The devil eventually gives up. Jesus, in his defiance of the devil, has corrected the original sin that brought death, ushering in a new salvation. Jesus then begins his public ministry. Those who believe in him can share in that redemption, so part of Luke's Christology goes.* The "fruit" represented temptation and apostasy from God; all other *modern* interpretations resting in an *Amanita muscaria* Christian art conspiracy? Fruitless.

God had sent Jesus to correct Adam's folly.

---

*It should be noted that Matthew draws this same parallel in his Gospel, though in a subtler fashion.

RADIX APOSTATICA

Understanding this context, we can now unpack those early Nazarene psychedelic mysteries I promised earlier. We only have two holy books that the Nazarenes themselves might have favored (a form of Matthew and 2 Esdras). Although Nazarenes had access to any number of available psychedelics, only *one* was considered sanctified. That plant is the highly psychoactive mandrake, a member of the Solanaceae family. Mandrake held a status of "orthodox" for early Nazarenes (and early Christians) because it appears twice in the Old Testament. It finds favor and allusions to fertility magic in both Genesis (30:14–16) and the Song of Songs (7:13). Furthermore, mandrake has a triune property: medium doses bring about a form of "pleasant madness," larger doses bring on a deep and lucid dream state, and very high doses—well, you're looking at death.[7]

All of these elements came together in what was perhaps the earliest Nazarene Christian psychedelic mystery: Adam, the *radix apostatica* ("the root of apostasy.")[8] Adam had been fashioned, not *ex nihilo*, but *ex terra*—"from the dirt of the ground" (Gen. 2:7). Pharmaka, too, came from the dirt. Older Jewish sources like the Wisdom of Sirach (c. 200 BCE) confirm that "the Lord hath created medicines out of the earth; and he that is wise will not abhor them" (Sir. 38:4). Whoever wrote Jubilees felt similarly, commenting, "And one of us He commanded that we should teach Noah all the medicines . . . and we explained to Noah all the medicines of their diseases, together with their seductions, how he might heal them with herbs of the earth" (Jub. 10:10–12).

Here is where the Nazarene apocalyptic symbolism meets ancient psychedelia: just like the chthonic plant mandrake comes from the deepest, darkest soils, so did God create Adam from that very ground. Aquinas was one of the first later Christians to uncover this most deep Nazarene occult symbolism:

The Mandrake herb has a root whose limbs resemble those of a human, though it lacks a head. This suggests the Jewish people who are still headless. However, at the end of the world, the Jews will inhale the word and the fragrance of the Church and they will finally be reunited with Christ, their head.[9]

But someone else, much earlier than Aquinas, had also understood this deep, primitive, messianic Christian psychedelic tradition. Esdras (late first century CE) had contemplated all this symbolism long ago. But he also knew shamanistic techniques of transcendence as well as the awesome power of visionary plants. All these he used to give us a portrayal of what a late Nazarene (or early Christian) looked like when using a psychedelic to uncover the deeper meaning between Adam's transgression, the Fall, the coming of Jesus, and the final judgment.

OPPOSITE IT, THE PARADISE OF JOY

Far outside the ruined Jerusalem city walls, entrenched in hostile wilderness, Esdras sat in a field among the flowers as he readied himself for the final revelation. After weeks in solitude, he had company: five selected companions, known to "write swiftly," waited patiently to record Esdras's prophecy.[10]

Esdras was perhaps one of the last of the dying Nazarenes, a Jewish eschatologist who nonetheless saw Jesus as the messiah who would bring the end-times. Esdras had already experienced quite the spiritual storm. Little more than a decade after the destruction of the second temple (c. 70 CE), his final vision stemmed not from simply taking some psychedelic pharmaka but rather from a series of ordeals: fasting, isolation, self-flagellation, and apocalyptic dream divination, which finally culminated in taking some kind of visionary potion. The story outlining how this all unfolded survives in the book 2 Esdras. The text presents both positives and negatives to the historian. As to the positive, the book shows a near-perfect meshing of customary Jewish eschatology with that new, rabble-rousing offspring of such doomsday schools: Christianity. As to the negative (which ironically reinforces the positive), the form of 2 Esdras that has come down to us has been touched and revised by several editors.[11] *That* is why the text merges so well the Hebraic traditions of yore with Jesus's preaching of the end-times. It is in this liminal space that Esdras has his psychedelic vision.

Esdras stood squarely in the line of Jewish prophetic apocalypticism. Jewish prophetic apocalypticism can be traced back to the spiritual beliefs of Zoroaster, who taught of a dualistic cosmos—the celestial fight between light and darkness. Such concepts can be seen in the Hebrews' ancient desire to isolate themselves from the pagan world. They were the children of light; Roman pagans were the children of darkness.[12]

Esdras's book weaves several narratives, one of which charts his development from a simple visionary to a bona fide prophet of the one true God. He must endure several psychological, physical, and spiritual trials, along with seven visions, before being admitted into a higher state of prophetic awareness via a drink that was, in all likelihood, psychedelic in nature. Esdras's seven visions dealt with the ultimate triumph of the Kingdom of God over the oppressive Roman state through the might of Jesus. Those who sided with the pagans would end up in the "oven of Gehenna,"* while those who were pious would sit "opposite it, [in] the paradise of joy."[13] It provides a myth for the age-old Abrahamic mystery: if Yahweh had chosen the Hebrews as his people, why were they constantly on the losing end of historical circumstance? The first vision seeks to answer this, referencing Adam, the first human, as the radix apostatica—the source of Jewish woes. Adam had corrupted all of Jewish lineage. So long as the Hebrews, the descendants of his seed, continued to transgress Yahweh's laws,

---

*Gehenna refers to an area in southern Jerusalem where heathenistic Hebrews sacrificed children. The area also served as a landfill for animal carcasses, the bodies of the dead, human waste, and other refuse. Here, it serves to contrast the spiritual Kingdom (the "paradise of joy"). It is, in fact, one of the earliest whispers of the spiritual Hell.

terrible calamities (say, a flood worthy of an ark) would befall them.

The second vision concerns those who have already died. Would they miss the rapture? As we saw with Paul's letter to the Thessalonians, 2 Esdras also shows that early transference from the physical Kingdom to the spiritual heaven: "I said: 'But then, lord, you give preference to those who are [alive] at the end; so what will those who precede us do, or we, or those who come after us?' God replied, 'I will compare my judgment to a circle: as there is no disadvantage to the slow, So there is no disadvantage to the fast.'"[14]

By this time, Esdras had been fasting a fortnight. Harsh as that ordeal was, it did result in his third vision, which asked why Hebrews suffered both the wrath of Yahweh and their earthly enemies. The answer came by way of comparison: How could humans possibly appreciate paradise if they never experienced the opposite?

Returning to another week of meditating and eating only "the wild plants of the land," Esdras had his fourth vision: that of a woman bemoaning the loss of her son. The woman served as a metaphor for the mother of Israel, whose son had recently "died," along with the destruction of the Temple. This son would be back, though. The *pieta* underpinnings here are unmistakable.

The fifth vision showed Esdras the rise of the Roman Empire in the form of a three-headed eagle coming out of the ocean. It was defeated by a lion waiting patiently in the bushes. The lion represented Jesus, "the anointed one whom the Most High has reserved till the end of days, who will arise from the seed of David."[15] The sixth vision, which occurred in a dream, outlined the actual combat between Jesus and Rome.

Now it was time for the final revelation.

Sitting under an oak tree, Esdras heard a voice coming from a shrub (recalling the story of Moses and the burning bush). The voice told Esdras to prepare for the final unveiling by ordering him to find five scribes to accompany him for his prophetic climax and record his words. Esdras found his scribes promptly; one does not take orders from a talking bush lightly! Together the six men returned to the forest of Ardat. The scribes sat with their writing tablets on their laps as Esdras took a drink from a cup whose contents he described as "fire-like." The potion had quite the impact on him. He tells us that as he imbibed, "My heart uttered understanding, and wisdom grew in my breast, for my spirit strengthened my memory. . . . The Highest gave understanding unto the five men, and they wrote the wonderful visions of the night" (2 Esd. 14:36–48). He spoke for forty days, sometimes staying up all night to tell of the wonders inspired by the fire-like cup.

This account reeks of ancient psychedelic magic.[16] It falls perfectly in line with the ecstatic techniques used by the earliest visionaries: prayer, fasting, dream divination, isolation, and psychedelic pharmaka.* But it also makes a subtle though very specific point. The pharmaka weren't necessary for spiritual experiences. Indeed, Esdras had *six* visions before the seventh and final, and only this latter one included a pharmakon. All the preliminary procedures had been met through other ancient mind-expanding methods. However, the compounded experience culminating from all of these visions required a psychic container that could only be reliably manifested through the awesome power of a psychedelic. More important, I think, we are witnessing some kind of ancient mystical Jewish apocalyptic shaman who understood the occult nature of the mandrake's associations, which tied together Adam, Christ, and the end of days. Might we assume that it was the mandrake that inflamed the fire-like cup?

Applying the word *entheogen*[17] to Esdras's experience, while initially useful to avoid a mischaracterization like "drug experience," now strikes

---

*Zoroaster was said to have used similar techniques (prayer and fasting) to enter the spiritual life. See Ankarloo and Clark, *Witchcraft and Magic in Europe,* 114.

me as somewhat debatable. It all comes down to this question (assuming the fire-like cup contained mandrake): Did Esdras believe Christ acted as the "head" of the plant? If so, his experience is purely entheogenic, for he drank the body of Christ. He certainly seemed aware of the occult understanding of Adam and Jesus. Had he bridged the two with mandrake? In the pursuit of truth, we must also admit that at no point did Esdras say he was taking Yahweh (or any other deity) into himself by drinking the fire-like potion. He drank it specifically to induce a revelation that would untangle the message of his previous visions of the final Christian crescendo—the coming of the Kingdom of God—so that he could record it, not in any kind of Cosmic Christ way (as a gnostic might) but as a celestial weapon, destroying the pagan oppressors and liberating the children of God for all eternity. This is, in my estimation, closer to a pythiagenic, not entheogenic, operation—especially when viewed in conjunction with the other magical techniques that Esdras endured (isolation, fasting, etc.).

Interestingly, two more branches of Christianity show evidence of psychedelic pharmaka usage via two totally different avenues, which we will wrestle with over the next two chapters. For now, we can say quite confidently that one of the earliest (and probably among the last surviving Nazarene Christians) managed to smuggle a pythiagen (or in this case, would it be a *pytheogen?*) into his account, drawing on Jesus's original message of the coming of the Kingdom. There were potentially a host of ways for obtaining apocalyptic visions, of which pharmaka represent just one avenue.* Of those prescriptions that survived the ruins of time (which we'll meet in the next two chapters), we see different *meanings* ascribed to a variety of pharmakon practices.

---

*There is no evidence, for example, that the Revelation of John of Patmos was inspired by a pharmakon.

And in these differences of intention and outcome, as demonstrated in 2 Esdras, we get a small glimpse into the beginnings of the ways psychedelic pharmaka were used among those third-generation Nazarene Christians still hoping for Jesus's return.

Desperately seeking a new spirituality to explain the failures.

7

DISCIPLES ⊙ OF THEIR OWN MINDS

Gnosticism and Primitive
Christian Psychedelia
c. 100–400 CE

Indeed, there have to be factions among you, for only so will it become clear who among you are genuine.
PAUL OF TARSUS, 1 CORINTHIANS 11:19

The poet Rutilius Claudius Namatianus (c. sixth century) hated Christians. They had stolen his good friend away into their fold with their weird mysteries. And what a loss it was! Rutilius's friend of "high descent" (he affiliated mostly with that kind) had fallen into such debauchery that it offended even conservative Romans. Daily, he would beat the sin out of himself, torturing his flesh with terrible punishments. Rutilius knew exactly what the problem was. He attributed the "bestial" behavior of Christians to the use of psyche-magical potions: "May I ask," he wonders, "if [these Christians] are more corruptible than Circe's magical pharmaka? . . . Once it was only the bodies that changed, now it is the souls."[1] When we consider that Solanaceae plants like mandrake were associated with Circe's potions and that that pharmakon had a long history in Judaism (thanks to the blatant use of love magic in Genesis), we may conclude that at least *some* Christians in the ancient world mixed mandrake (or other pharmaka) into their wines during ceremony.

At least enough to qualify both Rutilius's association and discontent.

❧

As outlined in the last chapter, Jesus and his followers had a reputation as an insurgent group—one of many in the eyes of the state. But accusations of insurrection weren't the only problem for those earliest proto-Christians.

Aside from the occasional charismatic radical, the ancient Palestinian landscape was also steeped in a cosmopolitan mysticism, providing the perfect environment for magicians, wandering wonder-workers, and every assortment of seer, dream interpreter, *pigmentarii* (drug dealer), and witch to peddle her or his services. Honi the Circle-Drawer,[2] Apollonius of Tyana,[3] the witch of Endor (1 Sam. 28:3–25), and scores of other magicians could be found in nearly every corner of the empire. These characters did not always attract the good graces of the townspeople. In an uncertain world plagued by any number of calamities, the slightest bit of queerness amounted to ostracism (at best) and condemnation (at worst).

The miracles Jesus performed opened him up easily to the charge of magic. For this fact, the gospel authors chose not to record a single medical technique that Jesus employed.[4] In fact, the Gospel of John openly admits that "Jesus did many other signs in the presence of the disciples, which are not written in this book" (John 20:30). But there might be some ancillary evidence outside the gospels: Jesus was well known for his ability to cast out demons with a word. And how did healers in those days, lacking the power of the one true God, handle these kinds of possessions? It is interesting to note that the first-century Jewish historian Josephus gives a long treatment to a plant called *baaras,* which was a local name for mandrake. Indeed, one of mandrake's long-known magical features was the root's ability to cleanse people of evil spirits. Such an observation did not escape the famed Jewish historian: "It quickly drives away those called demons, which are no other than the spirits of the wicked, that enter into men that are alive, and kill them."[5]

Additionally, mandrake turns up in Jewish mystical traditions, like the special root trapped in Solomon's ring, which drew out demons from the possessed. We can only speculate, but when we consider that the earliest charges against Jesus's followers involved magic, it makes sense that the Nazarenes would work quickly to disavow such an allegation.[6] Is it possible that Jesus used a similar technique with a similar pharmakon, which the gospel writers quickly discarded to avoid associating his miracles with the works of magicians?

Maybe.

Based on the tales about his incredible deeds, Jesus was one of two possible historical personas: either he was the only begotten son of the one true God or he was an insurgent who practiced magic. In the custom of his enemies, I tend to side with the latter description. After all, he cast out demons, healed the sick, and transfigured—all classic operations of the magician's practice. One noted scholar even felt Jesus's transfiguration scene (Mark 9:2–8, Luke, 9:28–36, Matt. 17:1–8) "reflects common experience in hallucinative rites."[7]

If Jesus really fiddled with some form of ancient magic cobbled from Jewish mysticism and apocalypticism, healing, and various exotic enchantments brought through Palestine via Egypt, it seems improbable that he would not have known *anything* about the pharmaka present in those latter two disciplines. An accusation of magic, expressly forbidden in Rome, could have landed Jesus in prison, his disciples mocked as followers of a criminal.[8]

Why *would* the gospel authors have written about Jesus's use of enchanted pharmaka?

Such a thing could get a person crucified . . .

Just prior to his arrest, Jesus ate a traditional seder meal with his twelve disciples to celebrate the Passover. Passover was always a hostile time in the Jewish lands, prone to inspiring outbursts and minor rebellions. Therefore, it was not unusual that Roman guards, who typically stayed away from the Holy Land, were present that weekend in full battle array. Tucked safely in an ordinary house away from the careful eyes of the Roman police, Jesus sat with his followers awaiting the coming Kingdom. He broke bread and poured wine, encouraging his twelve closest followers to eat and drink. Christians throughout the ages have referred to this meal as the Last Supper, as it was the final dinner Jesus shared with his disciples before his arrest hours later at Gethsemane.

Or so the story goes.

MYSTERY OF THE LORD'S SUPPER

Then as today, Jewish seders included the Kiddush, a prayer of thanksgiving to Yahweh, which is very different from what reportedly took place at the Last Supper. We today accept the historical concept of the body and blood of Christ (i.e., the Eucharist), even if we do not accept Christianity as a personal religion. And yet, as odd as it might strike the modern Christian (or for that matter even a pagan or atheist), the Eucharist held no place at the original Last Supper. That meal was nothing more than a traditional seder, complete with the Kiddush. Bread and wine were undoubtedly shared at the table, but the prayer was invigorated with nothing other than its usual role— to thank God for providing the meal. Indeed, the Jewish Kiddush holds no mystical or magical implications at all. So where did this idea of the body and blood of Jesus, represented by bread and wine, come from?

Maybe it was the blistering desert sun. Or road fatigue. Or nibbling an innocuous-looking (though poisonous) morsel as a snack. Whatever the prompt, Paul of Tarsus (mid-first century CE) toppled to his knees and had a vision of Jesus while traveling on the road to Damascus (Acts 9:3–9). Paul is important to our story because, if anyone, *he* can be credited with inventing a new religion out of Jesus's apocalyptic teachings, namely Christianity. One of the accoutrements Paul would later instill in this new religion included turning the Kiddush into the Eucharist. This perhaps helps explain why early Christians chose that particular word, for Eucharist means "blessing" in Old Greek. It was Paul who first saw the bread and wine as symbolizing the body and blood of Jesus. Paul placed the Eucharist at the center of the mystery, a way of signifying a new covenant between the Almighty and the people of Israel (1 Cor. 10:23–6).

A new covenant free from Adam's transgression.

The historical truth is unimpeachable: the very act of drinking the "blood" and eating the "flesh" of a deity lends itself to paganism, not Judaism (Gen. 9:4–6). Jesus, his followers included, would have abhorred such an act. Imagine their reaction: here, at the final hour before the revolution, their charismatic leader, Jesus, reveals himself to be a pagan?! Hell, had that happened, Judas probably wouldn't have been the only disciple to turn Jesus in to the authorities. Even most conservative Romans would be disgusted by the act. There is simply no historical way the Lord's Supper took place as first recorded by Paul. In fact, the Jerusalem church had never heard of the Eucharist. One would expect Jesus's followers to be familiar with this concept. And yet, they weren't, meaning that the meal and ritual must have come from somewhere, or *someone,* else.[9] Indeed, Paul tells us himself that Jesus revealed the mystery to him through a vision (1 Cor. 10:23–6).

As shown in previous chapters, ingesting a god (as an entheogen or otherwise) is, strictly speaking, a pagan form of devotion with no

Hebraic analogue. Indeed, Paul originally described the meal not as the "Last Supper" but as the "Lord's Supper" (*kuriakon deipnon*), the very term used for the sacred brew drunk by initiates of the cult of Mithra. Further, the Pauline association of the "blood of the vine" serving as a metaphor for wine is perfectly Dionysian in its implications.[10]

Paul knew *exactly* what he was doing.

This kind of Eucharist would certainly attract pagan converts.

But he wanted Jewish converts too.

And so he hatched a plan.

In his letter to the Christian community in Corinth, Paul says that the kuriakon deipnon represents a "new covenant" with Yahweh, immediately endowing the bread and wine with a numinous depth absent from the Kiddush (1 Cor. 10:25). The new covenant included eating the body and drinking the blood of Christ—oftentimes to excess. The upper-class Christians of Corinth often started the celebrations early, eager as they were to begin the festivities. They refused to wait for their lower-class sisters and brothers, who labored well after sunset: "As a result, one person remains hungry and another gets drunk" (1 Cor.11:20–22). Need I mention that Claudius Aelianus (c. 180–230) recalled that the "Corinthians have been reproached in Comedies for being intemperately addicted to wine"?[11] In fact, the familial bloodline that traced back to Dionysus himself, the Bacchiadai family, had once claimed residency in Corinth.[12]

But for that fact, the pride of the locals had never waned.

With a stroke of the quill, Paul took a regular Hebraic food blessing (the Kiddush) and, giving it a transcendental dimension, turned it into a pagan mystery ritual complete with Dionysian and Mithraic appropriations.[13] More importantly, he opened the door for pagan converts into Christianity to mix their traditional entheogenic and mystheogenic pharmaka into their Eucharists, whether this occurred at the Lord's Supper or not.

Jesus, and therefore salvation, could now be ingested.

The possible addition of pharmaka might also explain those incidents in Corinth when the more wealthy Christians greedily partook in the Eucharist celebrations while their lower-class brethren still labored in the fields. Apparently, they were getting so drunk off the Eucharist that some of them were weak, ill, and dying (1 Cor. 11:29–30). It's enough to make one wonder what pharmaka might have been in those early Corinthian Eucharists that would cause such diverse reactions. Truly, this is no ordinary wine, but a trimma. When we consider that some of these early Corinthian Christians were former pagans, we can conjecture that they brought their traditional pharmaka into their new faith and added them to their new Eucharists. They had precedent, too. As shown in the last chapter, mandrake had a long tradition in Judaism. And suppose Sula Benet is correct and the "sweet cane" of the Old Testament is an echo of cannabis?[14] Pagans who had converted may have been all too happy to add some kind of enhancing pharmakon to their Eucharists, whether it be mandrake, cannabis, opium, or psilocybin mushrooms. Intermarriage between Christian and pagan was one of many things the church fathers complained about.[15] We can only wonder about how many newlywed Christians engaged in the practices of their pagan spouses.

Working off this hypothesis, let's consider what Julie and Jerry Brown ask us in *The Psychedelic Gospels* about an intriguing passage from the Gospel of Thomas. Jesus asks Thomas to compare him (Jesus) to another person. When Thomas pleads ignorance, Jesus admonishes him: "Because you have drunk, you have become intoxicated from the bubbling spring which I have measured out."[16] This was one of those trick questions that Jesus was known for. The answer (i.e., who is like Jesus?) is Thomas himself. Through Jesus, Thomas had attained an equal standing with Christ after intoxicating himself from a spring. When we consider the pagan concept of ingesting entheogens as the bodies of gods,* the Browns' analysis of Thomas strikes this writer as most plausible. Indeed, within Thomas we also find evidence that both

---

*Specifically, the unmistakable Dionysian "blood of the vine" motif.

the physical Kingdom *and* the spiritual heaven have been modified. The *new* Kingdom is inside you—a sharp departure from Nazarene psychedelia.

But wait—*it gets even better!*

SACRED KNOWLEDGE

Differences among ancient Christian sects were numerous as this once apocalyptic faith slipped out of its Nazarene shell and into the wild world. Sometime around the middle of the first century CE, perhaps as soon as five or ten years after the death of Jesus, a particular brand of Greek middle-Platonism started to mingle with the apocalyptic Nazarene faith. Today, both academic and popular television and internet personalities refer to these middle-Platonist Christians as gnostics. *Gnostic,* from the Greek *gnōsis* ("to know"), denotes a variety of religious beliefs and practices that flourished in the first centuries CE, which sometimes did and sometimes did not hold doctrines contrary to those of the proto-apostolic. While gnosticism itself did not represent anything like a unified religious system, many gnostic faiths held some views in common, allowing for something like a fountainhead from which different sects drank. The very premise of chasing gnostic beliefs down historical rabbit holes promises a wonderland of possibilities, the truth of which will unfortunately forever remain unknown. What we can do, however, is descend as deep as possible into these Christological caverns and observe the gems of possibility poking out from the subterranean bedrock before the air grows too thin, the crawl space tapers, and all light fades to black, forcing us back to the surface.

Despite the doctrinal differences dividing diverse, competing gnostic groups, we can detect two overarching themes common to most that can give us an idea about the foundational elements of this multifaceted new Christological understanding. These two umbrella themes will be crucial for understanding how and why an ancient gnostic-leaning believer might incorporate psychedelic pharmaka into a ritual.

The first umbrella theme deals with a common gnostic theology: how divine entities (called aeons) of the universe formed. This theology held that all existence started with one Supreme Being.* This Being *was not* Yahweh. This Being existed outside space and time, beyond the material world, beyond anything a human is capable of understanding; we are no more likely to conceive the nature of this Being than a spider is likely to understand the rules of roller derby. This one unfathomable Supreme Being was all that existed. But since this Being was technically living, Living became something of its own entity. This Being was also able to think, and so Thought became its own entity. As more aeons (like Silence, Depth, and Word)† spilled out from the one Supreme Being into infinity, they created a divine realm called the Pleroma (or "fullness").‡

Aeons occupying the Pleroma also brought forth lesser-divine entities. In some traditions, Sophia or Wisdom, the twelfth aeon emitted from the Supreme Being, took to making love to and impregnating herself. Without her male counterpart to balance the cosmic coitus, Sophia brought forth a deleterious offspring called Ialdabaoth. Her intercourse with herself had "violated the harmonious nature of opposites," that is, the co-creative energies of the Sacred Marriage; she was subsequently kicked out of the Pleroma.[17] Ialdabaoth was, according to some of the

---

*One, that is, according to some gnostic traditions. Others, like that founded by Valentinus, proposed this deity was a dyad, a twofold being; something like conjoined twins, two separate individuals composing one whole person; see Irenaeus, *Against Heresy*, 1.11.
†The different divine "genealogies" are too numerous to catalogue here. Interested readers can check out Robinson, *The Nag Hammadi Library;* all references to gnostic texts in this chapter derive from that collection.
‡How interesting that our modern concepts of heaven as a place *out there* beyond the cosmos began with gnostic, not proto-apostolic, theology. Indeed, at this time, the Nazarenes still believed that God's physical Kingdom was *coming.*

more anti-Semitic gnostics, the God of the Jews:* a deformed bastard of the depraved aeon Sophia. After seeing how maladjusted and deformed he was, Sophia cast him into lower matter. Needing a way to occupy his time, Ialdabaoth created the material world that encases us all—the universe as we know it. Stuck in physical reality, the lowest plain of existence, Ialdabaoth was ignorant of the Pleroma, the divine, immaterial realm above. He thus erroneously declared himself to be the one true God, as recorded in the First Commandment to the Hebrews. However, the true Creator God—the one Supreme Being—had nothing at all to do with the physical existence of our observable universe. The result of such theological premises comes with an obvious conundrum: that is, all material objects are evil by the nature of their creation.

And humanity was no exception.

The second umbrella theme underlying most gnostic ideologies presents itself in a much less complicated way. It is, in fact, so precise, so exact in its implications, that we can easily reduce it to two words: *life sucks*. And why does life suck? Because we humans do not belong in this material reality. We are, in fact, alien to planet Earth, itself the result of Ialdabaoth's disastrous unraveling of the fabric of space and time. Our true home resides in the spiritual Pleroma, not on the physical Earth. Salvation could be obtained, so gnostic theology goes, by liberating oneself through the acquisition and understanding of secret knowledge. This knowledge had to do with the self—of knowing that you belong not to Ialdabaoth's material world but rather to the celestial race of the one Supreme Being to which you will someday rejoin in the glorious Pleroma. Well, some of you.[18] Indeed, many gnostics believed in an ascending hierarchy of humans (hence the Neoplatonism). At the top of the pyramid sat the "perfects," a rather elitist group that understood themselves as a naturally moral authority; they were, of course, part of

---

*And therefore the God of the Nazarenes and the later proto-apostolic movement.

the saved class. Beneath them were the "worthy." Although not fully cooked (from a divine standpoint), the worthy had souls and were contenders for a spiritual afterlife—depending on how they lived and what they believed in this life. Finally, there are people like *you*. Most of *you* are soulless—here merely for the entertainment of the perfects and the worthy. *You* will not return to the Pleroma when you perish. When *you* die, it is total reduction to nonentity; *you* will fall apart, decay under the pleasure of feasting maggots, rot into nothing, and soon be forgotten.

You will never be an ancestor.

All this valuable spiritual information tallying the worth of everyone's personal essence had been suppressed by Ialdabaoth. How could anyone know who was worthy of true gnosis? Or who was to be saved and who was not? Luckily, a divine ambassador from the Pleroma delivered this message just when humanity needed it most. That celestial man was Jesus Christ. To most gnostic faiths, salvation manifested through accepting that Jesus's teachings emphasized realizing that humans do not belong in the material world but rather belong to the Pleroma. Escaping one's material body opened the doors for deliverance. Jesus had not come to save humanity; he came to convey instructions to the worthy so they could save themselves. Part of that message seems to have had something to do with the nature of material existence and a single question: If humans are divine, *what are we to do with our earthly flesh*?

Some gnostic groups answered with asceticism. The Ebionites, a particularly conservative example, lived a life away from the hassles of the city in a state of perpetual purity. They did not partake in the pleasures of life, good food, wine, pharmaka, or sex—yes, even procreation struck the Ebionites as a sin that continued Ialdabaoth's evil plan to keep humans in subjugation and ignorance. They would have spurned the mystheogens found in the pagan temples. Needless to say, such a group didn't attract many converts. Even Irenaeus (c. 130–200) found their level of spiritual purity too extreme. While recording the different ways diverse gnostic groups might initiate a new member, he references the kind of gnostic who "maintain[ed] that the mystery of the unspeakable and invisible power ought not to be performed by visible and corruptible creatures."[19] In other words, human flesh and autonomy were both too dismal to administer any kind of sacrament to a believer. These kinds of gnostics would not have sought any kind of mystheogen for use in their rites.

Of course, not every gnostic Christian group was so austere.

And it is here where we will find the origins of various gnostic Christian psychedelic mystery traditions.

WHERE THE ROOTS OF THE UNIVERSE ARE FOUND

The first reported heretic, Simon Magus, came from Samaria, a region in the Holy Land near the eastern border of the Mediterranean. He was said to have operated within living memory of Jesus's disciples. Simon had been a working magician within his own influential spheres when he heard of a new religion that intrigued him. At the time, Jesus's followers remained in a state of collective shock and fear. They had been promised salvation. Promised justice. Promised the glorious return of their divine leader.

They had been promised paradise.

None of these prophecies proved accurate; the faithful grew restless. An uncertain and forced confidence might be easily swayed if the right person with the right answers to these pressing questions presented an alternative narrative. Simon Magus was such a person. We do not have any writings left by Simon or his followers, though we know that they did compose some form of sacred text. Part of the introduction of this lost Simonian tome was preserved in Hippolytus's (c. 170–230 CE) treatise *Refutation of All Heresies*. Therein, Simon claimed his book was "the revelation of the voice . . . of the great Infinite Force . . . where the roots of the universe are found."[20] With an opening like that, how regrettable it is that we do not have the complete manuscript! But alas, we are left only with the charges cast against Simon and his followers by his enemies. Still, we can gain some insights. For example, we know that his religion included recognizing and championing the divine feminine. In his attempt to bridge Greek philosophy with Christianity, Simon had deified Helen of Troy as the "mother of all." She was reborn ad infinitum, the Cosmic Graell incarnated in the great queen of yore. According to the Simonian school, she embodied all celestial knowledge.[21] She was, in effect, Sophia—mother of wisdom. Simon even traveled with a woman as his cosmic consort who would adopt this role as the living Helen.

Well versed in Greek philosophy, Simon appeared as a fantastic orator to the otherwise illiterate masses that gathered to hear his message. His religion is complicated, but one aspect of it made perfect sense to most people: "the necessity of promiscuous intercourse." Indeed, Simonians supposedly professed "all earth is earth, and there is no difference where any one sows, provided he does sow."[22] But the Simonian subscription to the more libertine forms of gnosticism also included use of psychedelic pharmaka.

Knowing full well the power of transcendent experience, Simon understood the most practical way to gain a following. He initiated members into his group by administering to them a mystheogen.[23] They, in turn, would use these same concoctions during "their more secret rites." Complete with "incenses, sacrifices, and libations," the Simonians worshipped Helen and Simon through sexual sacraments later denounced by Eusebius (c. 260–340 CE) as "the foulest crime"— though, he also gives us insight into the psychedelic powers of the libations. Indeed, according to Eusebius, inhaling or imbibing pharmaka (whether incense, wine, or both) left a person "wonderstruck . . . brimful of frenzy and lunacy and of such a kind that they [cannot] be put down in writing."[24]

Simon's other enemies were just as condescending, condemning the mystheogens as nothing more than recreational "love potions . . . and philters."[25] Epiphanius (310–400 CE) agreed with Eusebius; the Simonians's potions and magical operations caused mental derangement and hallucinations.[26] Simon's enemies' accusations cast his deeds out of a religious sphere and into the ready and waiting rubric of criminal magic.

But the proto-apostolic perspective of the pharmaka was not shared by Simon. For him and his followers, the coitus and mystheogen allowed some kind of vision that perhaps guided them down the root systems of the universe. And while we cannot be sure about the tales, songs, and rituals that accompanied the mystheogenic experience shared during the Simonians's conversion ceremonies, we can at least hear the echoes of the earliest non-Nazarene, gnostic-Christian use of psychedelics ricocheting off the centuries.

Other gnostic leaders like Carpocrates (d. c. 140 CE) followed suit. Admittance into his school demanded careful study that would ensure any neophyte's recognition of her or his celestial origins from the Pleroma. After all, as divine entities, should humans not embrace the joys of life? *Divinity cannot be defiled,* so went Carpocrates's logic. Church father Clement of Alexandria (c. 150–210 CE) answered this kind of rationalization with the ironic comment that these particularly hedonistic Carpocratians "would combat lust by enjoyment of lust!"[27]

Carpocrates placed Jesus among a Pleroma pantheon of other god-men like Pythagoras, Aristotle, and others.[28] Carpocrates admitted both women and men into his school. His son, Epiphanes, proclaimed "righteousness of God is communion with equality."[29] And while there is no evidence that Carpocrates worked the sacred feminine into his form of Christianity (as did Simon), he did manage to work in several forms of magic: dream divination and spirit invocation, operations the Carpocratians fulfilled through their use of psychedelic pharmaka.[30] In this case, the pharmaka were employed not as a Simonian mystheogen but instead for purely pythiagenic reasons.

As more people came to understand the revealed word through Carpocrates, some felt the need to proselytize. Marcellina from Alexandria (c. mid-second century) took up the task. With her branded right earlobe, she was unmistakably a devotee of Carpocrates at one point in her life. Alexandria was a hotbed of magical activity where psychedelic pharmaka could be found as easily as one can find cannabis today in Portland, Oregon. More importantly, it was a place where upper-class women could enjoy membership in any number of mystical conservatories.[31] Given her Alexandrian setting and her studies in the Carpocratian school, Marcellina was in all probability well versed in the fine art of psychedelic magic. Taking these skills with her to Rome sometime around 150 CE, she set about making a name for herself. Whether she promoted the views of her teacher or espoused some new faith remains uncertain. Also uncertain was whether she used psychedelic pharmaka; if so, were they used as mystheogens (as did Simon), as pythiagens (as did Carpocrates), or in some other way? What is certain is that she was fantastic at her job and ended up gaining a large following.[32] Indeed, women played an active role in the earliest developments of house churches, as is clear from the letters of Paul, wherein several women of wealth and status are mentioned by name as church leaders.*

Any number of them may have used theogens like (presumably) Marcellina.

---

*Examples include: Lydia, a merchant and landowner (Acts 16:11–15); Euodia, Syntyche, and a woman referred to as their "partner/coworker" (*syzuge*), who founded the church in Philippi (Phil. 4:1–3); Theomempte, a wealthy woman from Myndos (modern-day Turkey), also founded a church; an Egyptian inscription refers to a certain Paniskianes as a *presbytera* ("female elder"); see Torjesen, *When Women Were Priests,* 20. Interested readers might also enjoy the Acts of Paul and Thecla from the New Testament apocrypha. For gnostics, Marcion's church was egalitarian, though not necessarily lacking in misogyny; see Ruether and McLaughlin, *Women of Spirit,* 44–45.

MYSTERY OF THE LIGHT MAIDEN

Some of these licentious forms of gnosticism involved a truly sacred act, sexual union with the mother or personification of all wisdom, Sophia herself. Sophia, you will recall, had given birth to the demiurge, the false god, Ialdabaoth, the result of which found her booted out of the Pleroma. Her salvation and reentrance back into the Pleroma rested in sexual union with the Cosmic Christ. Afterward, she would be reborn as the Light Maiden. The mystery rite that accompanied the myth, the ceremony of the Bridal Chamber, was considered the pinnacle performance of a readied student, for Sophia herself selected those who may know her deeper mysteries.[33] How she tapped the worthy aspirants remains unknown. But those lucky fourteen (seven women and seven men) would engage in a spiritual orgy that honored Sophia's salvific intercourse with the Cosmic Christ, followed by her ascent back into the embracing arms of the Pleroma.

The bedchamber no doubt served as a terrestrial analogue of the Pleroma. A simple room or basement would not suffice for such a deed—*no*. Instead, a luxurious space, decorated with paintings, ornate pillows, flowing tapestries, and burning incense provided the setting for this glorious act; for therein, the fourteen chosen would transcend material existence into the realm of eternity, declaring in glorious triumph, "First take grace through me and from me. Adorn yourself like a bride who awaits her bridegroom, so that I shall be you and you shall be I. Let there descend upon Your bridal chamber the seed of light."[34] The seven women became Sophias, reborn as Light Maidens; the seven men became Cosmic Christs. This appears to be a gnostic form of the Sacred Marriage.

The mystery of the Light Maiden, as a rite in itself, *may* also point to one of our few references to psychedelic pharmaka in a gnostic ritual. Aside from the magnificent aesthetics of the room, the congressional chamber filled with fumigations of "balsam and sweet herbs . . . delicious scents of myrrh and other savory plants," as we read in the Ode to

Sophia. One noted scholar translates the savory plants as "Indian leaf," which has obvious inferences to cannabis.[35]

Another opaque reference that possibly points to ancient gnostic pharmaka use within a Bridal Chamber mystery can be found in the Nag Hammadi Library's *Authoritative Teaching*. The text opens with a passage that can certainly be interpreted as some kind of psychedelic experience, wherein a certain "bridegroom fetch[es] *it*." Unfortunately, we are not told what "it" is.

Trying a mystheogenic gestalt, the passage grows more tantalizing:

He presented *it* to her mouth to make her eat it like food, and he applied the word to her eyes as a medicine to make her see with her mind and perceive her kinsmen and learn about her root, in order that she might cling to her branch from which she had first come forth, in order that she might receive what is hers and renounce [material existence].[36]

See what I mean?!

Authoritative Teaching very well might have been describing precisely that—a truly ancient mystheogenic experience. Only this was not about meeting up with goddesses and gods as pagans would do; this was about a worthy woman surrendering her soul to the immaterial world, the Pleroma—the cosmic taproot from which she had first come forth.

Outside the actual gnostic texts themselves, church father Irenaeus references a "mystic rite" in his work *Against the Heresies,* which includes a "nuptial couch" used for a "sacred marriage" wherein the sexually conjoined participants mirror the aeons of the Pleroma. Irenaeus is undoubtedly referring to a personalized interpretation of the Bridal Chamber mystery. Some gnostics prepared for this rite by washing in a stream and then anointing themselves with an ointment of "that sweet odor which is above all things."[37] Other gnostics, he writes, find the preliminary soaking in water a superfluous endeavor, holding the true power to be found in the ointment alone—perhaps an indirect reference to the unguent's psychedelic properties?

Whether or not "Ode to Sophia," *Authoritative Teaching,* and *Against Heresies* are referencing cannabis (or any other pharmaka) hardly means that some gnostics didn't incorporate theogens into different interpretations of the Bridal Chamber mystery.

We have some pretty solid evidence, in fact, that some did.

PRECURSOR OF ANTICHRIST

No one took the pleasures of gnostic libertinism further than Marcus (c. mid-second century CE). Once a devotee of the Valentinian school, Marcus had a vision that would forever change his life when the "infinitely exalted Tetrad descended upon him from the invisible and indescribable places in the form of a woman . . . and expounded to him alone its own nature, and the origin of all things, which it had never before revealed to anyone."[38] Such a vision would not have been uncommon for a pupil studying under Valentinus; in fact, all Valentinians were expected to receive a revelation from the "living One," Jesus Christ.[39] Driven by this epiphany and also knowledgeable in ars magica pharmaka, Marcus eventually formed his own church, an institute equal parts Greek philosophy, pagan entheogenism, and sex magic.[40] Marcus's school differed from others like those of Simon and Carpocrates. In the former schools, members engaged in sexual spiritual rites *within the group.* On the other hand, Marcus's students were expected to find people *outside the group* to enchant with their charm, wit, and psychedelic Eucharists.[41] They would hit up local pubs and bathhouses seeking women and men to participate in their sexual-spiritual rites. Marcus had essentially appropriated Christianity into a cult of swingers and pickup artists.

It drove the church fathers crazy!*

---

*Irenaeus called him the "precursor of Antichrist"; see Irenaeus, *Against Heresies,* 1.13.

I am prone to believing that this gnostic troublemaker, Marcus, delighted in that.

Marcus's main mystery rite recalls something akin to the Bridal Chamber if only in its sanctification of coitus and pharmaka. However, instead of paralleling the sexual union of Sophia and Christ (as in the Bridal Chamber mystery), Marcus entheogenically awakened "Charis" in both women and men with a special trimma—a mixed wine. And here I do mean "entheogenic" proper. This was no mystheogen of the Simonians or pythiagen of Marcellina. For Charis, the goddess of grace, would spill her blood—her *essence*—into the Eucharist, making it accessible to anyone who partook, a use of pharmaka every bit as entheogenic as oracles "inhaling" Apollo or Bacchants "drinking" Dionysus.

All that Charis needed now was her Cosmic Christ.

Marcus eagerly filled that role. He would stir the potion before his disciple and ask her to drink it, saying:

> May that Charis who is before all things, and who transcends all knowledge and speech, fill your inner [person], and multiply in you her own knowledge, by sowing the grain of mustard seed in you as in good soil. . . . Receive first from me and by me [the gift of] Charis. Adorn yourself as a bride who is expecting her bridegroom, that you may be what I am, and I what you are. Establish the germ of light in your nuptial chamber. Receive from me a spouse, and become receptive of him, while you are received by him. Behold Charis has descended upon you.[42]*

In passionate frenzy, the two would then embrace each other. This may be perhaps the clearest example of a person mingling

---

*It seems the Charis cup was also pythiagenic, enabling whoever drank from it the ability to prophesy. Thus we see a magical potion said to possess two functions. Such was the complex nature of magic and spirituality in the ancient world.

Eastern pagan sex magic, aeon angelology (for lack of a better term), and Christianity. Indeed, the rite strikes me as very similar to one outlined in chapter 5, found in the *Demotic Magical Papyrus.**

Historians must appreciate the layers of historical social strata if we are to reach the truth. This kind of channeling works this way: 1. Around the rim of our funnel, there is a general gnostic belief that affirms that Jesus was an aeon, a purely spiritual being, the Cosmic Christ; 2. Within this broad framework, different schools adjusted their preferred tenants to the doctrine as seen fit; 3. Focusing even further, we find that some of those modifications included psychedelic pharmaka.

And these psychedelic pharmaka were themselves tailored to the individual within the broader range of beliefs. Here, among seekers of gnosis, we find quite the variety of uses. We saw how Simon Magus used his pharmaka as a mystheogenic Eucharist. Perhaps he guided his initiates through the visions as something akin to a modern trip sitter or ayahuasca ceremony facilitator? We can't say for certain whether or not the experience was properly entheogenic. There is simply no evidence to suggest that Simon had convinced his followers that by drinking from his cup they could somehow swallow divinity into themselves.

The mystery of the Bridal Chamber was a different story, serving as a way to generate the divine within by mirroring the sexual union of Sophia and the Cosmic Christ. In this way, certain selected worthy humans could find their way back to the Pleroma. As shown in an earlier chapter, some pagan religions incorporated pharmaka into their rites. Clearly these pagan converts, somewhat knowledgeable in philosophy and ars magica pharmaka, were bringing their personal forms of psychedelia into the Christian faith. Indeed, it is all too likely that some newly converted Christians took their pagan penchant for strong

---

*Only here, it is the blood of Osiris, not Charis, which gets poured into the cup (see page 86).

beer and wine, reinforced with pharmaka like opium, cannabis, mandrake, or henbane, into their new religion. The curious references to peculiar potions, odd oils, and mysterious morsels mentioned by the likes of Irenaeus, Hippolytus, Eusebius, and others certainly point in that direction. These church fathers' mentions of love philters and various poisoned cups were really different kinds of psychedelic Eucharists when viewed through the perspective of the people—the "heretics"—using them.

Such people like Simon, Carpocrates, and Marcellina demonstrate this. Gnostics came to incorporate entheogens, pythiagens, and mystheogens into their faiths through Paul's highly paganized Eucharist. Spiritual and magical intention seems to have made a very important difference from one experience to the next. We see an ancient awareness of "substance, set, and setting," even if these Christian gnostics never thought in such terms.

8

PATRONS OF THE SERPENT

Psychedelics and the Holy Doctrine
c. 30 CE–100 CE

<hr>

I will gladly burn a hundred if just one of them were guilty.
CONRAD OF MARBURG, PAPAL INQUISITOR

And my, did the church fathers ever react with such righteous venom! Such divine scorn! The infiltration of pagan elements into Christianity via gnosticism would have spelled doom for the new faith. And so apologists all came to rally behind a new paradigm of psychedelia. Far from the claims made by both bona fide scholars and conspiracy theorists banking on an outdated notion of ancient Christian mushroom-cult coverups, early Christianity in its numerous forms (as we saw over the last two chapters) had a rich and colorful psychedelic history.

What I hope to do in this concluding chapter about Christian psychedelic mysteries is demonstrate the *three* orthodox traditions—for they exist! But they have nothing to do with secretly painting *Amanita muscaria* mushrooms into medieval Christian art.

As more and more converts brought their psyche-magical traditions into the new faith, proto-apostolic Christians (that group that survived as orthodox) needed a way to keep the theogens out of private pagan worship—a fruitless task, as we have seen in prior sections of this work. Such psyche-magical plants had been employed by pagans for centuries.

The church fathers could do nothing about this.

So they simply appropriated it.

Leaders of the growing church hatched an idea: they would *Christianize* the way people sought direct experience of the godhead via theogens. And once again, they had an ancient magical plant, mandrake, to use as the vehicle for this new, Christian psychedelic mystery tradition.

THE SLEEP OF HEAVENLY CONTEMPLATION

The first orthodox psychedelic mystery tradition was a somnitheogenic one, which provided a way for good Christians to fall into oblivion in Christ. There, they could redouble their spiritual commitments to the Christian godhead. The idea was to drink or eat a strong pharmakon (in this case, mandrake), forget the material world, and become reunited with God in immaterialism—a somnitheogenic use of a theogen taken *directly* from pagan authors. In fact, the church fathers may have stumbled on the idea as expressed by Lucian of Samosata (c. 120–180 CE), who wrote, "Of course, wherever are you, asleep just as if under the influence of the mandrake root, which leads you to neither hear those who forswear, nor observe the committing of injustices, your eyes running and dazzled, blind towards anything discernible and your ears deafened just like those well past their prime?"[1]

Now compare this to a comment made by the first great Christian apologist, Origen (c. 180–250 CE), living only a few decades after Lucian. While discussing the mandrake found in Genesis, Origen accepts Lucian's prescription.

Medical experts tell us that the mandrake acts as a soporific but that, if taken in the right quantities, it is not poisonous. The Christian should follow the lesson contained in this: he must not kill himself, but he must fall asleep to sin. And even as those who have drunk of the mandrake no longer feel the movements of their body, so should those who seek to cultivate virtue empty the cup and thus lull their passions into quiet sleep.[2]

Basil (c. 330–379 CE) agreed. But he also felt that Christians need not limit themselves to just *one* theogen. After outlining the practical medical benefits of mandrake, hemlock, and opium, Basil remarks on the effects these plants might have on good Christians. For Basil, a mind turned to Christ would transform these poisons into spiritual medicines: "These plants, then, instead of making you accuse the Creator, give you a new subject for gratitude."[3] With these words, Basil allowed other theogens (besides the already consecrated mandrake) into Christianity.

Theodorat, the bishop of Syria (mid-fifth century), blended both the ideas of Origen and those of Basil into his treatment on the subject. For Theodorat, true Christian enlightenment came through reading scripture under the influence of pharmaka. Only, unlike Basil, who preferred mandrake, Theodorat was happy that opium was also considered sanctified: "An opiate [brings] . . . deadness to the world and sin, and tranquil sleep, free from all disturbances attained by quaffing the chalice of holy doctrine."[4] These all seem to deal with direct, personal experience of the divine—a subdued form of Terence McKenna's "heroic dose," wherein a person takes five grams of dried mushrooms and "lie[s] down in darkness and silence."[5] While Theodorat and McKenna had vastly different approaches and different psychedelics to work with, their goals remained the same: spiritual transcendence through theogens.

As usual for the church fathers, not everyone agreed with this assessment of the power of a theogenic experience. Ambrose (c. 340–400 CE), for example, wasn't having any of it. Borrowing a term first used by Philo, "sober drunkenness" (*sobria ebrietas*),[6] and reinforced with John 6:35,* Ambrose's reprimand is very telling: "Why need I speak of opium which has come to be used almost daily?"[7] He asks all who would listen to consider Jesus alone as the only "pharmakon" one need imbibe: "And Christ to us for food shall be, from Him our drink that welleth free, the Spirit's wine, that maketh whole, and mocking not, exalts the soul."[8]

Boethius (c. fifth century), a Roman statesman turned Christian, agreed. Boethius had inside knowledge of both the pagan use of theogens and how they had infiltrated Christianity. Apparently very upset about watching those in his new faith fall back into their old habits, Boethius eventually tried to warn the flock about pagan theogens: "This terrible pharmaka is so strong that it cuts to the core of a person's being. [The pharmakon] enters to the inner-essence of the self. Those pharmaka that destroy the body are not nearly as powerful as those that corrupt the mind."[9]

The opinions of both Ambrose and Boethius were quickly drowned out by others who felt abstinence too impractical. Indeed, in order to enter such a spiritual mental state necessitated a reprieve, if even momentarily, from the material world. Such a notion confirms that the theogenic use of pharmaka by pagan-cum-gnostic Christians had penetrated the minds of the orthodox.

St. Basil is a case in point. For it was Basil, not Ambrose, whose ideas won the debate. By medieval times, Lucian's idea had been completely Christianized. The unknown author of the Trudperter Hohelied (The Trudpert Song of Songs, c. 1160) puts the new Christian psychedelic mystery tradition on full display: "The bark of [mandrake] root brings stupefaction. This root denotes God, the image of whom was Christ. On earth he was a man. For us he is a medicine and a security for eternal life. He is the root. . . . The root's bark is the Holy Ghost, this means the numbing vapor which makes all lovers of holy Christ sleep."[10]

Wow!

---

*"I am the bread of life."

Even into medieval times, it seems that few churchmen cared about how Christians used these powerful plants, provided they used them in an *orthodox* manner: to escape the evils of materialism and fall into somnitheogenic bliss in Christ.

Let's invoke Thomas of Perseigne (d. c. 1190) to round out this first section of the orthodox somnitheogenic mystery tradition.

> For the mandragoras symbolize aspiration through contemplation. This tranquility makes it possible for a person to fall a sleep [*sic*] of such delightful sweetness that he will no longer feel anything of the cutting which his earthly enemies visit upon him, that he no longer pays attention to any worldly things. For the soul has now closed its eyes to all that is outside—it lies in the good sleep of the eternal.[11]

So long as Jesus remained copilot, a person's mind and soul could not be harmed by seeking spiritual oblivion in a draft of mandrake—or, as Basil adds, drafts of opium or hemlock.

And we mustn't ignore cannabis either. Many psychenauts these days are familiar with Herodotus's famous passage in *The Histories* where he describes the cannabis rites of the Scythians (*Histories* 4.75.1). But they may not know that *all* the earliest Christian writers were familiar with Herodotus, whose *The Histories* (c. fifth century BCE) was the standard text from which all authors learned to write. Without question, every gospel author (and Paul), and *all* their later editors, and every single church father, knew exactly what cannabis was and how it was used spiritually.* In a way, *The Histories* was ancient peoples' *Schoolhouse Rock!* If you could write in Greek and/or Latin, you learned how to do it by painstakingly copying out *The Histories*. We can therefore conclude that, had they not discovered cannabis elsewhere (doubtful), Christian authors certainly learned of it via Herodotus. In fact,

---

*Clement of Rome (*Epistle to the Corinthians*), Clement of Alexandria (*Stromata*, 1.14), Origen (*Contra Celsum*, 6.39), Augustine (*The City of God*), Athenagoras of Athens (*A Plea to Christians*, 17) and many others all show familiarity with Herodotus.

one medieval Jewish physician and biblical scholar, Rabbi Moses ben Maimon (popularly known as Maimonides, c. 1135–1205), named cannabis the "most frequently used" pharmakon of his day.[12]

Cannabis, at times, found use to ensure whole congregations would enter righteous entrancement. In an obscure text, *The Travels of Macarius* (c. mid-seventeenth century), we read, "The first thing our Lord the Patriarch took in hand, was three clumps of wood, three stalks of hemp . . . and he lighted up the fire in two grates." Once the fire was burning brightly, sending its magical cannabis fumes into the air, the priests would "read from the holy Gospels."[13] This was, in its essence, what Theodorat might have recommended—only not with opium in the privacy of one's home and inner space, but rather with cannabis in a collective spiritual setting. The nonchalance with which Macarius's biographer, John of Aleppo, (bolstered by Maimonides) wrote gives us clear evidence of cannabis as a tool of spiritual ascendance in orthodox Christianity. It seems unlikely that Macarius's congregation was the first of its kind. Most importantly, his anecdote gives extra precedent to Benet's translation of cannabis as kaneh bosm, meaning "the sweet cane."[14] Still more importantly, should Benet's theory prove incorrect, we still have direct textual evidence of at least one early modern Christian cannabis fumigation ceremony left to us by Macarius.

In these early and medieval "orthodox" uses of pharmaka, we can see plainly that the topic was addressed by the church fathers. It all began with mandrake, the *one* theogen with scriptural precedent. That soon changed when Basil added opium and hemlock into the mix, and those in Macarius's congregation (and probably scores of others throughout history) decided that Jesus could be realized in cannabis fumes. The use of pharmaka in ancient, medieval, and Renaissance-era Christianity wasn't covered up, or shunned at all, as conspiracy theorists ask us to believe in modern times—in fact, quite the opposite. Theogens were endorsed by several church fathers! Christians, it seems, were all too eager to employ these powerful spirit plants and discuss the benefits of such an experience.

But such concepts quickly led church leaders to develop a *second* Christian psychedelic mystery tradition.

A most disconcerting tradition . . .

CHRISTIANIZING PAGAN PSYCHEDELIA

The second proto-apostolic psychedelic mystery tradition is slightly less enlightening than the first. Some decades after Jesus's execution, his name began to appear in magical texts and curse tablets.[15] Additionally, as we saw in the previous chapter, Neoplatonists were also mingling Christian motifs with their gnostic rites.

This had to stop.

ॐ

Earlier, we saw how many Christian thought-leaders had identified the forbidden fruit as a metaphor for *all* temptation. But other early Christian writers like Tatian the Syrian (c. 120–180) advanced a totally different hypothesis. For Tatian in particular, eating the fruit meant becoming "sexually aware."[16] Both Clement and Irenaeus disagreed vehemently with this interpretation. People, after all, needed no further incentive to promiscuity other than their natural impulses. Unrelenting (as always), Irenaeus referred to followers of Tatian as "patrons of the serpent and death."[17]

But Tatian's views on the fruit of carnal knowledge would eventually be addressed in a more favorable light by other second-century contemporaries like the anonymous author(s) of *Physiologus*. Therein, the fruit from the Tree of Knowledge of Good and Evil is identified as the mandrake. Its role (according to *Physiologus*) was an obvious reference to the ecstatic effects of the plant when used during sex. Employing elephants as a metaphor, the female elephant (Eve) seduces the reluctant

male (Adam) by feeding him a mandrake.[18] We might well consider if
these "love apples," as the Hebrews often called them, formed the basis
for our later, more modern interpretation of the forbidden fruit represented as an apple.[19]

Tatian's identification of the forbidden fruit as a metaphor for sex
warranted quick response from his theological enemies. Furthermore,
Physiologus confirmed that some people were fusing Christianity with
paganism in the popular literature of the time. The fathers were out-
raged. What if good Christians used Tatian's interpretation of the fruit
from the Tree, along with *Physiologus,* to justify their own use of mandrake as a way for Jesus to fulfill the problem of Adam's transgression
through sex magic? Irenaeus (and most others) favored the original
Pauline interpretation as the Fall representing human temptation; all
this talk of mandrake and sex magic could only serve as a foundation
for the origins of free will and its byproduct—human depravity.

The magical and pagan influences that had already permeated
Christianity needed new arguments from the church fathers. The surviving apologetic literature demonstrates two key points: first, Jesus
was thought a magician since early times (hence, gnostic magicians like
Marcellina and Marcus); second, the church fathers worked desperately
to hide this matter. But in their efforts to account for all the discrepan-
cies between who Jesus was and who they thought he was, the fathers
developed an ingeniously sinister idea: these psyche-magical plants, it
came to be assumed, could be used to *depaganize* the masses. In fact, if a
newly converted Christian started to wax nostalgic for her former pagan
excesses, the church fathers recommended—*immediately*—a mandrake
potion. And they had a whole new Christian psychedelic mystery symbolism to couch their concerns. Apponius (c. fourth–fifth centuries)
simply took the radix apostatica from the Nazarene tradition (which
was concerned with Jews who had not yet converted to Christianity)
and foisted it on the pagan world. First, it was the "headless" Hebrews

who did not believe in Christ. Now, it was the pagan world that needed conversion.

Apponius outlines this new psychedelic orthodoxy clearly: "Mandrakes symbolize the pagans; until recently they were a wild sort living their lives sunk deep in the earth; thanks to the law of nature they were like people endowed with reason, but they lacked the head of faith, by which I mean him who is the head of man, namely Christ."[20]

In fact, a detail that escaped me while writing *The Witches' Ointment* deals with famed physician Hildegard of Bingen (1098–1179). In my last book, I took Hildegard's warning to wash mandrake roots before using them in love magic (to "cleanse them of their power") as a somewhat naïve, senseless superstition; Hildegard couldn't really believe that washing a mandrake root would take away all its (unknown to her) chemical properties, could she? My own anachronisms got the best of me. Now, with this new lens of what ancient and medieval psychedelic Christianity looked like, we can see that Hildegard was not washing the root but *baptizing* it. This baptism "washed away" the occult pagan notions of such a powerful theogen. After all, Hildegard was recommending mandrake not to excite the senses but to calm them. Her prescription sought to magically depaganize the root so that it would sedate the users, not excite them. Therefore, proper mindset was crucial when using mandrake: "The influence of the devil is more present [in mandrake] than in other herbs; consequently [a person] is stimulated by it according to personal desire, which may be good or bad."[21] A good Christian, pure in heart and clear of conscious, could now enjoy a once-deadly delight. Only Christians had the power (through Christ) to turn a pagan poison into a true theogen, or so the church leaders believed.

There is really no way to say this lightly: this second branch of the orthodox psychedelic mystery tradition is based entirely off spiritual bigotry. Psychedelic experiences were *fine*—provided you were a Christian. For the fathers were certainly working off 1 Enoch, the author of which declared that it was the fallen angels who taught humankind "charms and enchantments, and cutting of roots and made them acquainted with plants" (1 Enoch 7:10). But a mind purified by Christ served as the only way a person could take these powerful plants safely (as Basil assures).

This use of pharmaka to wipe out surviving pagan beliefs saw its most foul misuse centuries later in the hands of clergymen administering torture to an accused "witch." With much regret, Freidrich Spee von Langenfeld (1591–1635), the author of *Cautio Criminalis* (*Prosecutors' Manual*, 1631), spoke of a most disturbing use of these pharmaka— to dose women during torture in hopes of making them confess. He writes, "In some places the torture is permitted to drive out the sorcery of silence . . . by supplying some kind of potion." The ingredients of the draft, von Langenfeld did not know. But soon after the accused had drunk this potion, "they were confused, as if they were surrounded or besieged in the middle of a crowd of spirits." To stop this mental torture, those accused simply confessed their spiritual sins, whether real or imagined.[22]

Such was the culmination of centuries of divine chauvinism. What started as a bigoted (albeit essentially harmless) approach to reconfiguring pagan psychedelia in the first few centuries CE through medieval times had snowballed into such a horrific abuse of power by the Renaissance era.

And so passed away the Olympians of yore.

ECSTASY DRINKS AT THE FESTIVAL OF LAMPS

There is still a *third* orthodox psychedelic tradition that we may uncover (and it is far less evil than the prior)—that of intoxicated celebration. Interestingly, it is our modern ideas of Christian abstinence that have colored our views of the spiritual benefits of collective, festive celebration. Even famed mycologist Paul Stamets seems to be operating under this (relatively new) idea of Christian temperance. "I'm not into party-ing with psilocybin mushrooms," he said during an interview on *The Joe Rogan Experience.* "I think these are serious tools. When it comes to something that is so powerful, so important, let's not jeopardize its use medically, and the benefits of society in the future, by appeal-ing to the lowest common denominator."[23] Whether he realizes it or not, Stamets is operating under modern *Christian* assumptions when he suggests that mushrooms are not meant for collective revelry (or, as he might say, "partying"). We today separate the sacred from the pro-fane, carefully demarcated by that charged word *recreational.* But as we saw earlier with the rites of Dionysus, especially those pertaining to the Thracian Satrae, a psychedelic mushroom (psilocybin or otherwise) was almost certainly added to the wine. On a philosphical note, I do not see how eating mushrooms and dancing naked in a forest with friends and lovers in joy and gratitude constitutes the lowest common denominator.

To our modern sense, once something becomes recreational it ceases to be spiritual. But our ancestors, even our Christian ones, never made such a distinction, which can be seen in the liberal way Christmas was celebrated only a couple of centuries ago. Even just before America's emancipation from Britain, Virginian minister Samuel Davies (1723–1761) would complain that Christmastime served only as an exercise in "sinning, sexuality, luxury, and vari-ous forms of extravegnce, as though [people] were not celebrating the birth of Jesus but of Venus, or Bacchus, whose most sacred rites were mysteries of inequity and debauchry!"[24] When we consider the Bacchic tones out of which Paul crafted the new covenantal Eucharist, none of this should strike us as very surprising.

❦

There were other problems as well, which mostly have to do with the ambiguity of some of the earliest Christian writings on the subject. Take the Didache, a text that has been dated to the late first century CE. The anonymous author(s) felt the need to calm the drinking parties of the early house churches. But, she also knew that harsh proscriptions would not attract many converts.

Addressing all Christians, clergy, laity, and hopefuls: "We say this, not [that] they are not to drink at all, otherwise it would be to the reproach of what God has made for cheerfulness, but that they not be disordered by wine. For the Scripture does not say, [']Do not drink wine; but what says it? Drink not wine to drunkenness.'"[25]

I suppose the author(s) of the Didache decided it best to leave up to each individual to find the fine balance between "cheerfulness" and "disordered." For this admonishment, some Christians possibly abstained altogether; others might have drunk the wine pure, unmixed with either water or a pharmakon. Still others, especially converting pagans, probably interpreted the passage as including their traditional pagan psychedelic brews; so long as they remained cheery and not belligerent (as adding a pharmakon would certainly aid), they felt within the confines of the rule as outlined in the Didache. Therefore, a Christian could use a pharmaka-wine as long as it did not cause one to drift too deeply into an altered state.

But who then, exactly, would police this?

Today, we tend to see the phrase "good tidings and great joy" specifically tied to Christmas. But the concept originates in the Roman Saturnalia celebrations,* which were certainly current during the days of Jesus's ministry. At the time, Saturn had become a god of vegetation. During Saturnalia, friends, families, and neighbors lit the streets of Rome with rows of lamps, illuminating the cold, winter air. "Flute-girls" provided the music, and bonfires were ignited in more open areas so that those who so chose could undress and warm their dancing bodies beside the roaring fire. Celebrants added decorative wreaths and garlands of evergreen branches to their homes and streets—clear indications of life in

---

*The festival ran from December 17 to December 23.

the dead of winter. They then celebrated the joys of existence and the coming promise of Proserpine,* for it was Saturn himself who demanded it: "No one is to do any business, public or private, during the festival, except what pertains to sport, luxurious living and entertainment."[26]

It was a helluva week!

Beyond the festive revelry, the Saturnalia celebrations, interestingly, recognized something virtually unheard of in the larger Roman Empire: human dignity. Even the lowest of society deserved a chance to sit at a fine dining table and enjoy service from others. Indeed, social roles were reversed: masters would serve their slaves. This allowed the lower class to share in the pharmaceutically reinforced wines that fueled the celebrations of the upper class. As Lucian of Samosata commented, "[During Saturnalia] all shall drink the same wine, and neither stomach trouble nor headache shall give the rich man an excuse for being the only one to drink the better quality."[27] This is an indirect (though clear) reference to psyche-magical plant infusions. Indeed, what other kind of wine was used for head and stomach troubles in the ancient world besides those mixed with cannabis, opium, or mandrake? As shown above, all three theogens were expressly allowed for Christians to use. In fact, Lucian also makes reference to the "loving-cups" (i.e., love philters) passed around at dinner. When we also consider that Christianity served originally as a religion for the marginalized of society, we might possibly credit Saturnalia as the pagan festival that *most* introduced ceremonial, psyche-magical mixtures into the new faith.

But Saturnalia might not be the only place such pharmaka entered Christianity. There were also the Yule (or Jul) celebrations in northern Europe. We don't know much about how pagans celebrated Yule, as the only records we have of the festival comes from Christian authors eager to color pagan rites with Christian imagery.[28] We do know that those original celebrators of Yule had special beers they prepared (let's call

---

*Proserpine was the Roman analogue for the Greek Persephone.

them Julbeers for ease). One scholar of Norwegian folklore believes this kind of drink to have been shared among friends and family to obtain "ecstatic connection with each other and with the gods."[29] Should we really be surprised that such a Julbeer, such a "mead of inspiration,"[30] might contain cannabis, opium, wormwood, henbane, or even psilocybin or *Amanita muscaria* mushrooms?

When we consider the survival of these ancient rites into Old Germany, we can see the psychedelic magic of early Christmas traditions: "At Christmas time, especially in eastern Germany, people eat baked poppy goods and cake. . . . To eat poppy on Christmas Eve brings lots of money"—and merriment as well. Additionally, a young girl eager to know of her future bridegroom will bake an opium biscuit and feed it to her dog. The dog, now released into the yard, entranced by the opium and jumping around wildly, will tell the girl which direction her lover will come from (by hopping in his direction). Finally, due to the witches' penchant for opium, seeds of that plant should be dropped outside the front doors of houses. The witch will spend all her time counting the seeds instead of entering the home.[31]

Recall from the previous chapter that pagans and Christians intermarried—and quite often at that. Who's to say that newlyweds wouldn't celebrate Saturnalia one year and Christmas the next? Perhaps Yule the year after that? After all, David's church had not transformed into a Goliath yet. Church "authorities" had no actual power in the larger pagan landscape. They could merely complain. Only later, with Constantine's Edict of Toleration (311 CE), could Christians grow out of the house churches they had existed in for centuries and really compete for the minds and souls of the masses. In this process, they would baptize such pagan pharmaka-wines in the living waters of Christ, giving us a glimpse of our third and final peek into the earliest orthodox psychedelic mystery traditions: that of theogenic collective revelry.

THE TRUE STORY OF THE
PSYCHEDELIC SANTA

While we are on the subject of Christian entheogen usage in the ancient and medieval worlds, I feel the need to address a certain unsupportable meme that has taken the psychedelic renaissance by storm. Namely, that our modern notion of Santa Claus derives from an association with the *Amanita muscaria* mushroom. The idea seems to have grown out of the larger sacred mushroom theory discussed earlier. To recap: a few decades ago, philologist John Marco Allegro claimed in *The Sacred Mushroom and the Cross* (1970) that linguistic evidence found in the *Dead Sea Scrolls* demonstrated that Jesus's original ministry not only lacked its famed leader, but that said famed leader also was really a "cover story" for magic mushroom use.

How intriguing!

But most sadly, Allegro made it all up. The crucial vocabulary he employed in *The Sacred Mushroom and the Cross,* which was necessary to confirm his theory, was quickly recognized as unsound by other competent lingisuists of the day who were also working on the *Dead Sea Scrolls.** Most psychedelic social scientists, even those who still accept some portion of Allegro's *Amanita muscaria*–Jesus theory, will readily admit that Allegro's overzealous desire to give Christanity a psychedelic origin caused him to fudge the evidence to fit his conclusions.

But they never fully abandoned the theory; instead, they moved the goalpost away from linguistics and into art. Scores of recent books (from the scholarly[32] to the conspiratorially laughable[33]) now claim that—forget linguistics—the true story of psychedelic Christianity can be seen in stained-glass pieces, mosaics, and frescos found all over Europe. The theorists claim that mushrooms are hidden (or blatant— depending on convenience) in numerous works of Christian art. Along

---

*Godfrey Driver was not only Allegro's doctoral adviser but also held views more radical than Allegro's regarding the Qumran materials. Still, his career never fell to ruins like that of his former student. Baigent and Leigh, *The Dead Sea Scrolls Deception,* 63.

with this new art claim came the bold idea that *all things Christian* must have a psychedelic history.

Their next target was good old St. Nick, Santa Claus.

The most oft-heard claim holds that Santa Claus is based off Siberian shaman-reindeer herders. Reindeer, as noted earlier, eat the *Amanita muscaria* mushroom for its entrancing effects. It is claimed by the *discipuli Allegrae* that therein lie the origins of the "flying reindeer" that carry Santa Claus across the sky every Christmas Eve. This feeds into a second line of inference, which holds that traces of the *Amanita muscaria* can be seen in the red and white of Santa's outfit (the same colors as the mushroom). Let's take both those claims in turn.

Regarding the shaman-reindeer herder claim, there is an unnatural convergence of three historical lines necessary to make the theory work: (1) the history of St. Nicholas, (2) the history of Santa Claus, (3) the history of shaman-reindeer herders occupying the colds of Siberia. The correlation works in this wise: Santa is associated with reindeer (today). Siberian shamans eat *Amanita muscaria* mushrooms to fall into trances.[34] Reindeer also like *Amanita muscaria* mushrooms.[35] Reindeer live in Siberia—so case closed, right?!

Not quite.

All three lines are totally historically unrelated. When Santa (actually, St. Nick) made his way from Mira (modern day Turkey) into the colds of Russia, the locals saw him as a protector of sailors—*not* reindeer herders. On the other hand, for the poor of Russia, St. Nick was a symbol of protection from the cruel appetites of the czar.[36] The fact remains, Santa's association with reindeer is *specifically* an American thing, holding no historical Russian analogue with St. Nicholas or Siberian reindeer herders or otherwise.[37] Early depictions of Santa Claus show him traveling through a variety of methods, not just reindeer. On Christmas cards dating from roughly the late nineteenth century to the early twentieth century, he can be seen riding a sleigh not pulled by any animals; other times a lone donkey pulls his sleigh; other times Santa drives a car or rides a bicycle. In one of his earliest stories, Santa sailed a ship—no reindeer required. It's only in modern times that Santa became exclusively charioted by reindeer. There is no direct line of evidence to substantiate the flying Siberian reindeer–*Amanita muscaria* theory. It only works if we ignore the larger cultural development that created our modern ideas of Santa Claus and how he traveled.

But I should also note that St. Nicholas *did* have some shamanic powers according to at least one old folktale about him. And as we'll see, the story deals not with Siberian shamans but rather pulls from *global* shamanic traditions.

At a party for saints, St. Basil went to all the attendees and filled each of their cups from a "golden jug." The party continued. But while the others "talked away . . . St. Nicholas began to nod, and his cup tilted in his hand." The other saints put the party on hold and took note of Nicholas's pathetically low tolerance. Finally, St. John nudged the sleeping saint and inquired as to why he would fall asleep with a drinking vessel in his hand. The roused Nicholas replied, "St. John, since you ask—the enemy has raised a terrible storm in the Aegean Sea; so, while my body dozed here, my spirit was off to rescue all the ships and bring them to shore."[38] It turns out that Basil's golden jug contained some kind of theogen, the effects of which caused Nicholas, with his natural shaman inclinations, to astral project. No other saint at the party had this reaction. Thus, we see a dichotomy: Saints could enjoy their theogenic drinks in collective revelry. But only Nicholas, the shaman, would be unable to stop from falling into a trance under the awesome power of the theogen. Moreover, here he is (as expected) protecting *sailors,* having nothing to do with Siberian shamans at all. I think it also worth noting here that in this one premodern story outlining St. Nick's ability to astral project, flying reindeer play no role.

This is a universal shamanic tradition (i.e., a theogen causing astral projection); yes, it is found among *Amanita muscaria*–eating Siberian shamans, but it's also found in other parts of the world with other entheogens. So while St. Nicholas certainly falls in line with shamanism in this story, our modern Santa Claus has nothing to do with any of it historically. Now, it is certainly easy for us today to claim that St. Nick *is* Santa Claus, so the facts remain. But this mingling of St. Nick and Santa Claus happened in modern, not ancient nor even medieval, times.

Having grounded the flying reindeer, let's take a look at the second claim: that remains of the secret history of the *Amanita muscaria* can be seen in the red and white of Santa's costume—the very colors of that famous mushroom. The evidence the discipuli Allegrae marshal in support of this claim rests in two areas: a legend regarding the "flesh" of the German god Wotan and postcards first manufactured in Germany and Austria in the late 1800s.

To deal with Wotan's flesh first. Despite claims of the *Amanita muscaria* flowing into the Christmas season through Santa's mushroom-eating reindeer, it is more likely that they entered the holiday through the Northern European ecstasy drinks of Yule and New Year, though the best evidence for this comes from just east of the Italian peninsula. Murmurs of an old tradition in Kocevje, in southern Yugoslavia, tell a particular story about the Germanic god Wotan (Odin). One Christmas Eve, Wotan found himself rushing through a forest on his horse, fleeing a gang of devils that followed close behind. As saliva from Wotan's galloping horse hit the ground, the *Amanita muscaria* popped up. Since then, *Amanita muscaria* sprouts anew every year. Rumor has it that later on the mushroom was called "the flesh of Wotan" by some rural folk and was added to their Julbeers (and presumably their Christmas Eve beers as well).[39]

This claim is repeated often in both popular and scholarly literature.[40] But how true is it, and how far back into history does it go? All the references to this story originate from H. Kleijn, former president of the Royal Society of Natural History in Amsterdam in his book *Mushrooms and Other Fungi* (1962).[41] I can find no earlier reference to his assertion, and Kleijn doesn't cite anyone. He seems to have picked this up through travel or perhaps even through personal experience with the locals. Unfortunately, there is no hardcore evidence that the *Amanita muscaria* symbolized Wotan's flesh and was added to Julbeers until the modern era.

❦

The second line of evidence advanced by the discipuli Allegrae rests in Germanic postcards from the turn of the twentieth century. Now, this *does* have to be explained, as the postcards unambiguously show *Amanita muscaria* mushrooms. This, claim the discipuli Allegrae, proves positively that Santa and Christmas (and, ipso facto, Jesus) have psychedelic mushroom roots. At first glance, this seems plausible. But before we celebrate, it might be advantageous to ask how those mushrooms got on those postcards in the first place.

Let's look at the earliest of these German cards. We see some kind of association with pigs, the *Amanita muscaria,* and little elflike creatures (figures 8.1 and 8.2 on page 163). There are many more just like these. What you will have noticed immediately is that Santa Claus does not appear on a single one of them. That's because these aren't Christmas cards, they are New Year cards.* And these are not Santa's elves; at least nothing in the cards would lead one to think so. They seem to be autonomous little creatures unbound by the time-clock at Santa's workshop.

So far we have some very intriguing cards featuring the *Amanita muscaria,* but nothing to tie them to Santa Claus. Still, how did those mushrooms get on those cards in the first place? What do they mean?

Looking at some later cards, we get more clues. Here we see similar elf fellows with their mushrooms and pigs. But look closer. What else do you see? Horseshoes and four-leaf clovers, right? (See figures 8.3 and 8.4 on page 164.) They are not on the earlier German and Austrian cards.

Where did they come from?

As late as 1909, many Americans were asking that same question.

---

*Many of the cards read "Gelukkig Nieujaar," "Happy New Year."

Fig. 8.1. *Glücksschwein und Fliegenpilze.* Lucky pigs and the fly agaric: Germanic symbols of luck. They bring a chimney sweep (also a sign of good fortune), a letter (good news, perhaps?), and three baskets of flowers. The large number one on the *Amanita* house (ummm . . . *I want this house!*) represents the first day of the New Year.

At a congressional meeting that year, Francis Hamilton addressed the issue directly while discussing tariffs. It is here where the true history of the great *Amanita muscaria* postcard mystery unfolds. Taking the floor, Hamilton spoke:

The German post-card manufacturer suddenly realized that the demands for post cards was greater in the United States than in any other country. . . . The result of all of this activity was that for a long time the German and Austrian manufacturers were the only

Fig. 8.2. "Happy New Year."

Fig. 8.3. These fellows also want to wish you a Happy New Year, for they have traveled all the way to America and returned to Denmark with strange, new symbols of fortune: four-leaf clovers and horseshoes.

ones [producing cards] in this this country. The American manufacturer secured a small foothold by reason of the fact that . . . he knew American ideas, and produced cards to meet these ideas. . . . While in Europe, and especially Germany and Austria, Christmas and New Year's cards were printed with pictures of pigs and mushrooms, these being considered lucky omens, as horseshoes and four-leaf clovers are with us, and while at first foreign manufacturers sent us Christmas and New-Year cards of pigs and mushrooms the significance of which we did not know, they now print those cards

Fig. 8.4. This little gnome dude and his pig want to share their mushrooms and wish you all "Healthy Tidings and a Happy New Year."

Fig. 8.5. Angel with *Amanita muscaria.* During my debate with Jerry Brown (author, *The Psychedelic Gospels*), he projected this image as evidence for a tie between Santa Claus and the *Amanita muscaria.* But here we see that Santa Claus is not even present. In fact, he isn't present on any of the original cards. Moreover, this card reads not only "Merry Christmas" but also "Happy New Year," a holdover from its Germanic roots. It is closer to a secular "holiday" card than a specifically Christmas card.

especially for the American market with horseshoes, hollies, and four-leaf clovers; in fact, the American trade is so important to the European manufacturers that certain factories are printing no cards except those for the American market, and some factories have their entire output sold for an entire year to some one importer.[42]

And there you have it. The mushrooms that appear in early twentieth-century New Year postcards have nothing to do with Siberian shamanism, reindeer, Wotan's horse, or even Santa Claus himself, though they were certainly brought into Christmas via old-fashioned German winter-festival customs. And technically, Hamilton is somewhat mistaken when he speaks of "Christmas and New Year's cards . . . printed with pictures of pigs and mushrooms." There simply are *no* German Christmas cards that feature the *Amanita muscaria;* only New Year cards (and later American Christmas and New Year cards). The good luck pig (*Glücksschwein*) and fly agaric mushroom (*Fliegenpilze*) are symbols of *Glücksbringer,** an old German custom of good fortune when friends and families exchange small lucky charms. We begin to see the merging of the old Germanic with the new American luck motifs with this untitled card (figure 8.5).

*In some Germanic areas, a person of good fortune is called Glückspilz.

For starters, angels have replaced the elves (how American!). Along with the *Amanita muscaria* hung around the doorknob, the angel also comes equipped with distinctly American symbols of luck: horseshoes and four-leaf clovers. We see further evidence of this bridge in the accompanying text: while all the Germanic cards read only "Happy New Year," this American card reads "Merry Christmas and a Happy New Year." Other cards, however, feature all the symbols of luck and retain only the original Happy New Year.

And while we do not know exactly how the *Amanita muscaria* came to be considered lucky, perhaps there is an explanation that has to do with the deep pagan roots of the psychedelic experience. I speak of the fairy realms (which I will outline more fully in the next chapter). In the broad range of European pagan beliefs dealing with elves, fairies, other magically fun creatures, and the theogens used to access them, it is quite possible that some Europeans were opening these fairy realms through the *Amanita muscaria*.

Still, we are a long way away from Siberian shaman-reindeer herders.

Fig. 8.6. All four elements of symbolic fortune are present: pig, *Amanita*, horseshoe, and four-leaf clover. Interestingly, while the disculpi Allegrae claim that Santa's suit comes from the *Amanita*, here we see the artist had the same idea of decorating her elf in flora . . . only she chose to decorate him in clovers, not mushrooms! There are, in fact, no known versions of Santa looking so blatantly like an *Amanita muscaria* as this guy does dressed in clovers. I am very interested to hear how the discipuli Allegrae account for this . . .

Should my theory prove true, then we are indeed hearing echoes of the magical effects of the *Amanita muscaria*—echoes that eventually *did* sneak into popular Christmas traditions. But it happened in recent times, in the mid-twentieth century, as we saw with Kleijn and his exposé of Kocevje people in southern Yugoslavia. Perhaps *they* have *Amanita muscaria* holiday drink traditions extending back into the furthest reaches of history, but they remained local until the mid-twentieth century. And even then, when other Germanic peoples' *Amanita muscaria* tradition reached American shores, it did so as an ordinary symbol of luck, completely devoid of its theogenic associations. Mordecai Cooke's *The Seven Sisters of Sleep* (1860) had long been published outlining the Siberian uses of the *Amanita muscaria*. And yet, through the years of the great mushroom, pig, horseshoe, and clover fad in America, *no one* associated the *Amanita muscaria* with Santa Claus *or* Siberian shamans. Even John Marco Allegro, who unwittingly sparked this whole meme before his passing in 1988, never made such a connection.

This fusion is far from "ancient."

It happened in living memory.

This all helps explain why the earliest of these German and Austrian cards feature not Santa Claus but elves (sometimes solo, other times in pairs, other times in groups). These elves are the spirits from the otherworld, accessed through the ingestion of theogens like the *Amanita muscaria* (so I hypothesize). But they only found a place in the Christmas story much later (mid-twentieth century) when they became associated with an earlier, decidedly nonpsychedelic St. Nicholas and the German and Austrian postcards of the early 1900s.

Still, none of this explains where the red and white from Santa's outfit comes from.

If not from the mushroom, from where?

In the mid-1800s something happened that would change the colors of his wardrobe forever—the Civil War. The Civil War had more impact on Santa's attire than any other event in history. The Civil War holds the true story of how Santa's costume changed from brown fur to the familiar red and white. Take a look at this most early image of the jolly ole elf (figure 8.7). Here we see Santa Claus giving gifts to Union soldiers. His outfit (despite the black-and-white illustration) shows stars on his jacket and stripes on his trousers. The artist is clearly comparing Santa's outfit to the American flag, which waves gently in the snowy breeze above him. Santa was a sign of emancipation. He was feeding, protecting, and spreading goodwill to the Union soldiers fighting against the cruel injustice of slavery. The red and white came not from the *Amanita muscaria,* but rather stems from the red, white, and *blue* of the American flag. The illustrator of the piece, Thomas Nast, was an abolitionist, even going on to paint a striking mural titled *Emancipation* shortly after the war.

Years later, in 1931, when Coca-Cola adopted Santa as their spokes-

Fig. 8.7. Santa gives provisions to Union soldiers. His costume: a star-spangled fur suit complemented by the American flag.

elf, they dropped the blue from his Civil War outfit, as that soda company had already been advertising for years using the other two colors: red and white. That is the history of Santa's costume. It has absolutely nothing to do with the *Amanita muscaria,* and everything to do with the emancipation of an entire group of people unjustly enslaved in America.

Additionally, in the later decades of the 1800s and the first decades of the twentieth century (during the period of the great German postcard invasion), Santa's outfit went through a variety of changes. Sometimes his attire was red, white, blue, and green; other times it was red and black; other times it was red, white, and green; still other times Santa dons a long, brown cloak. At no point does he appear on any Christmas card that features the *Amanita muscaria* (or any other symbol of luck for that matter). Once Santa *does* start appearing on the cards, all the symbols of luck have been removed (figure 8.8). Simply try to find a single card that features both Santa Claus *and* the *Amanita muscaria* mushroom. None exist.

Fig. 8.8. The colors of Santa's outfit went through a variety of changes. In this postcard Santa's coat is red with a black trim. Notice that the card features reindeer, but the mushrooms (and other symbols of luck) are gone. If the mushrooms were truly meant to signify the flight of the reindeer, isn't it interesting that *every* artist who designed these cards during the twentieth century forgot to show them together?

INK INCLUSION

As I hope the last three chapters have demonstrated, Christianity absolutely had psychedelic mystery traditions throughout its history—nearly up to the modern day. From the Nazarene apocalypticists having visions of the end-times, to the various gnostic magic and mystery traditions, to the orthodox appropriation of various pagan theogenic experiences, to the collective revelries at Christmastime complete with theogenic Saturnalia wines and elf-invoking Julbeers, psychedelia has been a part of Christianity since its earliest days.

Most telling is what all this says about the so-called sacred mushroom hypothesis. Why would church leaders espouse their ideas about mandrake, opium, and cannabis, all the while never mentioning anything about an *Amanita muscaria* mushroom—least of which that they were painting them into art to teach illiterate people about Jesus?[43] The paintings supposedly feature *hundreds* of mushrooms, but the texts leave not a trace? Why wasn't the mushroom included?

Where's the ink?

It makes no sense.

Moving into the recent offshoot of this theory, I think Santa's suit is far better explained by the historical circumstances mentioned above rather than by any secret psychedelic reference (southern Yugoslavia notwithstanding). Our human history is rich with psychedelic history. Let's not desperately try to rivet *Amanita muscaria* customs onto Christianity where no evidence for them exists.

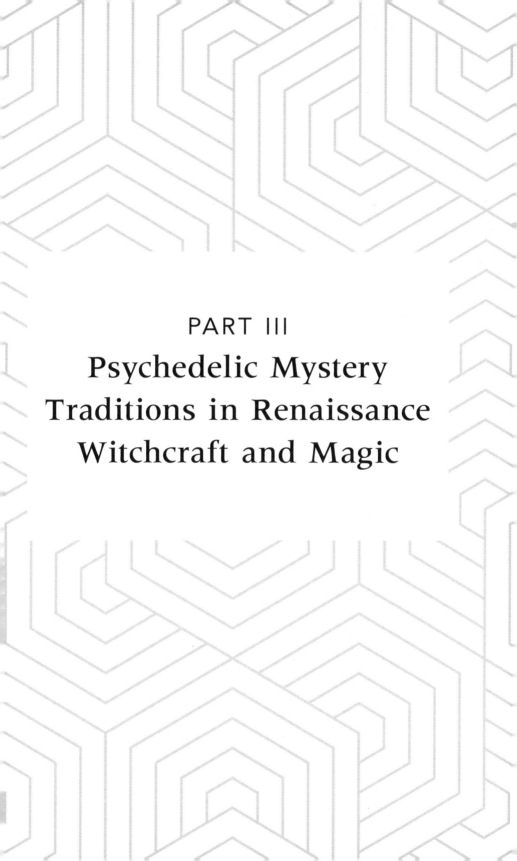

PART III
Psychedelic Mystery Traditions in Renaissance Witchcraft and Magic

How far this journey has taken us! Into the earliest somnitheogenic dreams to the rise of empires that could offer every theogenic mystery experience under the psychedelic sun.

But there is still more to discover. After the fall of Rome, these traditions carried on sporadically, in mutated forms, all over the crumbled landscape. During this time, infighting raged between clergymen for little reason other than unparalleled power. Not every priest was a scholar and gentlemen; many were lazy, fallible, dishonest hypocrites (to put it mildly). Of course, there were the good ones too. But when the differences in interpretation (and morality and competence) of the itinerant preachers met with the traditional folk beliefs of locals, the result was an odd mix of paganism affixed to shaky Christian ideas that even many clergymen could not properly explain.

The flock slowly fell away from the church, all the while happy to indulge in the magic of Christian sacraments. They wanted their Eucharists, but they wanted them in ways that made sense to them, ways the church would deem unorthodox. Everyone had an opinion on witchcraft and magic. And some who practiced those arts knew the secrets of theogenic plants.

Both magic and witchcraft were not necessarily targeted by the church immediately after the fall of Rome. In those centuries, the church fathers were still too busy organizing the most successful religious endeavor in history. They gave bread and medical care to the poor where and when they could, but mostly spent their time fighting with themselves, unconcerned with the neighborhood squabbles that occurred in the remote villages.

Furthermore, the going consensus in Christian Europe was that people *could* have theogenic experiences—provided they fell asleep from sin and into the Christian godhead. Those Christians who opposed the use of theogens could do nothing about it anyway. Consider this: with all our modern police efforts, surveillance, funding, and militarization, the so-called War on Drugs is still just a joke. A *cruel,* racist, time-and-money-wasting joke. Such unenlightened authoritarianism that we recognize today was no more successful (indeed, it was *far less*) in medieval times. This was a time before cameras, tape recorders, and other modern tools of investigation. For this fact, medieval scholars have noted a magical underworld that existed among both the laity and the learned.[1]

The next couple of chapters will take us into the psychedelic mystery traditions of witches and magicians. Witches were said to engage in "low" magic—the magic of the people, so to speak. These traditions might include fertility goddess worship. They were common traditions shared and passed down through the ages with no known recollection of origin. These beliefs were fraught with superstition. Before universal education and literacy, something like a crop failure had a supernatural origin.

Following the ancient ways discussed in earlier chapters and coupled with unambiguous Christian influences, the witchcraft and magic of medieval and Renaissance times that would echo into the Victorian period is most varied!

9

WYLD AND WYRD

--◆•◆•◆--

Fairy Ointments and Goddesses Worship
c. 10,000 BCE–Present

I have written of the "fairies ointment," which I set forth only in detestation of the frauds of devils and witches.

GIAMBATTISTA DELLA PORTA

Quiet.

The days grew longer, harder.

The crops had failed, and no one in the village knew why. Thankfully, a shaman resided in the vicinity. The villagers did not scorn nor persecute her. She was in many ways celebrated, for she was their spiritual guide. Though repeatedly warned by wandering preachers to not seek advice from this woman, the villagers nonetheless ignored the admonitions. Thinking back on their own lives, the villagers couldn't recall a time when she wasn't revered in the community for her magical abilities. Neither could their parents nor grandparents remember such a time. She had access to the divine realms beyond waking reality where prophecies stirred in an enchanted breeze, where cures for the crops could be found in the subtle whispers of moonlight.

She sprinkled some holy water on the edges of the fields, took a few snippings of wheat, and retired to her domicile. Grinding the grains and adding them to her psychedelic ointment, she then lathered herself up and down her arms, saving some for vaginal insertion as well. Slowly, the ointment overtook her, and she fell into a deep, lucid somnitheogenic state.

There, the Goddess appeared to her and told her how to save the crops.

*

A kind of ancient somnitheogenic experience that deferred to a goddess survived in some form from antiquity into the early modern period. In *The Witches' Ointment,* I hinted at the possibility that some of the experiences caused by psyche-magical ointments (set and setting, notwithstanding) might have been entheogenic. That is, if those ointment-using wise women believed they were in communication with otherworldly entities, particularly some echo of the Fireside Goddess, I suggested that a term like *entheogenic* would be a fitting moniker. I would like to update that statement by, instead, applying the term *somnitheogenic,* a neologism that didn't exist when I finished my previous book.

First, I think it important to define what I mean by "witches' ointment." A witches' ointment, in its finalized theologically contrived form, is an unguent composed of child's flesh that enables a person (usually a woman) to fly with other malefactors to the Sabbat, where the devil awaits their worship. They will collectively partake in a diabolical conspiracy against humanity. Anything less than that is not, strictly speaking, a witches' ointment. The point of my last book was to show how that *theological* concept—the diabolical interpretation of the ointments—came to pass. Here, I would like to do my best to construct the lost religion of these wise women. I am going to use many of the sources I used for *The Witches' Ointment,* supplemented here with new discoveries. I am also going to dissect them a little more fully than I had in my prior treatment. Finally, I would like to offer new insights as to why I believe that within the formulation of the witches' ointment we can see the gradual demonization of somnitheogenic access to the sacred feminine.*

When I first started my investigation into the origins of the witches' ointment, I was not exactly sure what I was looking for, nor did I know what said experience entailed. Some vague kind of flying sensation perhaps? To my surprise, I found that what I nebulously conceived as a flying ointment told only a small part of the story. Indeed, as I delved deeper into my research, I discovered that there were psychedelic ointments that had nothing to do flying, psychedelic ointments that didn't involve entheogenic experiences, and finally, somnitheogenic ointments that enabled a person to dream that she or he was flying in spiritual form with a divine entity. This chapter will focus on this last kind of ointment—the somnitheogenic-flying kind, as I theorize that it served as the foundation on top of which some theologians built their ideas about what would later be called a witches' ointment.

'Twas a gradual transformation: the reimagining in the public consciousness of these somnitheogenic ointments as witches' ointments took half a century to complete. But its very slowness allows us to catch up to, and ride beside, its historical development. To comprehend the process whereby these ointments evolved from somnitheogens to diabolical drugs, it is essential to understand the literary machinery through which some theologians interpreted them. Three major literary trends are important for understanding how the witches' ointment formed. Indeed, the witches' ointment first appears in theological treatises of the mid-1400s,† and that is where its mysteries will be uncovered.

The first of these literary trends has been dubbed by scholars the *interpretatio romana*.[1] The second has yet to garner a name from scholars; I therefore refer to it as *interpretatio heretica*. The third is often referred to as the *crystallization of the witch stereotype*.[2]

---

*I would also like to use this chapter to serve as an errata for mistakes I have come to realize I made in *The Witches' Ointment*.

†Not yet called a witches' ointment, the usual term in those early days was a "certain ointment" (*quaendam unguento*).

INTERPRETATIO ROMANA

The easiest way of understanding the interpretatio romana trend is to consider how the ancient Romans adopted and adapted the gods of their neighbors (particularly the Greeks). For instance, the Romans fancied a space for Ares, the Greek god of battle, in their pantheon. But instead of referring to him by his Grecian name, they preferred to call him Mars. Likewise, they renamed Artemis as Diana, Cronos as Saturn, Hades as Pluto, and so on.

The interpretatio romana in the early modern period worked similarly, only this time clergymen weren't reinterpreting Greek gods into Roman gods, but rather reinterpreting pagan religious survivals into a Christo-demonological framework. All pagan goddesses and gods would be consigned to the company of the damned, usually earning the designation of Satan himself.[3] This highly Catholicized interpretatio romana was an educated priestly class's construal of a peasant culture it did not fully understand.

The founding document for our medieval into late medieval interpretatio romana is the oft-cited *canon Episcopi*.[4] The canon, originally commissioned by Rathbod, bishop of Trier, was compiled by Regino of Prüm. It detailed beliefs held among commoners in the backwoods areas of Germany, one of which included "certain wicked women" who were deluded by fantasies produced by demons into thinking that they rode animals at night alongside the pagan goddess Diana. The canon is skeptical—never castigating people for actually journeying at night but rather condemning the *belief* that a person could potentially ride out at night. We might call it a "thought crime." Such restrictions on thinking had already been addressed as early as the Council of Paris in 829, when delegates determined that "the devil's illusions" could be inspired by, among other things, pharmaka.[5]

It is doubtful that Regino of Prüm intended to kick off a literary trend in 906 CE that would materialize five centuries later in demonology treatises. He was merely looking for a term of convenience. So many people worshipped this pagan goddess that Regino couldn't catalogue all the names by which she was known. Holda? Bertha? Fraw Holt? Holle? Pertcha? These and countless other designations for the goddess[6] meant that Regino was going to have to invest a considerable amount of money in buying extra parchment. Or perhaps instead of pinching some coins from the donation baskets to supply his parchment needs, he might designate one name that could serve as a *linguistic placeholder* for them all. He couldn't be certain who among his comrades had heard of which goddess, but he could be certain that they would all recognize one name: Diana, goddess of the hunt.

Goddess of the wild and weird women.

Confounding the matter was the fact that most people living in the backwoods of Germanic lands in the tenth century had probably never heard of Diana. These people had a host of different names for the goddess (besides the few mentioned above). But she wasn't just worshipped in the Germanic areas. She held a special place in the hearts and minds of most Western Europeans. In parts of northern Italy like the Fassa Valley, she was known as Richella; in other parts of Italy she might be called Madam Oriente, as she was called in Milano.[7] Over in France her ties to fertility origins are evident in two of her names: Satia and Domina Abundia.[8]

Even as Diana appears in the *canon Episcopi* by name, she is probably a clerical gloss for something closer to Holda or Berta (depending on one's location in the Germanic lands). Since Latin was the lingua franca of the time, all localized names of this Great Mother of fertility became Latinized, Romanized as Diana. She represents that archetypal Great Mother, whose worship survived the fall of Rome and the rise of Christian Europe. She was one of the most difficult pagan beliefs to eradicate.[9] Therefore, Diana is important in documents pertaining to folk traditions: her name serves as a linguistic placeholder, an interpretatio romana, for some obscure fertility goddess.

THE BLASPHEMOUS EUCHARIST

Witch literature also points toward another kind of *interpretatio*: an *interpretatio heretica*. *Heretica* may be called a list of church-conceived ideas about heretical activity enumerated centuries before theologians much cared about witches and witchcraft.* Two of these heretical attributes demand special attention for understanding how they influenced the concept of the witches' ointment in later centuries. The first included the sharing of an oath through ritual cannibalism, the second, worship of the devil. The idea of an oath made through ritual cannibalism makes an early appearance in the work of Polyaenus (second century CE). While describing the tyrannies of Apollodorus of Cassandreia (c. third century BCE), Polyaenus employs this stereotype. He claims that Apollodorus killed his friend Callimeles and gave his body over to a coconspirator, Leontomenes, who cooked him into a meal. He also mixed the sacrifice's blood into wine. He gave this blasphemous Eucharist to his comrades as part of an oath they would all swear before trying to seize power. The ritual cannibalism was said to form an unbreakable bond between the members.[10] Other ancient sources attest to this pre-Christian, pagan-against-pagan stereotype.[11]

But when that newest group of terrorists fearfully referred to by pagans as Christians appeared in Rome in the middle of the first century, something had to be done. Roman authorities, neighbors, and even family members castigated their fellow Christian neighbors as insurgents who feasted on murdered children during their ungodly rites.[12] After the triumph of proto-apostolic Christianity, now properly crowned orthodox Christianity, such ideas were taken from these earlier pagan sources and thrust onto Christian groups deemed heretical by those in power. Thus, we see St. John of Ojun slandering the Paulicians in such a way in 719 CE, referring to the group as the "sons of Satan."

---

*Which did not begin in earnest until the mid-fifteenth century.

The Paulicians were said to employ a Eucharist in their rites, which they may have used in one of the ways different gnostics employed them (as outlined in an earlier chapter). The slanders said about their holy drink show an early form of Eucharistic heretica: the Paulicians commit incest with their mothers. When a child is born, they throw it among themselves until it dies. They then mix the infant's blood with flour to make their Eucharist.[13]

The pagan-insurgent stereotype survived, but early medieval Christians added a second layer of depravity to it. They included in these congregations the worship of the devil, a figure that would obviously be absent from any earlier Roman pagan religions. Indeed, Roman pagan religions had no devils.

This inclusion of Satan meant an increase in the fervor with which some theologians went about stamping out alternative—heretical—Christianities. Now unconventional Christian groups, like the Waldensians living in the Cottian Alps toward the end of the fourteenth century, would be hunted out and forced to confess their errors. In one case involving a clandestine preacher, Antonio Galosna, interrogators pulled from him the name of Bilia la Castagna. Little is known of Bilia other than it was she who provided the Eucharist drunk by those Waldensians gathered in worship. Based on the effects of this potion as preserved in the records, there is little reason to doubt it contained some kind of pharmakon. The pharmakon listed in the dossiers is toad excretions. Now, this could have literally been the poison from a toad, or perhaps it was simply a general colloquialism for "poison." One scholar has even toyed with the idea that the toad Eucharist might be a veiled reference to a toadstool—a psychedelic mushroom like the fairytale *Amanita muscaria*.[14] Plausible, for certain. But we will likely never really know. Regardless of the pharmakon in Bilia's potion, the psychedelic Eucharist was slowly becoming the blasphemous Eucharist in the eyes of some theologians.*

---

*Interested readers may refer to chapter 3 in *The Witches' Ointment*.

The clergy's distaste for entheogens, pythiagens, or whatever the heretics used would carry over into their ideas about how wise women accessed the sacred feminine.

THE SATANIC WITCH STEREOTYPE

The third literary trend in ecclesiastical history, the crystallization of the witch stereotype, was cobbled together by theologians in the early 1400s while obsessing about the following: fears of heretics, fears of Satan, fears about ceremonial magicians, and, finally, fears about the beliefs and spiritual practices of commoners. Pretty much, they were scared of everything that wasn't *them*. All of these worries seemed to stem from the calamities (war, famine, plague) Western Europe endured during the late 1300s. Some theologians started to reason that the only explanation for these societal catastrophes in the face of a supposedly loving God must have been a supernatural source. The best explanation they could conceive was that God was abandoning his people because clergymen were not doggedly eradicating the worship of pagan deities—pagan deities that the church had decided were satanic.*

All this came to a head in the 1430s; the interpretatio romana and the interpretatio heretica finally fused into one idea: the satanic witch. And perhaps it was the viscous nature of the ointments themselves, but some kind of adhesive wed the blasphemous Eucharists of heretics with the shamanic experiences of fertility goddess worshipers. The infamous (and anonymous) *Errores Gazariorum* (c. 1438) contains our earliest description of the Sabbat. This author had obviously taken her or his ideas from ancient works pertaining to the heretical stereotype. From the author's description of the Sabbat we see the earliest merging of the interpretatio heretica with the new witch stereotype—the psychedelic

---

*Seven centuries later, the late Jerry Falwell would make a similar claim. After the tragedies of 9/11, he inferred that the event was God's punishment for Western civilization's toleration of homosexuality. Rest in hell, asshole.

Eucharists of the "heretics" became the infernal ointment of the witches:

> The wretched person who has been led astray worships the presiding
> Devil. The devil gives the newest heretic an ointment and a stick so
> as to return to the Sabbat. The ointment is made by secret method
> of diabolical malice, from the flesh of roasted children.[15]

An interesting detail about this document is the use of the word Gazarii to describe the witches. Gazarii comes from the name of the Cathars, a heretical sect that flourished in Albi, southern France, stomped out of existence during the Albigensian Crusade in the middle 1200s. Further, the slang word Gazarii originated from northern Italy, near Savoy. Did some Cathars really survive the crusade against them and relocate south of the Alps, in Italy? While this seems a plausible explanation, the true story reveals a different narrative, for by the early 1400s, the term Cathar designated a witch, a fact that can be seen in the full title of the work.*[16] The idea that the flying ointments contained the remains of murdered infants stems from interpretatio heretica merging ever so slightly with the interpretatio romana.

The result was the witches' ointment.

FAIRY WOMEN

Medieval and early modern preaching manuals were filled with *exempla*. Exempla, or "stories of virtue," played an important role not just as tales of morality but also as news reports to warn congregations of the necessity of a pious life and the consequences of depravity.[17] Most exempla derived from the minds of those who wrote them; they are fictional stories. However, like much creative writing, the stories were based on real events, real moral and ethical dilemmas, and real beliefs found in every-

---

Errores Gazarii seu illorum, qui scobam vel baculum equitare probantur, which translates to *The Heresy of the Gazarii* [or *Witches*], *Meaning Those Who Are Known to Ride on Brooms and Staffs.*

day life. One of those everyday life beliefs, that which revered a fertility Goddess, seems to have been fairly widespread, as evidenced by the ideas first outlined in the *canon Episcopi* finding expression in some exempla from centuries later. I think that by examining the ointments through these literary lenses—romana and heretica—we can actually uncover an obscure rite existing as a substratum of a larger magical worldview. This rite involved astral projecting to distant locations and engaging in bacchanalian revelry by using psychedelics somnitheogenically.

Along with this widespread European belief in traditional pagan deities came the belief that there was some enchanted realm in which they dwelled. These realms were populated by supernatural creatures like elves and fairies. It was these fantastical creatures that some theologians reworked into demons—that is, strictly speaking, the interpretatio romana. These fairies and elves didn't just cross between our world and theirs willy-nilly. They had human contacts on our side of the veil, the fairy women, who collected medicinal and psychedelic herbs for use in healing and magic.[18] Interestingly, Satan plays no major role in the earliest records pertaining to witches. His appearance in the ceremonies evolved in heretica, not romana. In Burchard of Worms's *Corrector* (c. 1000 CE), he writes that the worshippers of the Germanic fertility goddess Holda were really demons transformed into the likeness of women. The message is clear: worship of fairy-like fertility goddesses rests in the province of false, even demonic, hallucinations; therefore, should a person stumble on Holda's congregation, they should not join the rites. Indeed, they would only be enjoying the company of the damned.[19]

Mingling around the atrium before entering the larger house of historical witchcraft, one will find a pastoral handbook, *The South English Legendary* (c. 1270 CE), eagerly waiting to make company. Here, one anonymous author who contributed to the larger work wrote on the folk belief of certain elves, called *eleuene,* who could magically take on the appearance of women. The writer cautions his readers (and his readers' listeners in the pews) that these women are not really elves in disguise but demons instead.[20] The reason is fairly obvious: ecclesiastics were hesitant to believe in fairies, pixies, elves, and the like; these creatures were mere superstitious holdovers from the days when paganism corrupted the minds of future Christians.

But these men certainly needed no encouragement to believe in demons.

As time went on, concepts like the Diana-fied fertility goddesses (i.e., those bastardized by the *canon Episcopi*) and the accompanying belief in supernatural beings like fairies and nymphs were condemned, courtesy of clerical ignorance and prejudices, as evidenced by the publication of another preachers' handbook, *Fasciculus Morum* (c. fourteenth century), written by an anonymous Franciscan friar. *Fasciculus* discusses, among other topics, spiritual idleness in the form of sloth, one of the seven deadly sins. He wrote of some "superstitious wretches who claim that at night they see . . . queens and other girls dancing in the ring with Lady Diana." These people, the author tells us, are called elves. They can change women and men into other creatures and transport them to "elvenland." The author is quick to warn that such feats are "nothing but phantoms shown to them by a mischievous spirit."[21]

Despite the convergence of romana with heretica, there are some noticeable differences between the women mentioned in the *canon Episcopi* and those mentioned in *Fasciculus*. For starters, the women of *Fasciculus* "see" these elves dancing with Diana. They do not participate; they do not traverse the land with the goddess the way the women did as described in the *canon Episcopi*, which leads us into the second noticeable difference: they aren't traversing at all. They are dancing—carousing. It should also be mentioned that, like the *canon Episcopi*, *Fasciculus* does not say anything about an ointment (or potion, powder, etc.) necessary to transport to elvenland. How the women in *Fasciculus* came to see the dancing and merriment is anyone's guess. But an answer might be found in another text. *The Book of Oberon* (fifteenth century) recommends mixing an ointment that "will make open the air unto thee, that thou mayest see spirits in the clouds of the heavens, and all so there by though mayest go surely." This ointment allows anyone who uses it not only to see these supernatural beings but also to actually join in their divine activities. Should we be surprised that *The Book of Oberon* includes as an ingredient for this ointment the highly psyche-delic mandrake?[22]

We will return to the incontrovertible psychedelic nature of these ointments in just a bit. For now, *Fasciculus Morum* shows that such beliefs found favor among a large cross-section of the population. Some believers could fall into these states quite naturally, no somnitheogen required. Others used the kinds of psychedelic* ointment found in *Oberon*. Both procedures (pharmakon-less or not) show a broad-ranging belief in these pixie realms. Otherwise, why do they keep coming up over the centuries in various forms? And how do we account for the changes over time? One of the arguments I made in *The Witches' Ointment* (and worth repeating here) is that texts like *Fasciculus Morum* demonstrate a decisive datum: at least according to pre-1400s literature, there was no need to posit a magical ointment as necessary to transform or fly to some enchanted gathering. And yet, in the texts we are about to meet, the ointments are absolutely necessary for achieving those very feats.

Why?

SPIRIT FLIGHT

We know few things about her.

She is found in one of Johannes Nider's (c. 1380–1438) sermons—a sermon on the First Commandment, which is part of a larger hom-ily anthology titled *Predigten* (*Sermons*). Fortunately for us, Nider gave this oration to a lay audience, meaning he was speaking in a lan-guage and conveying ideas that would have made sense to regular peo-ple. Any hint of *romana* or *heretica* would have gone over the heads of the largely illiterate congregation. And even those who could read

---

*There is no hint that the *Oberon* ointment was intended to be used as a somnitheogen. It may very well have been extheogenic (should the entities appear while the user of the ointment is awake).

would mostly have had a handle on the vulgar languages, not the complex Latin script of the theological writers. In any event, there was little reason to warn the people about things they didn't believe existed.[23]*

She was evidently some kind of healer-sorceress whose cures had caused some trouble in the community. Most importantly, she was a fertility goddess worshipper, a fairy woman, as we may infer from Nider calling her an "unhold(en)" (i.e., "a servant of Holda"). This is a real treat; the text clearly comes from a time *before* the Diana-fication of the various offshoots of this goddess. The unhold has no relations with demonic powers; she isn't called a witch; and most importantly, the ointment that Nider describes clearly contains some kind of narcotic pharmakon, as evidenced by the fact that applying it to her skin knocked her out cold.

Her ritual of spirit flight is also interesting—the kind of practice I find it difficult to imagine Nider (or anyone else) simply inventing: the unhold props a kneading bowl on a stool, climbs inside, and rubs her body with an ointment while singing incantations. She falls into a deep sleep, believing that in this trance state she is able to fly to the Heuberg (meaning "Hay Mountain") in Bavaria, perhaps intending to, while there, astral project and commune with Holda.[24] Indeed, the few references to that mountaintop suggest a place like elvenland; there is usually a "fairy queen" or some kind of strong female lead who presides over the realm. In the case of the *Fasciculus Morum,* this female character was eschewed in favor of the more easily recognizable Diana, the fertility goddess linguistic placeholder.

---

*One of the critiques conservative historians have against the idea that maybe—*just maybe*—someone before the 1960s took a pharmakon rests in their position that medieval and early modern exempla represented false stories dealing with morality, intended only to confer proper behavior on the faithful. If this is true, then the conservative historians would have to explain why, aside from psychedelic ointment use, the following topics are also found in Nider's exempla: thievery, infidelity, murder, lying; I suppose that none of these immoralities existed either, as they appear in one exemplum after the next. Joan of Arc also makes an appearance in Nider's exempla; by conservative historian logic, Nider must have invented her as well.

Nider's later work, *Formicarius* (1438), allows us to see more clearly how the interpretatio romana colored the folk belief in spirit flight by sheer linguistics alone. Recall that when giving sermons, Nider spoke in vulgar German (as reflected in *Predigten*), a language his audience would understand. *That* is why the story of the unholden and her ointment in his sermon is so unencumbered by demonological theory. At the time, such theological literary concepts had not yet seeped into popular Christian culture. Nider himself may not have even known about these ideas yet. And they certainly would not have made sense to his congregation.

But *Formicarius* was different.

Since *all* of Nider's peers understood Latin, he chose to write *Formicarius* in that language, which immediately made the story susceptible to the interpretatio romana. We today are all too aware of how translating a text from one language to another can result in a change of the meaning of the words from one culture to the next. For example, Nider couldn't call the woman an unholden—many of his non-Germanic colleagues would not have known to whom or what he referred. Nider therefore called her a *vetula,* which has a variety of meanings but here most probably means "deluded woman."[25] But such subtle linguistic shifts necessarily changed the unholden's character from that of a fertility goddess worshipper into that of a depraved fool. Further, Nider can't call the goddess Holda for the same reason. He therefore settled on the *one* name for a goddess that he could be certain all his peers would recognize.

You guessed it: Diana.

The vetula in *Formicarius* engages in the same flying ritual as that recorded in *Predigten* (placing a kneading bowl on a stool and rubbing herself with the ointment while chanting). Only instead of soaring away with Diana, the woman falls into a deep sleep and dreams of flying to Venusberg,* so strong were the pharmaka in her ointment. Here

---

*Venusberg was the term used by the literate class to refer to Heuberg. In Teutonic mythology, Venusberg ("Venus Mountain") was believed to be the peak that housed a subterranean temple to Venus.

it should be noted that while *Predigten* remains absent of the two literary trends, and there is clear evidence of romana in *Formicarius,* there is no heretica found in either text. Nothing in Nider's writings colors this woman with any kind of stereotypical accretion. She is not yet evil; she is not yet the satanic witch.

But the step that finally brought these fertility goddess worshippers from being merely described as depraved fools to the devil's whores appears in another set of texts written by the Spanish theologian and bishop of Ávila, Alonso Tostado (c. 1400–1455). Tostado was a biblical literalist, meaning he took the stories in the Bible to be true. But not true based on faith; rather true based on objective observation. In such works, we see the first whispers of what we might call scientific methodology—applied to theology. And so Tostado set about using crude Christian logic to rationalize biblical marvels. It is here where we find Tostado pondering over one of the first miracles found in Genesis. After God crafts Adam, he decides to create a companion for him. God casts Adam into a deep sleep and removes one of his ribs, from which he fashions Eve. Adam apparently felt no pain during this celestial surgery. We today may pass off this detail as a *so-what.* But it deeply troubled the biblical literalist mind of Tostado. It was a hiccup in fifteenth-century theo-logic. *Could God really cast Adam into such a deep sleep that he wouldn't feel the pain of having a rib removed?*, Tostado surely wondered, as he wrote his *Commentary on Genesis* (1435).

But there was hope.

Tostado decided to rest his argument in medical science—specifically pharmaka, noting that God must have anointed Adam with one of those "medical ointments" normally handled by physicians. Countless recipes from the era leave no room to doubt that these ointments contained powerful narcotics like opium, mandrake, henbane, and such.[26] Therefore, when Tostado turns his attention away from Adam to a woman who supposedly used one of these medical unguents to transport to a mystical realm so she could meet with others, he cares not about any kind of moral or spiritual implications. He mentions it purely as a way to bolster his literalist interpretation of God using one of these ointments on Adam.

Some of these [ointments] are the kind used by doctors to facilitate a deep sleep in a patient so they can operate. Such anointing causes the mind to detach from the body, so for a short while a person [thoroughly anointed] will not feel any sensation. There are certain women that [we theologians] call "witches" who claim to use these same medical ointments in conjunction with magical words to transport whenever they desire to diverse places to meet with other women and men. There, they will indulge in all sorts of foods and pleasures.[27]

You will have noticed that not a trace of romana, heretica, or the witch stereotype appears anywhere in this description. What makes it so fascinating is that Tostado inserted it in the commentary *not* to convince people that these ointments existed, *not* to convince them that they should fear women who use them to astral project, *not* to warn people about these ointments' association with Satan, *no*. He only brings it up to bolster a totally *different* point—the object of his query—namely, to demonstrate that, yes, God could have taken Adam's rib without causing him any pain. Indeed, even human physicians could achieve this miracle. With that, Tostado's literalist mind could rest comfortably, and as a by-product of his meticulousness, we get deeper insight into how these magical pharmaka, like the mandrake ointment in *Oberon,* ended up in the demonized witches' ointment.

But the insight gained only shows its fullness from marking Tostado's *Commentary on Genesis* against a later commentary he wrote, this one on the Gospel of Matthew. Having solved the rib crisis of Eden, Tostado aimed his finely calibrated mind toward other pressing matters. In Matthew, we find the story of Jesus fasting in the wilderness for forty days and forty nights, after which the devil makes an appearance. The devil tempts Jesus three times: first with asking him to perform a miracle by turning a rock into a loaf of bread to feed himself. Jesus was hungry, but not so hungry that he would fall for such a tasteless (and quite frankly insulting) ruse. After the bread ploy didn't pan out, Satan transports Jesus to the pinnacle of the Jerusalem Temple. Looking down on the bustling city below, Satan again asks Jesus to worship him. Jesus again refuses. Undaunted by this surprising turn of events, Satan pulls out all the stops, flying Jesus to a high mountaintop in the desert wilderness and showing him "all the kingdoms of the world (Matt. 4:8)." *Forget mere Jerusalem. Every knee on earth will bow before you.* As expected from the omnipotent son of the all-powerful Creator, Jesus was not impressed with mortal kingdoms. For the real kingdom, the Kingdom of Heaven, would soon arrive anyway. Although not recorded in Matthew, we may infer that at this point Jesus told Satan to "go to hell." Defeated, the devil does so.

It is the last two devilish tempts in the Matthew story that caught Tostado's attention. Could Satan really fly people across the sky? And not just anyone! If he could transport Jesus, then no one was safe from possibly earning sky miles with the devil. Again, we find Tostado's biblical literalist mind trying to untangle this problem. And again, we find Tostado placing his answer to this problem in the use of medical pharmaka: *flight must be achieved from using those magical ointments.* As ever, Tostado was resolute, quickly writing, "A person who believes [in spirit flight] . . . belongs not to [Jesus], but . . . to the devil. They believe Diana is a goddess and yet she is the devil. . . . It should not be denied that female and male sorcerers engage in wicked rituals with these ointments allowing demons to carry them away. . . . They revere these demons by indulging in lust and sexual indecency."[28]

Like in the *Fasciculus* and *Formicarius* of earlier days, Diana appears in Matthew to serve as our linguistic placeholder, no doubt covering for some local Spanish fertility or fairy goddess with which Tostado was familiar. Like two perpendicular lines finally meeting, Matthew finally introduces romana to heretica.* Each interpretatio reinforces the other, creating that newest accoutrement of the stereotypical witch—the stereotypical witches' ointment.

An additional curiosity of the two texts: The *Commentary on Genesis* does not hint at a religious experience by the women using these ointments. But the mention of Diana and the devil in *Commentary on Matthew* gives the text a spiritual dimension. We only have enough evidence for two possibilities to explain this discrepancy: either Tostado colored the once-secular experience mentioned in Genesis in spiritual terms when he composed *Matthew,* or he came to realize (after writing *Genesis*) that the astral projection had a spiritual dimension all along. I tend to side with the latter option for two reasons. First, I read it in light of Nider's description of an unholden, a name that certainly signifies spirituality: that of fertility goddess worship. Second, Tostado didn't necessarily have to spiritualize the concept to make his point that using these ointments led to depravity. He need not have mentioned Diana or the devil at all, and he still could have ridiculed the practice the way Nider did in both his works. The fact remains that Tostado had decided that some people using these ointments had been duped into believing in Diana (or whatever fertility goddess she stood in for).

And that such belief represented satanism.

DEMONIZING THE SACRED FEMININE

The evidence suggests that there existed a general background of beliefs pertaining to transformations, flying to supernatural lands with magical creatures, and courting fertility goddesses who appear under that universal linguistic placeholder "Diana." Within this broad framework, we narrow our search, trying to find who among those held such notions and also used psychedelic pharmaka to practice them. When we put these texts of Nider and Tostado on a time line, we can watch

---

*As in: "They believe Diana is a goddess and yet she is the devil."

it happen: the demonization of the somnitheogenic flying ointment morphs into the witches' ointment right before our eyes. *Predigten* (c. 1420s) presents the ointments in a truly untouched, somnitheogenic form. Commoners living in Western Europe were using the unguents to put themselves into a deep trance to travel "in spirit" to places like elvenland or Heuberg. Likewise, by 1435, Tostado not only gives us a relatively unbiased* report of these ointments' actions but also confirms that it is indeed medical pharmaka that cause these surreal experiences. But by 1440, after the new witch stereotype had infiltrated theological literary culture, Tostado has lacquered the somnitheogenic experience with a demonological polish. In the process, he opened the door for future churchmen to paint this survival of pagan fertility goddess worship with all the fiery colors of hell.

Kramer and Sprenger, who authored *Malleus Maleficarum* (1486), were only too enthusiastic to take up this task. Their excruciatingly misogynist tract put the final condemnation on top of the fairy ointments. Wise women do not exist; only witches do. Their ointments do not contain psychedelic pharmaka, only the boiled flesh of murdered children.[29] Any mention of medical pharmaka is gone, replaced with the ghastly remains of nurslings—ideas taken straight from the dossiers of heretica. Interestingly, the *Malleus* authors were not only familiar with Nider's *Formicarius* but even cite him as one of their sources several times.[30] And yet, they *chose* to leave out any indication that the unholden's ointment contained psychedelic pharmaka. The reason is obvious: if the experiences really derived solely from the actions of pharmaka, then the role of the devil becomes redundant. If the devil becomes redundant, then his opposition, the stalwart employees of the Catholic Church, become unnecessary.

And they couldn't allow that.

Another obvious attempt at a demonological explanation comes from Jean Vincent, writing just a few years before Kramer and

---

*Referring to wise women as witches, notwithstanding.

Sprenger. In his book, he recognizes all the psyche-magical potentials that prompted wise women to apply these potions and ointments: spirit flight, animal transformations, pythiagenic magic, and more. He further notes the psychedelic pharmaka as the enabling ingredients in all these mixes. But he cannot rest credit in the actions of pharmaka, for what place would the devil have if these experiences were all just drug induced? His (il)logic is quite telling.

> Poison witches . . . mix pharmaka into love potions and ointments which cause bizarre psychological reactions, transformations, and usually end up killing the user. [Wise women] claim to be transported far away at night to demonic Sabbats by using the aforementioned pharmaka. The correct deduction, however, [is that] none of these [magical feats] should be attributed to the natural powers found in the pharmaka, but instead to a shrewd demon . . . who is the true operative cause; [whereas] the pharmaka is only the secondary cause.[31]

Vincent's spiel hints at certain aspects of fertility goddess worship: spirit flight and animal transformations. So what exactly was this religion like? *The Witches' Ointment* opens with the story of Italian sorceress Matteuccia di Francesco (d. 1428). Let's put an even more finely calibrated microscope on her activities than I did before.

We today tend to think that the conflagrations of Europe began with the rise of Christian Europe. Not so. Matteuccia enjoyed a fine career as a wise woman in Todi, central Italy. She mostly dealt in love magic: her more popular spells ranged from taking revenge against abusive husbands who mistreated their wives to concocting pocula amatoria for use by lonely hearts. But during her interrogation by inquisitors for these operations, Matteuccia revealed that she also mixed an ointment that allowed her to astral project in the form of a mouse. Now, this transformation holds a deep meaning to it. One of the far-reaching tenets of this fertility goddess religion was that access into the spirit realm was denied to mortals in human form. Such transformations were necessary, such as into animals but also into zombified versions of the goddess worshipper.

Sometimes these transformations held a special meaning religiously. The need to turn into a zombie is obvious: it recognizes the nature of the world beyond the veil as the realm of the dead. In other cases, when the transformation was into an animal, we can guess endlessly as to why the zombie form alone wasn't sufficient to enter the spirit world. What we do know is that the wise woman had a host of beasts to choose from. For example, a cunning woman or midwife might turn into a cat,[32] a horse,[33] a fox, or a donkey.[34]

For Matteuccia, however, the preferred animal was a mouse; we are left with no explanation as to why. In any case, she rubs the ointment on her flesh and sings magical words in the process. Recall the texts of Nider and Tostado, who mention the need to sing magic words in order to complete the spell. We are fortunate to have preserved the actual magical words sung by Matteuccia as she applied the ointment to her skin. The historian now approaches an emotional dilemma, for the record has left us a real treat. But it is a treat that must also solemnly recognize the fear and pain that produced it. We are at once fortunate to have this real piece of psychedelic-magical history while simultaneously feeling both sadness and contempt: sadness for poor Matteuccia and contempt for the bastards who had her tortured and executed. Perhaps we can do her a service by letting her psychedelic-magical words reach us today: "Ointment, ointment take me to the Night Doings in Benevento, over water, over wind, over all bad weather!"[35]

I call her words "psychedelic-magical" because it is clear that Matteuccia placed her powers of astral projection in the ointment (when coupled with the correct chant). It was the ointment that would take her to Benevento, where stood a walnut tree that supernatural creatures liked to gather around in revelry, broadly similar to elvenland or

Heuberg. It was here that Matteuccia would meet with others in the spiritual shape of various animals (or the dead) and celebrate her faith.

Now here's where it gets interesting.

The record of Matteuccia's confession represents a microcosm of the shift we saw between Tostado's commentaries on Genesis and Matthew—a leap from ordinary spirituality to *diabolical occultism*—for Matteuccia's confession exists in two parts: The first half deals with folk magic and the kinds of secular spells Matteuccia would perform.* These included the love magic rituals and psychedelic potions used to terrify deadbeat husbands. With regard to the latter, one of her more popular spells included selling abused housewives a pharmakon and an incantation. The wife would surreptitiously slip the pharmakon into her husband's dinner and wait about an hour. Just as her husband started to feel the first effects of nausea, vertigo, muscle discomfort, and the hallucinations that followed, the wife would sing the incantation as her husband cowered, terrified in a corner. He would believe that her magic words were causing the physiological and psychological reactions he felt. Such a spell caused many an abusive husband to rethink his actions the next time he felt like raising his hand to his wife.[36]

The second part of Matteuccia's confession comes after a break in the questioning, during which time she was tortured. Thus, it is this second part of the record that is colored by the new satanic-witch stereotype. The latter half of the document reads very differently from the first part. Through the reliability of torture, guaranteed to make a person confess to just about anything, the inquisitors riveted their beliefs onto Matteuccia's religion.

---

*Interestingly, some of these secular spells included literally using the Lord's name in vain. One of her love magic spells required reciting magical words that are downright Christian. Matteuccia would weave hair around parchment (whether anything was written on the parchment is unknown) and place the bundles under the beds of her clients. Her client was to think about the man (or woman) and say the words: "I do not see you; but that one be seen, that one which is the hidden heart of the body; stay enclosed, as Christ stayed in the tomb; stay fixed, as Christ stayed crucified; return to my homeland, as Christ returned to his mother." See Jansen, Drell, and Andrews, *Medieval Italy,* 206.

Now, here's where it gets *really* interesting.

The break in the questioning whence Matteuccia suffered torture appears *right* at the moment that her psychedelic ointment is mentioned. The ointment literally straddles the record between the true folk spirituality of Matteuccia on the one side and the theologically contrived demonism on the other. Let's look back at Matteuccia's magical chant and place it within the larger context of how the man who "corrected, translated, and published" the document,[37] Novello Scudieri, interpolated it.

'Ointment, ointment take me to the Walnut Tree in Benevento, over water, over wind, over all bad weather.' And then, after they* had assembled, they invoked Lucifer by, by reciting the words, 'Oh Lucibel, demon of hell, after you were released you changed your name and have the name of Great Lucifer, come to me or send me one of your servants.' And a demon would immediately appear before her in the form of a goat, and she herself would turn into a mouse.[38]

For Matteuccia, we will never know the name of the goddess she sought to meet. Even Diana is skipped over. She had gone to the walnut tree to meet with "other witches, enchanted people, and hellish demons" and worship the "the Great Lucifer who presided over them."[39] She would be executed for this crime. And for the first time in history, we watch the psychedelically inspired religious experience of a fertility goddess worshipper who accessed the spirit world through psychedelic pharmaka suffer condemnation as evil by the Catholic Church.

---

*This is a curious statement about the text that I didn't unpack in *The Witches' Ointment* and would like to redress here. In none of Matteuccia's preserved magical deeds do we ever see any indication that she worked with other wise women. The fact that here, as the scribes feverishly inked Matteuccia's words, we finally hear that there were other "witches" operating in Todi reeks of *interpretatio heretica* and the theological fears over insurgent groups gathering collectively. Indeed, despite Scudieri noting that "they" would meet up to astral project and meet the devil, there is no indication or even a shred of evidence that anyone else was executed alongside Matteuccia.

In their efforts to stomp out this fertility goddess religion (whether a believer used psyche-magical ointments as a form of worship or not), some theologians inadvertently introduced these pharmaka to the wider public. Let's end this chapter by reviewing how later people would adopt this kind of psychedelia long after the witch stereotype formed.

In my earlier work, I discussed an eyewitness report of these ointments found in *The Book of Abramelin*. The author of *Abramelin* claims to have lived in the early 1400s (this, it turns out, is untrue), which would place him at the dawn of the witch stereotype. While passing through Linz, he meets a woman who claims to be able to astral project. His account of the ointment (he even tried it himself) is uncolored with diabolism and the new stereotype of the satanic witch. For that reason, and the fact that the latest editor of *Abramelin,* occult scholar Georg Dehn, dates it to the mid-1400s, I felt that the earlier dating was accurate. Since publication of *The Witches' Ointment,* however, I have come to agree with those who date *Abramelin* to at least two centuries later, the early 1600s. And while I do not agree with my critics that the incident in *Abramelin* is necessary to my overall theory,[40] I do agree that *Abramelin* shows what common magicians were doing with these ointments by the seventeenth century.

This conjurer of Linz told Abraham that she could transport him across the sky to check on friends of his who lived some distance away. Intrigued, Abraham joins the woman at her house, where she anoints them both. Once the somnitheogenic ointment takes effect, Abraham believes he is flying through the air to visit with his mates. But when he and the woman awake and she tells him of their journey, he grows confused. He was certain that the experience was real, and yet, he and she had dissimilar accounts of what happened while entranced. Abraham chalked up the experience to one of those "good and fantastic sleeping ointment[s] that make all imaginations appear as realities."[41]

The magic in Abraham's account is secular. It is a somnitheogenic ointment, but not one used for fertility goddess worship.

But what of the spiritual survival of these psychedelics (as entheogens) in popular early modern culture?

BEST SEEN IN TWILIGHT

As some of the earliest New World witch trials were taking place overseas in Salem, Massachusetts, a folklorist was fervently collecting traditional accounts of fairy encounters from the Scottish Highlands. Robert Kirk (1644–1692), a minister, died at the young age of forty-eight while investigating second sight (i.e., divination or clairvoyance). For Kirk, second sight included any and all techniques that permitted access to shamanic worlds. It was rumored that Kirk's early passing had to do with his impiety of revealing the secrets of the fairy realm to mortals, for part of his treatise on second sight, *The Secret Commonwealth,** dealt with using such mental magic to see and interact with those fairies and elves from the otherworld. Rumors circulated that the fairies brought him to their realm to prevent him from further revealing what occurred there. He did manage to describe the nature of the entities before joining them forever: "Fairies . . . are said to be of a middle nature betwixt [hu]man and Angell (as were daemons thought to be of old); of intelligent studious Spirits, and light changeable bodies (lik those called Astrall) somewhat of the nature of a condens'd cloud, and best seen in twilight."[42]

Kirk also differentiates between genetic second sight (i.e., naturally gifted) and voluntary (i.e., those who used magic techniques to achieve a visionary state). One of the voluntary methods of which Kirk was aware included use of an ointment that sounds remarkably similar to the one found in *Oberon*:

Yet it were more fasable to imput this Second Sight to a qualitie infused into the Eye by an unction: for Witches have a sleepie oint-

---

*Compiled between the years 1691 and 1692 but not published until 1815.

ment, that when applyd, troubles their fantasie, advancing it to have unusual figures and shapes, represented to it, as if it were a fit of Fanaticism Hyprocondriack Melancholly, or possession of some insinuating Spirit; raising the Soul beyond its common strain.[43]

Other times renaissance psychenauts relied not on ointments to enter spiritual worlds but rather would astral project by eating a psychedelic confection. Such was the case when a group of teenage girls gathered in a strawberry patch to eat magical bread brought by one of them, Magdalena. Magdalena had learned how to cook this "peculiar" bread by a certain Mrs. Hansen, deceased at the time of the incident. After eating the bread, one of the girls, Margaretha, experienced what we would call a bummer. She lost control and started crying and acting out until two women found the distressed girl and took her back to their village. Margaretha eventually recovered and told what had happened. Based on her testimony, it seems that Magdalena had either heard of this fertility goddess religion or was a practicing member of it. Accordingly, eating her magical bread would turn the girls into cows, enabling them to fly to Heuberg in animal form.[44]

In Andy Letcher's book *Shroom: A Cultural History of the Magic Mushroom* (2007), the author makes the case that three criteria must be in place for any culture to "centralize" psychedelics: (1) the pharmakon must be available, (2) the people using it must know that the pharmakon has the actions it has, (3) there has to be a cultural context in which people can couch their otherworldly experiences.[45] Here, though, I do not mean to claim that psychedelics were central to the widespread fertility goddess religions of Western Europeans. In fact, I think the practice of cooking psychedelics into breads and ointments for occult uses was just that, *occult*—relatively unknown until theological and, later, medical and literary culture popularized it over the fifteenth through seventeenth centuries. Many people no doubt accessed this realm without the use of ointments, potions, or confections.[46]

Regardless, the fairy goddess ointment meets all three criteria: first, the pharmaka were certainly available in apothecaries and could also be found growing wild all over the European landscape. Second, the countless references to these and other psychedelic pharmaka in both ancient, medieval, and early modern medical texts show a general knowledge of the effects of opium, mandrake, and so on. Additionally, it is clear by the reports of Tostado, Vincent, and others that wise women were perfectly aware of the occult nature of these magical plants. Finally, there is no doubt that an obscure, though nonetheless common, belief in fairy women and goddesses pervaded Europe. The evidence suggests that it was access to this supernatural world that some fairy women understood their psychedelic experiences to provide. And it was this very world of fairies and goddesses that theologians redefined as hell.

Wise women were far from the only people to dabble in psychedelic magic in the medieval, early modern, and Renaissance periods. Let's now meet their highly educated counterparts, who would often give lectures freely discussing the magical arts and the psychedelics that can be used to strengthen their practices.

10

ONE CONSTANT STORY

◆•◦•◆

Psychedelia in Medieval
and Renaissance Ceremonial Magic
c. 1100–1900 CE

*There is no grass or herb that grows in which G-d's wisdom is
not greatly manifested and which cannot exert great influence
in heaven.*

ZOHAR 2.80B

WISE MEN FROM THE EAST

Crawling aloft the glowing coals, the magical smoke permeated the
small chamber in which the magician had locked himself. All the
cleansings had been satisfied; all the prayers had been said. All the tools
had been sufficiently fumigated with precious incense. His eyes watered
as the fumes first scratched his corneas and then crept down his throat;
he perspired—his heavy ritual regalia sweaty and cumbersome in the
small, stuffy chamber. Maybe he was even a little nervous, for he was
opening a portal to worlds beyond sight, into the heavens—indeed,
divine knowledge and inspiration were obtainable to those who knew
how to access them. The smoke billowed around his head, picking the

locks deep in his psyche, gently caressing both the wounds and the redemptions found in the abysses of his mind. He was seeking that most sacred connection housed in his deepest self, a mere mortal hoping he was worthy of grace.

And then, the visions!

A strip of gold expanded over his head as if the angels themselves had drawn a blade across the air from the other side of infinity. The gilded line swelled, opening an aureola—a gateway—a luminous expanse that within moments had eclipsed the darkness of the chamber with the light of the holy. Spirals of clouds housing the heavenly hierarchy ascended far into eternity, stopping only at the throne of the Lord and Creator of it all—God. Trumpets sounded from every direction, welcoming this learned practitioner into angelic resplendence.

He was home.

Our magician's journey had started a thousand miles to the East; the reintroduction of pharmaka (especially cannabis) en masse entered medieval Europe around the eleventh to twelfth centuries through the cultural collision of an Eastern-expanding Christendom with a Western-expanding Islam. Or at least those whose lives straddled the border between a Christian world and an Arab world leave us our earliest clear records of cannabis's psychedelic potential in medieval Europe. One such mention survives in Simeon Seth's *Lexicon on the Properties of Food*. Born circa 1000 CE in Constantinople, Seth was raised in a city caught between two worlds. Islam claimed huge swaths of the Eastern Church in the mid-seventh century; additionally, Syrian forces made their way from the north, into the eastern Mediterranean coast through modern Israel and into Egypt. The so-called cradle of Christianity spent several centuries steeped in Arabian culture.

And the influence of the learned and creative Muslims on Western civilization was far from negligible.

A mere forty years before Seth's birth, the Byzantine Empire would once again regain Antioch and the surrounding lands; it is therefore not surprising that Seth could read and write in both Greek and Arabic—skills that fed his passion for medicine. He was therefore linguistically proficient and understood cultural dietary and drug differences when he sat down to write his *Lexicon*. While noting that taking too much cannabis could be "harmful," the *Lexicon* openly addressed the "remarkable intoxication and bewilderment" for which cannabis is today known and loved, revealing that it can be prepared several ways: "in a drink, as powder form, or most advantageously, as powder mixed in a drink." He writes that Arabs use cannabis in lieu of wine to intoxicate themselves.[1]

Little by little this use slinked back into Western civilization thanks to Muslim scholars who preserved such information after the fall of Rome. As Europeans toiled through those precarious centuries following the toppled Roman empire in the mid-sixth century, the East, under the banner of Islam, pushed westward. Beginning in 635 CE with the claiming of Damascus from the Byzantines, the spread of Islamic culture penetrated France by the early eighth century. Defeated by the Belgium-born Charles Martel (remembered as Charles the Hammer) at the Battle of Tours (732 CE), the Islamic advance was successfully stymied for the while. But other Arabian forces had set their eyes south, taking Carthage (North Africa). From there, they headed north to Castile (modern-day Spain) and successfully took that peninsula, thus founding Al Andalus (which included the areas already occupied in France), the first successful Islamic, Jewish, and Christian state in history. Advances in mathematics, poetry, music, philosophy, and many other arts owe their origins to the cosmopolitan intellectualism found at Al Andalus. Especially popular in Al Andalus was the thriving literary culture, which promoted linguistic education. Arabic translations of originally Greek and Latin manuscripts were painstakingly copied by some of the most etymologically fluent scribes.

Greco-Roman culture had volleyed back home.

Only this time, it was furnished with an exotic new look. And with it came an originally Arabian text that would have a major impact on Western high magic and alchemy.

THE GREATEST OF SECRETS

Of all the magical arts practiced by the learned class, truly the most opaque was alchemy. Beginning in China around the first century BCE, alchemy dealt first and foremost with transmutation: crude metals into refined gold, base minerals into salvific medicines, and, most importantly, the transformation of the alchemist into a higher form—a godly form. Alchemists hypothesized that all materials began in a lower state and over time slowly evolved into something of value: a metal like lead had the potential of becoming gold if the alchemist could discover the natural way of speeding up the evolutionary process that allowed such accretions. Liu An (c. 180–120 CE), a leading Daoist philosopher, remarked, "Gold grows in the earth by a slow process and is evolved from the immaterial principle underlying the universe, passing from one form to another up to silver, and then from silver to gold."[2]

This principle applied to the alchemist, referred to as *hsien,* was the idea that "the body could be so rarified that it took on the attributes and possibilities of the spirit."[3] The hsien were benevolent spirits of mortals who had transcended to a higher immortal state. The alchemist could speed up this process of spiritual enlightenment by giving an individual an immortality elixir, also called hsien. An individual so transformed would never grow old but instead could enter the spirit world and live perfectly well there as a hsien. And it is in this subdivision of the alchemical arts and the attainment of hsien where we will find references to psychedelic pharmaka. Indeed, this aspect of alchemy can be broken down into two kinds, *nei tan* and *wei tan,* the pursuit of which was the development of magical potions to achieve hsien.[4]

Such evidence can be seen in one of the oldest folk legends of the art, that of the alchemist Wei Po-Yang (c. fourth century BCE). In order to mix his elixirs without any interferences or annoyances,

Wei Po-Yang took to the mountains with three of his students and his dog. After concocting his pharmaka elixir, he fed the mix to his dog, who promptly died. Deciding he would rather die himself than face the dishonor of returning home without the immortal cup, Wei Po-Yang drank the potion; one of his pupils followed suit, while the other two decided they would rather live. They returned home to tell the news of their master's passing and prepare a proper funeral. But Wei Po-Yang rose from the dead in their absence. He restored both his student and his dog with some kind of magical medicine. Due to their journey into death, the three became hsien.

Contemporary sources make clear reference to the following pharmaka used in ancient Chinese alchemy: cannabis, aconite, arsenic, and foxglove. Some have speculated that the purpose of concocting these potions was "to produce death itself or a period of profound insensibility mimicking death, on the grounds that physical death is the gate to immortality."[5] Should this be the case, then Wei Po-Yang's tale points toward another ancient form of death and rebirth through the use of psychedelic pharmaka. This time, within the alchemical arts.

The biggest makeover for alchemy would emerge as it trudged through the Middle East on its way westward and met with some of the greatest minds Persia had to offer. These men were by and large polymaths, interested in mathematics, astrology, poetry, medicine, and music, among other endeavors. One walking encyclopedia in particular, Jabir Ibn el-Hayyan (b. c. 720 CE), developed alchemy further than his predecessors by adding both vegetable* and animal matter to his elixirs. Now, Chinese alchemists had already experimented with plants, specifically psychedelic ones, as we saw with Wei Po-Yang's return from the grave having achieved hsien. But they mainly stuck to minerals and metals

---

*Aconite, one of the ingredients found in some medieval fairy ointments, is mentioned specifically by el-Hayyan.

when it came to heavier transformative Chinese alchemical elixirs.[6]

Jabir Ibn el-Hayyan, the son of a pharmacist, was also (in manners unspecified) in good relation with Sufis.[7] Much like the various gnostic traditions in relation to Catholic Christianity, Sufism, a mystical branch of Islam, developed just as suddenly as the generation after Muhammad (d. c. 630 CE) passed on. Although, where Christian gnostics tended to fall into one of two categories, ascetic or epicurean, Sufis seemed to have relished both principles simultaneously. They preferred an austere lifestyle, though they regularly used hashish as a means of praising Allah. This, of course, was derided by orthodox Islam. One Persian poet and religious critic, the famed Khwaja Samu d-Din Muhammad Hafez-e Sirazi (or Hafez, 1315–1390), had this to say about the Sufis:

> It is this berry the Sufis eat
> When they would fall into an ecstasy
> And tell their precious lies to you and me
> A little hasheesh is the whole big cheat.[8]

Sufis also ascribed to Neoplatonist philosophies (like most Christian gnostics), which El-Hayyan would accepted doctrinally, bringing a hierarchy of spiritual entities into alchemy. His astrological affinities also aided alchemy, for he believed that when certain heavenly bodies aligned, the sulphur and mercury found deep in Earth's Kore moderately materialized many metals. He was clearly familiar with hash due to his ties with Sufism and was the first Persian to comment on its psychoactive effects, [9] concocting several recipes that included it.[10]

Another Persian polymath, Hakim Ibn Sina (Latinized as Avicenna, c. 980–1030), considered the Prince of Physicians, once even laughed that studying and understanding medicine was too easy. His work, *The Canon of Medicine,* occupied space on every physician's bookshelf in the Eastern and, later, Western worlds. Listed specifically within the pages of the *Canon,* such pharmaka like opium, mandrake, hemlock, and cannabis could be used for any number of health reasons.[11]

Avicenna certainly used these pharmaka himself. He seems to have done so to enter a higher state of mental acuity. Therefore, we can probably call his academic exercises a form of poetigenism. One medieval author even commented on Avicenna's poetigenic practices.

> I found in the words of one of the great philosophers of his generation, namely Ibn Sina, in which he said he would concentrate while composing his great works . . . if the matter was still too difficult, he would continue to think about it and drink a cup of strong wine, so as to fall asleep . . . and the difficulty in that subject would be solved for him.[12]

Avicenna was a huge fan of opium and added it to his "strong wine" to use when he sat down to tackle and contemplate his own philosophical musings. Unfortunately, this would also prove Avicenna's undoing; he would later die from an opium overdose. His experimental take with pharmaka, along with that of many other Arabic physicians, doctors, and magi, would have a major impact: first on Western medicine and then on Western occultism.

The most celebrated Arabic magical manuscript in the West was undoubtedly *Ghāyat al-Hakīm* (*The Book of the Wise*). First copied into Spanish in Castile (the last European stronghold in the Al Andalusian interior) under the orders of Alfonso X (c. 1220–1280), *The Book of the Wise* would later be Latinized to the designation it retains popularly today, *Picatrix*. The text stormed the Renaissance magic scene in the thirteenth through fourteenth centuries. Within *Picatrix,* one will find an open acknowledgment to the occult uses of pharmaka. Several psychedelic recipes place a heavy emphasis on the use of mandrake and opium to make "very powerful mixture[s]," one of which should be drunk with caution "because . . . the spirits in it are very effective."[13] The author also had a penchant for another popular herb: "The Indian cannabis has so many functions and the Indians use it mostly in their temples and some people prefer it more then [sic] the dregs of wine."[14]

Alchemy returned to Europe in the early twelfth century as an amalgam of ancient Grecian notions, commented on and supplemented by Arab intellectuals, along with Chinese, Egyptian, and Indian proscriptions. Under express protection by the church, which saw value in both limitless gold and immortality,[15] Western academics embraced the discipline with all the enthusiasm with which they had welcomed the magical arts of astrology and Arabic medicine. Alchemy used exotic symbols, diagrams, and (most especially) concealed language to initiate the eager student into the "secret of secrets."[16] Like the arts of necromancy and astrology, alchemy, too, existed in cultural limbo when it reached the West in the early twelfth century. Some universities shunned the alchemical arts, while others like Oxford and Cambridge actively encouraged them.[17] Praised in one place and spurned in another, alchemy was constantly trying to shed the lowly reputation of an *ars* (any craft) to prove itself a legitimate *scientia* of intellects.

By the time alchemy arrived in Europe, it required knowledge of a host of disciplines that it had picked up along the way. Crude forms of chemistry mixed with medicine, geology, Neoplatonist philosophy, and theology all found a place in Western alchemy. Astrology was also a large part of the art, as the creation of transmuting potions could be redoubled in efficacy if they were mixed under opportune celestial conditions.

Aside from Solanaceae herbs and cannabis, we also see in the annals of Western alchemy specific references to the use of a nonflora poison—notably that from a toad, which the alchemist George Ripley (1415–1490) references. But this alone raises some issues: Would an alchemist really disclose such a bold admission in an otherwise cryptic art?* Perhaps the alchemist here is referencing not the toad but something else, something

---

*Although that could also itself be the cover—actually putting the truth in plain sight.

that has had a long history of association with the toad—the toadstool or magic mushroom.

Indeed, Ripley's famed poem of toad poison as the chief ingredient in an alchemical elixir could possibly be a guised reference to a mushroom.

> *A toad full red I saw did drink the juice of grapes so*
> *   fast,*
> *Till overcharged with the broth, his bowls all to brast;*
> *And after that from the poisoned bulk he cast his*
> *   venom fell,*
> *For grief and pain whereof his members all began to*
> *   swell*
> *. . . Then of the venom handled thus a medicine I did*
> *   make.*
> *Which venom kills and saveth such as venom chance to*
> *   take.*[18]

A "red" toad drunk off the grapes of wine might indicate a red mushroom like the *Amanita muscaria,* famed shroom of children's books and Christian entheogen conspiracy theories. That Ripley makes sure to mention that his elixir can both save and kill also points (along with toad poison) to a possible mushroom. Now, during my research for *The Witches' Ointment,* I came across scant mention of mushrooms.* Though it should also be noted that most inquisitors and secular authorities usually didn't care much about the pharmakon used *but the magic* enacted. Therefore, most of the time the records rely on a single word, *vene* (poison), and instead of getting into botanical classifications (that didn't really exist until the sixteenth century), authorities focused more on what exactly a person was doing with them.

---

*With one notable exception from 1619 in Jean de Nynauld's *De la lycanthropie transformation et extase des sorciers*; see Hatsis, *The Witches' Ointment,* 199.

THE PHILOSOPHER'S STONE

But all these arts and sciences somehow all danced around one central idea: that of finding the legendary philosopher's stone. Although some have hypothesized that a psychedelic played a role in the so-called philosopher's stone,[19] I have a different interpretation. The philosopher's stone seems to have been some hypothetical substance that could turn *any* material into gold. Alchemists based the notion on the four elements of Aristotelianism. All material was composed of earth, water, fire, and air. An alchemist tried to find the "proper" stone for which each elemental need would be met to transmute a particular substance into gold. At the right moment during the circuitous alchemical process, the stone would be cast into the smelting furnace and turn that particular metal into gold. This same process, however, would not work for a different metal, which required a whole other set of meticulous instructions. The philosopher's stone circumvented all that, turning *any* substance into gold.

There doesn't seem to be anything *psychedelic* about this at all.

What *does* seem to have been psychedelic was the way all this processing of raw materials in stuffy, not properly ventilated labs contributed to the spiritual elation under the effects of all the burning minerals. Though it should also be noted that these spirits sometimes greatly toppled the mind of the alchemist, and she or he slowly went mad.[20]

This could have been supplemented by taking additional pharmaka in a poetigenic form of creative problem solving. For example, like Avicenna, the infamous Paracelsus (1493–1541) used opium regularly and never hid his use.[21] His assistant, otherwise critical of his ill-tempered and thin-skinned master, nonetheless said this of Paracelsus in a letter to Johannes Weyer (1515–1588): "Nevertheless, when he was most drunk and came home to dictate to me, he was so consistent and logic that a sober man could not have improved his manuscripts."[22] Possessing the keen and creative mind of a weird scholar, such bouts (whether of opium, cannabis, alcohol, or—knowing Paracelsus—most probably some combination thereof) didn't seem to dim either him or Paracelsus, nor a host of other brilliant though troubled minds at the time.

Therefore, while I do not believe the so-called philosopher's stone was a mask for a psychedelic, I do feel that there is evidence of alchemists taking psychedelics (sometimes involuntarily through fumes, other times voluntarily with theogens) while they contemplated unlocking the mysteries of alchemical transmutations.

We see such avenues of pythiagenic visions in order to gain deeper wisdom in other areas of the learned arts. A perfect example would be Abraham Abulafia (c. 1240–1290 CE), the Jewish mystic who wrote the first book of the *Zohar* (1280 CE). Abulafia used a visionary pythiagen, a cup of opium wine,* to have a vision of the "secret of secrets":

> *Out of the scorching noon of Isaac,*
> *Out of the dregs of wine,*
> *A mushroom emerged, a cluster,*
> *Male and female together,*
> *Red as a rose,*
> *Expanding in many different directions and paths.*[23]

Of course, Abulafia had his own culture's psychedelic mystical operations to consider as well. Hebraic magic texts had also infiltrated Western occult(ure). One of these books, a truly ancient work, *The Key of Solomon,* offers a rather cryptic passage that alludes to visionary magical experiences at the end of a long ritual.

> Let [the magician] also renew his fumigations, and offer large quantities of Incense, which he should at once place upon the fire, in

---

*Abulafia refers to the drink as a "strong wine of Avicenna," implicating opium. See Ruck and Hoffman, *Effluents of Deity,* 6.

order to appease the Spirits as he hath promised them. He should then cover the Pentacles, and he will see wonderful things, which it is impossible to relate, touching worldly matters and all sciences.[24]

Although the text isn't exactly clear about what kind of incense to use or what fumigations to inhale, the result of breathing smoke to produce visions of "wonderful things . . . impossible to relate" might speak to a pythiagenic operation of some kind.

The historical reality seems unimpeachable: many magicians read and used *The Key of Solomon*; many different kinds of incense, psychedelic or not, were employed.

THE MISTRESS OF INEQUITY
AND MALICE

Most magic fell into one of two categories in the ancient through Renaissance West: natural magic and daemonic magic. The former employed all the occult virtues of herbs, stones, charting the heavens, and dream divination. Today, we call natural magic science. Daemonic magic circumvented the natural energies of the universe. It was "religion that turned away from God and toward demons for their help in human affairs."[25]

However, this should not automatically imply that the magician was a satanist (in our modern sense of the word). Recall that a daemon was a neutral spirit whom magicians invoked to perform a host of tasks—everything from sending a storm at sea to sink a ship to helping an elderly person cross the street with groceries. In fact, some readers might be struck by the paradox of the need to first revere the Christian God in order to invoke demons. However, several prologues to magical books cannot be clearer: a good magician was *first* and *foremost* a good Christian.[26] Before exploring how and why these courtly magicians used psychedelics in their magic, let's briefly tour the legal history of this most controversial discipline.

❦

Magic of all kinds was illegal in Rome centuries before the rise of the Church. In the third century BCE (three centuries before the advent of Christianity), the Teian state outlawed "harmful spells and poisons." The penalty was severe: the family was executed along with the spell-casting magician.[27]

Roman law in those ancient days quashed magic as well, which the archaic *Twelve Tables* addresses (c. 451 BCE).[28] In the last century before the Common Era, the pagan emperor Augustine burned hundreds of magical books in 31 BCE.[29] And did not Agrippa, one of Augustine's closest allies and friends, expel all the magicians and astrologers he could find from Rome two years later? These kinds of people, Agrippa claimed, "introduce foreign elements into our religion . . . and from this are born conspiracies, and gatherings and secret clubs."[30] In the second century CE, Hadrian of Tyre addressed women burned at the stake by the Roman guard for the practice of witchcraft. In one particular case, a rival witch asked if she could have the honor of igniting her competitor![31] The very Celsus who wrote passionately against the Christians wrote just as enthusiastically against magic.[32] Emperor Diocletian (c. 240–310), the last great Roman persecutor of Christians, also had Egyptian magical books burned.[33]

Ironically, the first legates to loosen these laws against magicians were *Christians*. Some early Christian thoughts pertaining to magic were surprisingly laid-back. Historian Julius Africanus (c. 150–250 CE) found no problem with using magic for love, agriculture, and medicine. None of these operations involved calling up demons so far as he was concerned. Firmicus Maternus (c. fourth century) urged the Roman guard to arrest and prosecute temple diviners, but still considered pagan astrology a legitimate form of science.[34] The emperor Valentinian (c. 320–375), while intolerant of astrologers, judged that "soothsaying has nothing in common with the cases of 'evil-doing.' . . . [W]e do not reprove soothsaying, but we forbid that it should be practiced to do harm."[35] This effectively overturned the laws of one of his predecessors, Constantine. Later, the emperor Theodosius eased sanctions against astrologers, offering those convicted to "transfer their faith to the Catholic religion and never to return to their former error."[36] A bigoted ultimatum no doubt (forced conversion), but it also seems preferable to the earlier pagan alternative: execution. In a broad sense, the earliest days of Christianized Rome essentially adopted the pagan legal stance on magic; the only major difference was an easing up of these laws by Christians.[37]

Of course, not everyone agreed with such leniency. Disapprovals against magic could still find an audience with later, less compassionate Christian authors. Isidore of Seville (c. 560–636 CE) came from a deeply religious family. His brother had been the previous archbishop of Seville, while his sister Florentina, an anti-Semitic nun, had earned the privilege and position of overseeing forty convents. Spain had been overrun by Goths after the fall of Rome in the early fifth century. Therefore, Isidore rejected both the pagan beliefs they brought with them as well as the Arianism they picked up once they reached Rome. For Isidore, magic involved the calling of not daemons but "bad angels."[38] This is important because it shows a shift in Christian attitude absent from earlier pagan notions of magic. Explicitly, that daemonism was innately *evil,* no matter the reason for invocation. Perhaps the magic-wielding gnostics like Marcellina and Marcus had something to do with this new assessment.

Nonetheless, the magical arts thrived alongside the rise of the European university in the eleventh through thirteenth centuries. Far from the secrecy surrounding these arts that is imagined in popular culture today, magic of all kinds was once openly taught in the university. Here, a polymath student might take a course on medicine, grammar, and logic, and then head straight into alchemy 101. Indeed, the so-called *Scholars Guide* (*Disciplina clericalis,* 1106 CE), written by Pedro Alfonso, outlines the seven liberal arts, two of which affect magic: astronomy and necromancy.* Later that century, the archdeacon of Toledo, Dominicus Gundissalinus (c. 1110–1180 CE) would produce his *Branches of Philosophy* (*De divisione philosophiae,* 1140 CE), where he would remain neutral on the question of magic. For him, the magical discipline was just another of many "worldly vanities" that didn't, in and of itself, cause any harm. As a modern analogy, a Second Amendment absolutist faults the individual using the gun, not the gun itself.

But Gundissalinus's opinion was not the only option. According to others—let's call them the "gun grabbers" of the medieval world— magic was wrong, no matter who pulled the trigger. Writing at the same time as Gundissalinus, philosopher and mystic Christian (and killjoy) Hugh of St. Victor went on a tirade against magic in his *Didascalicon* (1141).

> Magic is . . . the mistress of every form of inequity and malice, lying about the truth and truly infecting a person's mind, it seduces them from divine religion, prompts them from the cult of demons . . . and impels the minds of its devotees to every wicked and criminal indulgence.[39]

Still, this was only Hugh's view. He could do nothing to stop the spread of magic, which, due to its acceptance in the university, flourished in medieval academic life. A major area of contention for both sides of the magical coin revolved around the biblical interpretation of the magi who appear in the gospels of Luke and Matthew. We know these magi popularly as the "three kings" of Christian folklore who visited the infant Jesus by following a star to a manger in Bethlehem. Medieval Christians interpreted this passage one of two ways. One side (the pro-magic side) saw this scene as one of devotion: both Luke and Matthew

---

*The other five are geometry, physics, dialectics, arithmetic, and music.

depicted the magi as upright individuals. Neither gospel author openly condemns the magical arts; ipso facto, they meet Christian approval.

Au contraire said others. The magi, in fact, were not revering Christ as an equal, but instead bowing—*abdicating*—before the newborn king. Magic was passé to these Christians, who felt that Jesus's birth signified its end. This shouldn't surprise us. As shown earlier, the need for Christians to distance themselves from accusations of magic began almost at the start of Jesus's public ministry. We could have predicted the attitudes of later Christians like those of Isidore of Seville and Hugh of St. Victor.

Compounding the problem of magic was the development of cities, which naturally extended from the increase of universities. So-called college towns are not new, and neither is the availability of pharmaka in and around them. A short stroll outside any evolving city or large town would turn up henbane growing wild from the detritus cast to the wild by the population; mushrooms likewise smiled freely atop animal dung; and cannabis, one of the most gloriously adaptive plants on the planet, grew *everywhere*.

Returning to the city and ambling through the downtown streets, after one passed a leather shop, a bookseller, and a butcher, one would likely stumble on an apothecary. Apothecaries housed the kinds of exotic florae like opium and mandrake that wouldn't ordinarily be found in the colder regions of Europe. In fact, one poem written by John Taylor, "The Praise of Hempseed" (1630), placed an apothecary's success on the higher strains of cannabis not usually found in the forests and fields.[40] Further still, physicians often kept personal gardens of psychedelic pharmaka.[41] By the beginning of the early modern period, any curious enchanter not only had access to magical plants (and biblical justification for using them) but also a professor of magic from whom to learn.

Therefore, we see neither an acceptance nor a "coverup" with regard to the magical arts in medieval Europe. Psychedelic pharmaka were openly written about by upper-class magicians (and their critics). In a previous chapter, we explored the grassroots magic of the Western psychedelic witch. Her arts differed from those of the learned gentry (divination, love magic, and necromancy, which were universal, not-withstanding). Indeed, practices like astrology, alchemy, and daemon invocation, while absent from witch accusations (except where there is an obvious theological interpolation with regard to the latter) appear in trials against upper-class male magicians. Some of these upper-class magicians dabbled in the art of invoking otherworldly entities through the use of psychedelic pharmaka.

EXTHEOGENS IN MEDIEVAL MAGIC

Extheogen, as I define it, is the use of a psychedelic to generate divinities not *within* the self but *outside* the self. Such entities could be daemons, angels, and the souls of the recently (and not so recently) deceased. Medieval and Renaissance magicians seemed to have mastered such practices. Some of the incense and perfumes used in their ceremonial magic have long been recognized by medievalists to contain psychedelic pharmaka.[42] Not every magician employed a pharmakon, of course, but the anonymous hand that authored the thirteenth-century Kabbalistic magical text *Sefer Raziel* knew all about the occult use of cannabis. The author recommends "the Juse of cannabis" as oil. A person should stand before a "mirrour of stele" and anoint the body. If called on, spirits will manifest and give the magician the ability to bind and loosen "deuills & other things."[43]

Solanaceae plants like henbane and mandrake and others like opium were also employed to summon mystical entities. One of the most famous Renaissance magicians and alchemists, Heinrich Cornelius Agrippa von Nettesheim, certainly used these pharmaka extheogeni-cally. Lighting the herbs and other pleasant fragrances to produce a bil-lowing suffumigation, Agrippa would inhale the psychedelic spices and invoke spirits. He makes reference to the "strange shapes" that appear alongside the apparitions under the influence of these extheogens.[44] Considering how popular his *Three Books of Occult Philosophy* was, we can comfortably imagine scores of novices and seasoned magicians locking themselves in small chambers and inhaling the sacred fumes of magical plants.

❧

Necromancers might also use extheogens to supplement the art. An ancient reference mentions "Scythian drugs" (probably cannabis) as a way to call up ghosts.[45] Albertus Magus specifically named henbane as the magical flora of necromancers. To raise the dead using henbane, one must first draw the proper magical symbols or sigils on the leaves of the plant.[46] From there, a necromancer may add them to a suffumigation and inhale the burning leaves. Or, she or he might crush up the sigil leaves and add them to a potion or use them in any other way the operator desired. Mirror magic (captromancy) also at times included the use of pharmaka: Caesar Longinus's *Trinum magicum* (1630) recommends a suffumigation of sesame grains and opium poppy for divining otherworldly entities in captromancy.[47]

Pythiagenic dream divination experiences were also readily available. The Sultan Bahadur, king of Cambaja (d. 1537), would dose himself with hash and dream of going to battle against the armies of Arabia, Persia, and Portugal, among others.[48] Despite the *magic,* the generating of visions, happening in Badur's sleep, the experience would not, in my opinion, be called somnitheogenic. As this work comes to a close, I think it best to recall the grand diversity of magical and spiritual practices found throughout the ancient world. I mention Badur's "sleep fighting" in that spirit.

Deep discipline and a primed mind preceded these kinds of experiences; those unprepared lacked a psychic container to hold and later interpret the visions. Magical rituals usually included one or two assistants. And sometimes those helpers weren't properly vetted to make sure they could handle the psyche-magical experience. Once, when an unnamed young boy participated in a magical ritual with the Renaissance mannerist painter Benvenuto Cellini (1500–1571), the fuming pharmaka overwhelmed him with terrifying visions, resulting in what we would refer to as a bummer. In fact, because this particular ritual included pharmaka, the lad was still in a visionary state of awareness hours after the ritual was terminated. Indeed, after all the other entities had fled, two demons remained. The boy could see them "skipping along the road or on the rooftops" as he made his way home that evening.[49]

Treasure hunting also provided a way for a learned magician to make extra income. Treasure-hunting rituals made use of everything from Christian objects like holy water and small crosses to more involved items like an iron stake that had impaled the head of a criminal.[50] Scrying (divination with a crystal ball) was a common magical technique used to find treasure.

Treasure was believed to possess a spirit. This spirit could relocate the treasure wherever and whenever it wished. Therefore, treasure-hunting rituals both sought to discover the location of the booty *and* bind it to the area before it could move. Treasure hunting, like all magical operations, did not rely on any kind of psychedelic to achieve the desired aim. However, also like all magical operations, this did not preclude a spell caster from employing a psychedelic plant. Since treasure had a spirit, a magician might use a pharmakon to put her or him in touch with that entity. In one case from Germany dating to the mid-1700s, a treasure hunter first smoked a powder "so that his evil spirit would come to him." This spirit would guide the magician to the loot. In another instance, a hunter also used a psychedelic extheogenically; only this time, instead of smoking it, the hunting party leader "snorted [it] like tobacco."[51]

There unfortunately remains no way of knowing what the spirits envisioned while taking a psychedelic pharmaka were like or how the magician might interpret them. We merely have passing and cryptic references to such substances found in medieval and Renaissance manuscripts. Even those manuscripts that do not mention using psyche-magical incense, potions, and ointments leave us no guarantee that a magician didn't employ them anyway. For example, "divine frenzy" fell under the dominion of Saturn.[52] Psyche-magical plants like deadly nightshade and henbane came to inhabit Saturn's sphere by Renaissance times.[53] Cannabis, too, fell under Saturn's rule.* Thus, even if a particular spell for generating divinities inside or outside the self withholds any reference to cannabis, this should not be taken to mean that a magician (one familiar with the occult use of cannabis, anyway) would not employ it in a Saturnine spell.

THE FORBIDDEN ARTS

The kind of magic we have the most information about is that which was used to cause harm against another person or animal. The reason for this discrepancy in sources between the ceremonial magician and the wicked magician was that the former worked privately (or with an assistant), while the other's misdeeds might leave a paper trail of legal dossiers. Those upper-class persons with access to these psychedelics didn't always use them in ways we would consider moral today. In fact, they weren't even considered moral in their own time. In Bern, 1509, four friars found themselves burned for playing around with a psychedelic pharmakon. No, they weren't taking the pharmakon themselves but instead conspired to use it against one of their order. They drugged the poor brother until he grew "dazed and immobile." Then they lifted him onto the altar in their monastery's chapel and hammered nails into his wrists and ankles, impressing on him the "wounds of Christ." One of the friars then sneaked behind a statue of Mary and dialogued with the bewitched brother as if he were the Mother of God.[54] Unrecorded is why the quartet perpetrated such an offense. Revenge? A practical joke? A way to get rid of a political rival?

Aside from the obvious horrors of the experience, the episode also

---

*According to *Culpeper's Complete Herbal,* cannabis fell under Saturn's domain. Here we may also possibly see the consonants *s, t, r* in *Saturn.*

tells us something about the friars who committed the crime. They knew that this kind of pharmakon (whatever it was) would put the victim in such a suggestive state that he would believe that Mary spoke to him. Perhaps one or two of them had used this pharmakon himself and had something like an extheogenic experience with it? If not for the serious bodily injuries they caused to their brother, we might even be tempted to think they attempted to give him an otherworldly experience. But that was probably not the case.

The perpetrators were all consigned to the flames for this transgression.

Physicians, too, obviously had access to these plants and sadly used them to violate women by dosing and then raping them. One man, a doctor from Gelders (unnamed in the records), used the medicines he found in the apothecaries for more sinister occult purposes. When one of his patients complained about an illness, the physician told him that a cure could be found by sending his (the patient's) daughter to come see him (the physician) at his home. Once the girl arrived at his house, he recited a "secret prayer" and gave her "a morsel to eat" that caused her to grow "disturbed and confused [and] . . . los[e] control of her senses."[55]

It takes no stretch of the mind to imagine what happened next.

Poisoning was also used among the gentry to acquire land and power. The Petrini family of Bologna had apparently come to squabbling about the family fortune that 1536. Two brothers both felt he had earned the estates. The elder brother had been a successful family man; the wealth should thus fall to him. The younger brother had not been very successful at all and felt that his older brother had already received enough good fortune. He, therefore, deserved to also live the good life. Apparently, the executors of the will had decided in favor of the elder brother. The younger, feeling slighted by this, opted to poison the entire family, leaving him the only living heir. He put arsenic in their wines, but apparently not enough. While the family suffered convulsions, hallucinations, and other unpleasant physiological symptoms, only two actually perished (the men's mother and a young sickly lad). The crime was uncovered when neighbors who had drunk the same wine (without the younger brother's knowledge) also experienced these symptoms. Fearing exposure, the younger brother fled, never to be seen or heard from again.[56]

Women, too, used these pharmaka to have what appear to have been lesbian affairs with young girls. Called *sahacat** in vulgar Italian, these women dosed themselves with psychedelic perfumes and "claim[ed] that they are then receiving the demon; then with altered voice, they pretend[ed] that the demon is speaking to them."

The sixteenth-century physician Johannes Weyer records:

> If on occasion attractive women come to them, the [sahacat] are inflamed with love . . . and in the guise of a demon, they ask that the women lie with them as payment. And so it happens that while the women think they have obeyed the words of a demon, they have actually had relations with witches.[57]

In other cases of black magic, women and men might take advantage of a natural disaster and gratuitously add to the body count. When the plague had ravaged Lombardy in 1477, spoiled children of the area saw the pestilence as an opportunity. Heirs to family estates paid a group numbering around forty women and men to finish the job that the plague had started. The group concocted poisonous ointments and smeared them across various objects in town (doors, gates, locks)—anything that a person might come into contact with. They also hired a hermaphrodite (probably a physician) to spread the poisons

---

Fricatrices in Latin. From *fricare* ("to rub," i.e., masturbate). This may also speak of the vaginal insertion of pharmaka, akin to how some shaman women ingested their fairy ointments.

in households as well as public facilities. But when everyone is dying except *you,* authorities are bound to look into the matter. The conspiracy was uncovered, and the members of the group experienced torturous endings.[58]

AN EARLY MODERN POETIGENIC DIGRESSION

But psychedelics didn't just find their way into medieval magic; evidence suggests that with the growth of universities came the spread of medical knowledge and the creative arts. As stated earlier (and worth repeating), I am not taken by the Allegro school of medieval Christian art—theorists who believe "enlightened" Christians were secretly placing mushrooms in paintings and stained-glass windows. This should not be taken to mean that I do not accept that medieval Christians ingested psychedelics, mushrooms included; it just means that I see no evidence for the claim that this practice appears hidden in Christian art.

During my research for *The Witches' Ointment,* I came upon a rather delightful manuscript illumination that I didn't exactly know how to properly present back then. I would therefore like to dissect it here briefly, as a sad lack of evidence means leaning on much speculation. However, allow me to suggest that the following image was created by a person, probably a Christian, who I believe had eaten a magic mushroom. This image is not found in any fresco or anything relating to Christianity or Jesus at all. It is instead from a medical text, *The Book of Poisons* (*Liber de venenis*), first published in the 1430s.* Therein, one will find all the soothing, medicinal, and psychedelic florae known to medieval writers. Each flora description begins with an ordinary looking chapter title. And yet, when we see a subchapter title like this one

---

*The edition I used was from 1492, accessed via https://digitalis-dsp.uc.pt/handle /10316.2/36030.

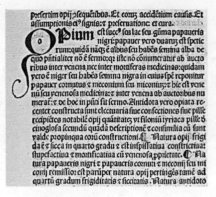

Fig. 10.1. Opium subchapter from *Liber de venenis* (1492). Here we see a slight embellishment on the lettering, absent from nearly every other chapter title in this text (notwithstanding f. 47 and 51).

for opium (figure 10.1), we can't help but notice the slight embellishment of the lettering. Most every title appears nondescript (with the exception of opium and two others on folio 47 and folio 51). There is nothing unusual about the text.

But let's take a look at another image from the 1492 edition of *The Book of Poisons*—that of mushrooms (figure 10.2). Notice anything? The title for mushrooms is *so* artistically embellished that when I saw it, I couldn't help but think that this dude, whoever she was, used a mushroom to excite her artistic imagination. Should this be the case, then we are looking at a medieval example of a mushroom used poetigenically. There is no conspiracy here; there is no imagined Allegroian coverup.

Fig. 10.2. Poisonous mushrooms chapter from *Liber de venenis* (1492). Perhaps here we are seeing the poetigenic residue of a magic mushroom experience.

There is just a person who ate mushrooms and decided to express the experience attractively while copying this edition of Santes Ardoyni's *Liber de venenis.*

No stretch of the imagination required except his—after maybe ingesting some *Psilocybe cubensis.*

THE ANSAIRETIC MYSTERY

Napoleon Bonaparte's campaigns into the East found him and his troops in Egypt between the years 1789 and 1801, where marksmen fired at the nose of the Sphinx for target practice. The soldiers also discovered a new use for an old pharmakon. Cannabis, long known in the West for its occult, medicinal, and commercial value, suddenly had some competition with a by-product of its own evolution—hashish. Farmers and apothecaries regularly stocked both cannabis and hash, depending on the strength a person required.

Other adventures in Algeria under the flag of France exacerbated the flood of hash into Paris. By the end of 1841, nearly forty thousand French soldiers had colonized Algeria, bringing knowledge and use of hash back home once discharged. The influx was noticeable. Poet and novelist Théophile Gautier (1811–1862) observed rather quickly that in France "hashish [was] replacing champagne . . . we believe we have conquered Algeria, but Algeria has conquered us."[59] Therefore, hash took root in intellectual and artistic circles by the time a practicing spiritualist named Paschal Beverly Randolph (1825–1875) arrived on the shores of France.

Born in New York and residing in the rough Five Points area (popularized by the film *Gangs of New York,* 2002), Randolph's life was sadly typical for the time. His father had abandoned him as a child, and his mother died during the cholera epidemic between 1831 and 1832 (the shock of which turned Randolph into an atheist for a brief spell).

Usually left to his own devices, he befriended ghosts and regularly found himself in a tug-of-war with spirits trying to claim his bedsheets as he tried to sleep. Randolph would later write that all the loneliness of his youth left him "love-starved" as an adult. By the time he was ten years old, he already felt that he had firsthand experience with "the shady side of human nature."[60]

After bumping around from one place to another seeking work, Randolph ended up in upstate New York, which at the time nourished a community of spiritualists. The movement had been kicked off by the Fox sisters, who claimed the ability to speak with the dead.[61] Spiritualists tended to be feminist, abolitionist, and champions of natural health remedies. They did not advocate for the personal experiences of spiritually inclined people. Early spiritualists had no program for obtaining and understanding transcendental experiences.[62] They were social reformers who would invoke such agents of change as Benjamin Franklin and Thomas Paine in their meetings. It would not be within this liberal milieu where Randolph would first discover hashish, but rather from his introduction to secret magical societies that populated England and France when he traveled to Europe early 1855.

Across the ocean, scores of magicians had benefited from the influx of hash, particularly in Paris, where the Club des Hashischins held their monthly meetings. The person who supplied the hash to the club, Dr. Jacques-Joseph Moreau de Tours (1804–1884), oversaw countless painters, poets, philosophers, rebels, freaks, and prophets on heroic doses of that pharmakon. And while he can certainly be credited with igniting some of the finest examples of Victorian poetigenism in the likes of Yeats and Baudelaire, such was not Moreau de Tours's ultimate goal. Instead, he hoped his experiments would demonstrate the reality of the soul and its ability to transcend time and space through magic and hash.

His work would have a tremendous impact on Paschal Beverly Randolph.[63]

Randolph was no stranger to psychedelia before taking his first dose of hashish. He had been practicing medicine at least a year prior to his European trip and had sampled elixirs he concocted out of opium and Solanaceae flora.[64] Hash blew them all away; Randolph even referring to it as "the medicine of immortality."[65] He quickly set about incorporating hash into such magical practices as scrying, publishing several works on his findings. One of Randolph's ointments shows the unmistakable influence that Moreau de Tours had on him. Randolph used the ointment to unlock the gates to the otherworld by generating apparitions in mirrors. The recipe for the salve consisted of 50 grams of henbane, 20 grams of belladonna, 250 grams of opium, and a staggering 300 grams of hashish.[66]

Randolph's enthusiasm would redefine ideas like clairvoyance. At the time, clairvoyance referred to nothing more than a slightly elevated awareness that allowed the clairvoyant to read the contents of a letter in an unopened envelope or play chess while wearing a blindfold. For Randolph, clairvoyance was much greater than that; it was a science cobbled from the magical arts and pharmaka that could be tested with repeatable outcomes. It had nothing to do with chessboards, but instead was closer to what we call astral projection. Under the guidance of magical techniques and hashish, Randolph would send his soul soaring through the cosmos, seeking divine wisdom.

He began to sell hash elixirs at his shop back in New York at a hefty price. He would advertise boisterously that buying hash from him came with a bonus: "full directions how to secure the celestial, and avoid the ill fantasies." Again we are seeing deference for proper set and setting within magical traditions when incorporating a pharmakon. Randolph was very aware of the way human duality played out in the expanse of the universe. He was also aware of how hash, with fair certainty, could open the doorways to the soul, letting the sunlight shine upon it.

Look sharp, be steady, for there's a power at work within you, capable of plunging you into thick gloom, elevating you into the bliss of paradise, and of leading your soul through the shadow, into regions of ineffable light, and glorious, illimitable, transcendent beauty. . . . It will burst upon you like the crash of ten thousand thunders, and for hours you will be the sport of imaginations turned to realities of the queerest, strangest, weirdest, and perhaps terrific kind.[67]

Such was the need for magical practice before taking a psychedelic like hashish.

But Randolph's real interest lay in another ancient magical art that we have become quite familiar with by this point: sex magic. Randolph *looooved* sex magic. Following in the tradition of magician-alchemist Agrippa, who used mandrake potions in his love magic,[68] Randolph's wedding of magic, hash, and sex was the culmination of one man's quest for perfect, heavenly rapture. Randolph's time among the spiritualists in upstate New York appears to have had a positive influence on his notions of feminism. He not only vehemently decried rape but also clearly recognized the divine role of feminine energy in the Sacred Marriage. He admonished men who treated women like "mere nervo-vital machine[s] for [their] especial pleasure and use." It was imperative, wrote Randolph, for not only women to achieve orgasm but to do so in unison with the man. Only then "do the mystic doors of the soul open to the spaces."[69]

Randolph believed that seeds of knowledge floated around Earth and that people in certain moments of heightened awareness could tap into those celestial juices. Sex was the oldest and most certain method. Blissfully heightened with one of his pocula amatoria, it is no wonder Randolph tapped into the godhead at the moment of sexual ecstasy.

Such was the secret of the Ansairetic Mystery: appreciation and recognition of women as the "gem[s] of God's own Aural crown."[70] A form of the Sacred Marriage rite, complete with psychedelic pharmaka, had survived not just the normal wear and tear of relentless time but also the attempted eradication courtesy of patriarchal Christianity.

THE THELEMITE

Perhaps the coincidence escaped Aleister Crowley, but the overlooked similarities between him and Jesus Christ are quite remarkable. Much like Jesus, Crowley was both precocious and rebellious.

Precocious: Jesus knew the Bible—the Torah anyway—at least as well as Crowley (though Crowley was equally at home with the New Testament). Jesus had a knack for this uncanny Abrahamic theosophy, demonstrating such aptitude early on when his parents famously found him talking shop with rabbis (Luke 2:41–51). If Jesus was illiterate, and he might very well have been, he certainly *knew* the Torah even if he couldn't read it. Born into especial poverty, his reading options would have been limited anyway.

Crowley, born into a wealthy family, had the world's libraries at his fingertips. Only he couldn't indulge. His strict religious upbringing— his parents were members of the Plymouth Brethren—meant that Crowley's options were simple (though somewhat limited): he could read either the Old Testament or the New Testament; the choice was his.

Rebellious: Jesus was a nuisance to those around him. Even Mary, Jesus's mother, thought her son crazy. Similarly, Crowley's own mother, Emily Bertha Bishop, referred to him as "the Beast." And while no one crucified Crowley, there were more than enough people who would have loved to have gotten their hands on him.

Finally, both the Nazarene and Crowley practiced magic—though of starkly different kinds. The former was a wonder-worker whose feats were either called "miracles" or "sorcery" depending on who held the quill; the latter was a ceremonial magician—the kind of which Jesus might have heard as stories of this kind trickled out of Sepphoris and into Nazareth. Indeed, such avenues are likely where Jesus learned his own magic. And while Jesus certainly had a thing for wine, Crowley could choose from a smorgasbord of exotic pharmaka. Crowley's own biographer claimed that some of Crowley's "finest writings" concern the use of either ether or hash as a means to "catapult the psyche headlong into the mystical experience."[71]

That is where the similarities end.

❦

Crowley was born into a different time and place than Jesus. By his birth in 1875, magic had all but been discredited—nothing more than a form of entertainment for audiences who *knew* they were witnessing illusions and tricks. And while such forms of prestidigitation existed in Jesus's time, so did *legitimate* forms of magic. To differentiate from the theater variety, Crowley called his legitimate rituals "magick," perhaps a borrowing from a mid-seventeenth century English translation of Giambattista della Porta's *Natural Magick* (1558).

He as well engaged in his own kind of Rites of Eleusis, and like the Greeks incorporated a pharmakon into the ceremony. Only this time, we know what that pharmakon was: cannabis. Such was his dedication to this particular psychedelic that by the time he was thirty-four, Crowley had completed a booklet titled *The Psychology of Hashish* (1909). The volume can be excused for its brevity due to the nature of its contents. Indeed, his association with certain occult groups, who believed that secrets revealed equaled power lost, meant that he had to "keep the paper within limits," using information that was already widely available to the public.[72]

But that clearly didn't stop him from referencing the occult use of hashish, indicating that such knowledge was not that big a deal. The war against cannabis waged by Harry Anslinger (1892–1975) was still decades in the future. In fact, Crowley's use of cannabis (and mescaline) did not single him out at all among other practitioners of the time.

But it is in *The Psychology of Hashish* that Crowley, no doubt reflecting on his years of occult studies, begins to ponder that "one constant story" central to mystic anecdotes.

Stripped of its local chronological accidents, it usually came to this—the writer would tell of a young man, a seeker after hidden Wisdom, who, in one circumstance or another, meets an adept; who, after sundry ordeals, obtains from the said adept, for good or ill, a certain mysterious drug or potion, with the result (at least) of opening the gate of the other world.[73]

Having experimented with "every drug in (and out of) the Pharmacopoeia," Crowley became convinced that the "certain mysterious drug" was *Cannabis indica.* A magickal mind, according to Crowley, was imperative to overcoming the stronger mental effects of cannabis, which might overwhelm the user.

As such, Crowley presents a brief survey of how and when the gentry of Europe, from the rise of the medieval university to the end of the Victorian era and into the modern age, incorporated these powerful plant allies. And maybe Crowley was right. We do, indeed, see here a continuation, a constant story, of the use of psychedelic pharmaka by Western magicians to achieve pythiagenic, entheogenic, extheogenic, and poetigenic states of consciousness.

AND UPWARD
The Psychedelic Renaissance

We have toured many lands and many peoples throughout Western civilization that, influenced by the magical cultures of Persia and China, employed psychedelic pharmaka for both spiritual and magical reasons.

Beginning in prehistory, our ancestors, fraught with all the sadness and horror that came with life at that time, experimented with the wild foliage that covered the world. Such excursions turned up culinary, medicinal, and psychedelic florae, the latter evidenced by numerous artifacts scattered across Eurasia that we considered in chapter 2. Also explored were the theories of Edward Tylor and the possibility that humans' first contact with otherworldly realities occurred once we became cognizant of, and could talk about, our dreams. As shown, early humans most likely recognized those pharmaka that lulled a person into a lucid dream state as some kind of vector to access those areas of the subconscious that tapped the realms beyond the veil. Here, psychedelics like mushrooms, mandrake, opium, and cannabis make their first appearance on the historical stage in both cave art and ancient myths about Egyptian goddesses. We also see nods not to divine masculine deities but rather divine feminine deities. Tracing historical lineages back to Africa, we find the Divine Mother, the Fireside Goddess, she who taught humans to tame the vegetation of Gaia. When the few thousand–numbering tribes of people that would one day become *all* of us fled the plains of Africa and spanned the globe, the mysteries of this Divine Mother took two distinct paths: one in the West, which retained the original matrifocal version, perhaps first conceived before humans understood the male's role in creation; the other one in the East, which acknowledged the male's role in creation.

This common belief in a Divine Mother would contribute to Europe's highest level of persecution of wise women, from the 1400s to the 1700s. Due to a series of natural disasters (famine, plague, syphilis outbreaks), clergymen debated and eventually decided that the somnitheogenic (and otherwise theogenic) experiences of local wise women and men marked the greatest threat to Christendom. In the process of this most heinous kind of bigoted eradication, both theologians and physicians (and theologian-physicians) would introduce the secrets of these arts to a wider audience.

Also buried in the deepest recesses of history is the mystery of the Sacred Marriage. Probably beginning when humans first noticed their connection with all creation, the Sacred Marriage offered the perfect myth to explain the dualism of divine feminine and divine masculine energies in the act of creation. As time progressed, this wedding would take on at least two distinct forms: Sometimes an immortal merged with a mortal, as with the pythia priestesses at Delphi. Other times two mortals might take on the roles of god and goddess and copulate ritualistically, such as the Dionysian revelers did. That these extremes found housing in the same temple (at least in Delphi) speaks volumes to the ancient recognition of substance and especially set to ensure two different religious experiences in the same setting.

But both pharmaka and wine, while celebrated in some places, came under fire in others. The fall of the spiritual use of pharmaka came largely from two places (broadly speaking, of course): first, from authoritarians who wanted to control the spiritual behavior of others; and second, from those incidental mistakes made by a priestess who trusted the wrong person (and the misogyny that perverted all justice once she stood trial). One fed the other.

The pagan use of psychedelic pharmaka for entheogenic and mystheogenic ceremonies did not escape the earliest forms of Christianity. Adherents of various kinds of gnostic belief employed psychedelic pharmaka in a number of ways (notwithstanding those that have been lost to us). Indeed, considering the fluidity of religion in those days, any pagan cum Christian might have readopted her religious use of pharmaka into her new Christian faith in some queer way. Indeed, the very nature of the Lord's Supper (ingestion of a god) waxes pagan—ideas absent from the Jewish apocalyptic motifs of Jesus's earliest followers.

However, it should be noted that the use of pythiagenic pharmaka survived in some of those apocalypticists' later writing. Some, like whoever authored the text of 2 Esdras, openly acknowledged the use of some kind of visionary drink that allowed her or him to sort and interpret the wave of visions endured leading up to the final revelation.

If the earliest Christians had the right to use such pharmaka in their personal experiences of the risen Jesus, then no Christian today should feel guilty about having experimented with a psychedelic. In the first few centuries of the Common Era, this mingling of psychedelics with Christianity does not seem to have been a bother to the Roman guard—only a bother to *other Christians*. Some of those early Christian views even reserved an aspect of the Divine Feminine. Historically, the antignostic view of Jesus won out. Still, that did not at all stop alternative Christianities from using psychedelic pharmaka to better understand what the person of Jesus meant to our human story and the possibilities of salvation. And while I do not think Christians would have fetishized a mushroom (an *Amanita muscaria,* no less) to the point that they secretly (and not so secretly when convenient) inserted mushrooms in their art, I do accept the historical fact that some Christians used psychedelic pharmaka.

Magical traditions that began in the days of ancient Greece and Rome survived the fall of the Western Roman Empire due to the copying and commentary efforts of both Persians and Muslims. When magical and medical texts returned to Europe in the early twelfth century, they featured a depth of wisdom and, in some cases, spiritualism that polished the ancient Western traditions. The successful spread of Islam westward created an atmosphere of cultural diffusion, such as we saw with Al Andalus. The pharmaka not only regained a home* in Western necromancy, alchemy, astrology—the learned arts—but also survived in underground vaults and hidden chambers up until the Victorian era.

Today, we live in the warm embrace of the psychedelic renaissance. Practitioners of almost every kind of magical or religious discipline incorporate psychedelic pharmaka into their own systems and practices. Some of those magical orders, first attended by not a few people who had sampled some kind of psychedelic in a mystical setting, like the Thelemite Church, *Ordo Templi Orientis*, survive to this day.

Throughout our history, Western peoples have struggled to fully comprehend the psychedelic experience—this fire, so inexpressible. But it is not just Western peoples, of course. Indeed, from the farthest reaches of every corner of Earth, beacons of the psychedelic renaissance light up those perfect orange and purple skies—nights perfect for magic. The ability to experience and contemplate the psychedelic state, in whatever way one sees fit, is part of the *human* tradition. And so, let's pass the pipe. Let it go around the whole of Earth to every psychenaut gathered around a fire to share their stories, their insights, their experiences with the otherworld.

And how inseparable these experiences are from the human experiment.

---

*At least one detectible by the unbreakable standards of history.

So should you need a hug and an inviting place to sit, just look sky-ward for the embers glowing in the last echoes of sunlight, for others are waiting around that fire, keeping a seat warm for you.

Standing tall against the winds of mystery as though the future of the tribe lay in the balance.

Loving and commenting on every weird idiosyncrasy of cosmic humor and sadness.

Holding tight against the storm.

Sending songs alongside the ashes to their final resting place in the heavens.

Huddling close to protect the light.

Guarding the flame.

N⊙TES

ONWARD

1. "Ellis: No-Hitter while on LSD," *Register Guard.*

1. GENERATING DIVINITY

Epigraph. Baudelaire, *Artificial Paradise,* x.

1. Osmond, "Review of the Clinical Effects," 429.
2. Wasson, Hofmann, and Ruck, *Road to Eleusis,* 33.
3. Newberg, D'Aquili, and Rause, *Why God Won't Go Away,* 73.
4. Ruck, Staples, and Heinrich, *Apples of Apollo,* 12.
5. Ogden, *Magic, Witchcraft, and Ghosts,* 282 *ff.*
6. Hillman, *Chemical Muse,* 2.

2. THE FIRST MYSTERY

1. Campion, *Dawn of Astrology,* 7–8.
2. Eisler, *Chalice and the Blade,* 10.
3. Eisler, *Chalice and the Blade,* 3.
4. Wright, *Evolution of God,* 17–19.
5. Chris Bennett, personal communication.
6. Other scholars have noted this; see Merlin, "Archaeological Evidence," 35.
7. Rubin, *Cannabis and Culture,* 305.
8. Bennett, "Scythians Ancient Ritual," in Estren, *One Toke to God,* 46.
9. Attrell, *Shamanism and the Mysteries,* 29.
10. For an oppositional perspective, see Letcher, *Shroom,* 25 *ff.*
11. "We Drank the Soma, We Became Immortal."
12. Diodorus of Sicily, *Library of History,* 1.81.

13. Diodorus of Sicily, *Library of History*, 1.22.

14. Bennett, "Scythians Ancient Ritual," in Estren, *One Toke to God*, 45–46.

15. Rudgley, *Alchemy of Culture*, 24–27.

16. Letcher, *Shroom*, 132–34.

17. Eliade, quoted in Wilson, *Occult*, 145.

18. Diodorus of Sicily, *Library of History*, 1.25.2.

19. McCabe, *Examination of the Cult of Isis*, 20.

20. Fox, *Spatula*, 212.

21. Diodorus of Sicily, *Library of History*, 1.81.

22. Pindar, *Pythian*, 3. 50.

23. Merlin, "Archaeological Evidence," 302–3.

24. Spence, *Ancient Egyptian Myths and Legends*, 167.

25. Riddle, *Goddesses, Elixirs, and Witches*, 59.

26. Spence, *Ancient Egyptian Myths and Legends*, 168.

27. Riddle, *Goddesses, Elixirs, and Witches*, 59.

28. D. Lit, *Mystery Religions and Christanity*, 133.

29. Remondino, in Wooster, *Pacific Medical Journal*, 527.

30. St. Basil, *Letters*, 387.

31. Plato, *Symposium*, 67.

32. Apuleius, *Apology*, 43; *cf* Luck, *Arcana Mundi*, 483.

3. COSMIC GRAELL

Epigraph 1. Quoted in Schmitt, "Ancient Mysteries," 113.

1. Danny Staples, trans., "Homeric Hymn to Demeter," in Wasson, Hofmann, and Ruck, *Road to Eleusis*, 69.

2. O' Reilly and Habegger, *Travelers' Tales, Thailand*, 398.

3. Wasson, Hofmann, and Ruck, *Road to Eleusis*, 77.

4. Wasson, Hofmann, and Ruck, *Road to Eleusis*, 79.

5. Otto, "Meaning of the Eleusinian Mysteries," 23.

6. See Wasson, Hofmann, and Ruck, *Road to Eleusis*.

7. Noconi, "Entheogens and the Eucharist: Altered States and the Origin of Sacrament."

8. Otto, "Meaning of the Eleusinian Mysteries," 26

9. Wasson, Hofmann, and Ruck, *Road to Eleusis*, 89–90.

10. Webster, "Mixing the Kykeon," 4–5.

11. Rinella, *Pharmakon*, 100.

12. Peter Webster, "Kykeon Chemistry," in Wasson, Hofmann, and Ruck, *Road to Eleusis,* 156.

13. Albert Hofmann, "A Challenging Question," in Wasson, Hofmann, and Ruck, *Road to Eleusis,* 43.

14. Burkert, *Greek Religion,* 285.

15. Plutarch, *Life of Phocion,* 28.3.

16. Burkert, *Greek Religion,* 287.

17. Goodart, "Lesser Mysteries of Eleusis," 21.

18. Otto, "Meaning of the Eleusinian Mysteries," 23.

19. Pseudo-Plutarch, *De fluviis,* sec. 3, "Herbus."

20. Bennett, *Cannabis and the Soma Solution,* 256.

21. Electronic Text Corpus of Sumerian Literature, "Inanna's Descent into the Underworld," 102–7.

22. Electronic Text Corpus of Sumerian Literature, "Inanna's Descent into the Underworld," 108–13.

23. Kleps, *Millbrook,* 71.

24. "Electronic Text Corpus of Sumerian Literature, "Inanna's Descent into the Underworld," 282–89, 354–58.

25. Coudert, "Elixirs," in Eliade, *Hidden Truths,* 249.

26. Broad, *Oracle,* 27.

27. Wasson, Hofmann, and Ruck, *Road to Eleusis,* 48, 97.

28. Ruck, "Wild and the Cultivated," in Wasson et al., *Persephone's Quest,* 183.

29. For an opposing view of my theory, see Raine, *Blake and Tradition,* 170.

30. Wasson, Hofmann, and Ruck, *Road to Eleusis,* 54.

31. Newman, *Alchemically Stoned,* 55.

32. Clement of Alexandria, *Exhortation to the Greeks,* 2.22.

33. Wasson, Hofmann, and Ruck, *Road to Eleusis,* 92–93.

34. Hippolytus, *Refutation of All Heresies,* book 5, chap. 3.

4. CELEBRATIONS OF THE LIVING FIRE

Epigraph. Homer, *Odyssey* 4.219–39.

1. Origen, *Contra Celsum,* 7.4.

2. Broad, *Oracle,* 35–39.

3. Strabo, *Geography,* 9.3.5.

4. Plutarch, *Moralia,* 51.1; *cf* Plutarch, *De defectu oraculorum,* 51.

5. Diodorus of Sicily, *Library of History,* 4.5.1.

6. Diodorus of Sicily, *Library of History,* 3.64.2.

7. Diodorus of Sicily, *Library of History,* 3.70.3.

8. Zosimos of Panopolitanus, *De Zythorum confectione fragmentum,* 102: "*Certe coctoribus zythi non desuerunt fraudulentae pessimaeque artes, quibus is et potentior, et ad ebrietatem inducendam aptior fieret.*"

9. Wasson, Hofmann, and Ruck, *Road to Eleusis,* 51, 99.

10. Ruck, Staples, and Heinrich, *Apples of Apollo,* 12–13.

11. Broad, *Oracle,* 42.

12. Pliny the Elder, *Natural History,* 14.18, 14.15.

13. Diodorus of Sicily, *Library of History,* 4.6.

14. Ruck, "Wild and the Cultivated," in Wasson et al., *Persephone's Quest,* 185.

15. Thorwald, *Science and Secrets of Early Medicine,* 60. For my thoughts on this, see Hatsis, *Witches' Ointment, 76 ff.*

16. Plutarch, *Roman Questions,* 112.5–6.17.

17. Ruck, "Wild and the Cultivated," in Wasson et al., *Persephone's Quest,* 183.

18. Burkert, *Greek Religion,* 163.

19. Astour, *Hellenosemitica,* 187.

20. Ruck, "Wild and the Cultivated," in Wasson et al., *Persephone's Quest,* 183.

21. Herodotus, *Histories,* 7.111.1.

22. Ruck, *Dionysus in Thrace,* 259–60.

23. Herodotus, *Histories,* 7.111.2.

24. Macrobius, *Saturnalia,* 1.18.1–2.

25. Ruck, *Dionysus in Thrace,* 79.

26. Titus Livius, *History of Rome,* 39.18.

27. Plutarch, *Roman Questions,* 112.

28. Oisteanu, *Narcotice în cultura român,* 48.

29. Yasna, 32:13; *cf* 48:10, reprinted in West, *Hymns of Zoroaster,* 74.

30. Diodorus of Sicily, *Library of History,* 4.4.1; *cf* Oisteanu, *Narcotice în cultura român,* 101.

31. Ruck, "Mushrooms and Philosophers," in Wasson et al., *Persephone's Quest,* 163.

32. Herodotus, *Histories,* 5.67.1–5.

33. Herodotus, *Histories,* 4.79.4–5.

34. Herodotus, *Histories,* 4.80.5.

35. Diodorus of Sicily, *Library of History,* 3.65.2.

36. Herodotus, *Histories,* 4.95.

37. Lewin, *Phantastica,* 133.

38. Quoted in Kirton, *Temperance Handbook,* 176–77.

39. Riddle, *Goddesses, Elixirs, and Witches,* 12.

40. Finkelstein, "Inanna and the God of Wisdom."

41. Griffiths, *Origins of Osiris and His Cult,* 163.

42. Ruck, "Wild and the Cultivated," in Wasson et al., *Persephone's Quest,* 186.

5. THESSALIAN ROOTS

1. Lucan, *Pharsalia,* 6.434–507.

2. Virgil, *Eclogues,* 8.95.

3. Virgil, *Eclogues,* 8.95.

4. Quoted in Ogden, *Magic, Witchcraft, and Ghosts,* 178.

5. Ogden, *Greek and Roman Necromancy,* 141.

6. Pliny the Elder, *Natural History,* 24, 102.

7. Diodorus of Sicily, *Library of History,* 4.45.2.

8. Diodorus of Sicily, *Library of History,* 4.45.2; *cf* Rinella, *Pharmakon,* 176.

9. Valeriano, *Hieroglyphica, sive, de sacris Aegyptiorvm aliarvmqve gentivm literis commentari,* 431.

10. Pliny the Elder, *Natural History,* 25.5.

11. Hatsis, *Witches' Ointment,* 15-16.

12. Liberalis, *Metamorphosis of Antonius Liberalis,* 188.

13. Ankerloo and Clark, *Witchcraft and Magic in Europe,* vol. 2, 249.

14. Dioscorides, *Pharmacorum simplicium,* 238: "*Mandragora . . . Circeon dixeruint; huius radicem ad amorem multi dant.*"

15. Diodorus of Sicily, *Library of History,* 1.7.

16. Homer, *Odyssey,* 4.220–235.

17. Ogden, *Magic, Witchcraft, and Ghosts,* 111.

18. Plutarch, *Conjugalia Praecepta,* sec. 5.

19. St. Basil of Caesarea, *Letters,* 188.8.

20. John Chrysostom, "Homily 17," in *Fathers of the Church,* 236.

21. John Chrysostom, "Homily 16," in *Fathers of the Church,* 212–13. *Italics mine.*

22. Hanz Dieter Betz, *Greek Magical Papyri,* 69–71.

23. Quoted in Smith, *Jesus the Magician,* 170.

24. Ogden, *Magic, Witchcraft, and Ghosts,* 111.

25. Theocritus, "The Spell," *Idyll* 2.48.

26. Ogden, *Magic, Witchcraft, and Ghosts*, 160.
27. Ogden, *Magic, Witchcraft, and Ghosts*, 58.
28. Colavito, *Argonautica Orphica*, 34.
29. Ovid, *Metamorphosis*, 7.179.
30. Dioscorides, *De materia medica*, book III, pages 165, 534.
31. Hillman, "Pre-Christian Sacraments and the First War on Drugs," in Estren, *One Toke to God*, 64–5.
32. Lucian of Samosata, quoted in Goodrich, *Priestesses*, 56.
33. Lucian of Samosata, quoted in Goodrich, *Priestesses*, 59.
34. Lucian of Samosata, quoted in Goodrich, *Priestesses*, 56.
35. Lucian of Samosata, quoted in Goodrich, *Priestesses*, 59.
36. Lucian of Samosata, quoted in Goodrich, *Priestesses*, 56.
37. Colavito, *Argonautica Orphica*, 36–37.
38. For different kinds of divination, see Luck, *Arcana Mundi*, 309 *ff*; on libomancy, see del Rio, *Investigations into Magic*, 160.
39. Luck, *Arcana Mundi*, 485, 491.
40. Virgil, *Eclogues*, 8.82.
41. Ruck, "Cultivated and the Wild," in Wasson et al., *Persephone's Quest*, 184.
42. Aristophanes, *Wasps*, 1; *cf* Ruck, *Road to Eleusis*, 103.
43. Pliny the Elder, *Natural History*, 2.106.
44. Quoted in Luck, *Arcana Mundi*, 364.
45. Luck, *Arcana Mundi*, 364.
46. Webster, "Mixing the Kykeon," 11.
47. Luck, *Arcana Mundi*, 304.
48. Pausanias, *Geography of Greece*, 9.39.13.
49. For the latest argument in favor of this hypothesis, see Brown and Brown, *Psychedelic Gospels*, 35.
50. Polyaenus, *Stratagem*, 8.43.
51. Polyaenus, *Stratagem*, 8.39.
52. Plutarch, *Moralia*, 3.20.
53. Polyaenus, *Stratagem*, 8.39.
54. Betz, *Greek Magical Papyri*, 233–34.
55. Apollodorus, *Bibliotheca*, 1.9.26.
56. Plutarch, *Alexander*, 77.4.
57. Polyaenus, *Stratagem*, 8.38.
58. Ogden, *Magic, Witchcraft, and Ghosts*, 80.

59. Justin Martyr, *Dialogue with Trypho,* 85.3.
60. Demosthenes, *Against Aristogiton,* 1. 80.
61. Quoted in Mirecki and Meyer, *Magic and Ritual in the Ancient World,* 172.
62. John Chrysostom, "Eighth Homily on Colossians."

6. THE FIRE-LIKE CUP

1. For Jesus as religious extremist, see Ehrman, *Jesus,* 126–28; for Jesus as wonder-worker, see Smith, *Jesus the Magician,* 195 *ff.*
2. Josephus, *Antiquities of the Jews,* 18.1.
3. Ehrman, *Jesus,* 77.
4. See Brown and Brown, *Psychedelic Gospels;* Ruck, Staples, and Heinrich, *Apples of Apollo.*
5. Wasson et al., *Persephone's Quest,* 74–75.
6. See Hatsis, "Dogmatists' Debacle."
7. della Porta, *Natural Magic in XX Books,* 197–98.
8. Augustine, *Enchiridion,* 26.
9. Quoted in Aquilecchia "La favola Mandragola si chiama," 94: *"Per il quale mandragora e un'erba la cui radice ha membra simili a quelle di us essere umano acefalo; questo significa il popolo ebraico che e ancora senza capo; ma alla fine del mondo gli Ebrei riceveranno la parola e la fragranza della Chiesa e saranno finalmente riuniti a Cristo, loro capo."*
10. Myers, *I & II Esdras,* 66.
11. Myers, *I & II Esdras,* 253.
12. Luck, *Arcana Mundi,* 300.
13. Myers, *I & II Esdras,* 209.
14. Myers, *I & II Esdras,* 187.
15. Myers, *I & II Esdras,* 286.
16. Brown and Brown, *Psychedelic Gospels,* 20–21; Bennett, *Cannabis and the Soma Solution,* 374 *ff.*
17. Brown and Brown, *Psychedelic Gospels,* 21.

7. DISCIPLES OF THEIR OWN MINDS

1. Rutilius Claudius Namatianus, *On My Return,* 811: on self-flagellation: *"Infelix putat illuvie caelestia pasciseque premit laesis saevior ipse deis";* on Circe's pharmaka: *"Num, rogo, deterior Circaeis secta venenis? Tunc mutabuntur corpora, nunc animi."*

2. Josephus, *Antiquities of the Jews*, 14.2.1.
3. See Philostratus, *Life of Apollonius of Tyana*.
4. Key, *Medicine, Miracle, and Magic*, 79.
5. Josephus, *Jewish Wars*, 7.6.3.
6. Origen, *Contra Celsum*, 6.11.
7. Smith, *Jesus the Magician*, 169.
8. For an overview of Roman laws regarding magic, see Hatsis, *Witches' Ointment*, 14–16.
9. Maccoby, *Mythmaker*, 113–14.
10. Burkert, *Greek Religion*, 164.
11. Oisteanu, *Narcotice în cultura român*, 47.
12. Burkert, *Greek Religion*, 290.
13. Burkert, *Greek Religion*, 116.
14. For an extensive argument in favor of Benet's translation, see Bennett, *Cannabis and the Soma Solution*, 353.
15. Justin Martyr, "Urbicus Condemns the Christians to Death."
16. See Thomas O. Lambdin, *The Gospel of Thomas*, in Robinson, 1990; *cf* Brown and Brown, *The Psychedelic Gospels*, 202.
17. Pagels, *Gnostic Gospels*, 54.
18. Søren Giversen and Birger A. Pearson, "The Testimony of Truth," in Robinson, *Nag Hammadi Library*, 449–50.
19. Irenaeus, *Against Heresies* 1.21.4.
20. Hippolytus, *Refutation of All Heresies*, book 6, chap. 9.
21. Nigg, *Heretics*, 19.
22. Hippolytus, *Refutation of All Heresies*, book 6, chap. 14.
23. Theodoretus, "Hæreticarum Fabularum Compendium," 1.1; Epiphanius, "Contra Hæreses," 2.2, in Mead, *Simon Magus; cf* Irenaeus, *Against Heresies*, 1.23.4.
24. Eusebius, *Ecclesiastical History*, 2.12.
25. Eusebius, *Ecclesiastical History*, 2.12, book 1; Irenaeus, *Against Heresy*, 1.23.4.
26. Epiphanius, *Panarion*, 21.2.1.
27. Quoted in Nigg, *Heretics*, 37.
28. Irenaeus, *Against Heresies*, 1.25.6.
29. Quoted in Ruether and McLaughlin, *Women of Spirit*, 46.
30. Irenaeus, *Against Heresies*, 1.25.3.
31. Torjesen, *When Women Were Priests*, 20.

32. Irenaeus, *Against Heresies,* 1.25.6.
33. Mead, "Ode to Sophia," 213 *ff.*
34. Quoted in Nigg, *Heretics,* 38.
35. See Bennett, *Cannabis and the Soma Solution,* 403.
36. *Authoritative Teaching,* in Robinson, *Nag Hammadi Library,* 305.
37. Irenaeus, *Against Heresies,* 1.21.3.
38. Irenaeus, *Against Heresies,* 1.14.1.
39. Irenaeus, *Against Heresies,* 1.21.5.
40. Irenaeus, *Against Heresies,* 1.13.1–7; *cf* Ruck, Staples, and Heinrich, *Apples of Apollo,* 187.
41. Irenaeus, *Against Heresies,* 1.13.6.
42. Irenaeus, *Against Heresies,* 1.13.2.

8. PATRONS OF THE SERPENT

1. Lucian of Samosata, *Timon the Misanthrope.*
2. From Origen's Lost Commentary on Genesis, quoted in Collins, *Bodies, Politics, and Transformations,* 88.
3. Jackson, *Nicene and Post-Nicene Fathers,* 78.
4. Littledale, *Commentary on the Song of Songs,* 339.
5. Quoted in Davis, "Terence McKenna's Last Trip."
6. Merkur, *Psychedelic Sacraments,* 21.
7. Theodorat of Cyrus, "On Divine Providence," 193.
8. St. Ambrose, "Splendor paternae gloriae."
9. Boethius, *Consolatio philosophiae,* 4.3: "*Haec venena potentius, detrahunt hominem sibi, dira quae penitus meant, nec nocentia corpori mentis uulnere saeuiunt.*"
10. Van Arsdall, Klug, and Blanz, "Mandrake Plant and Its Legend," 316.
11. Quoted in Rätsch, *Encyclopedia of Psychoactive Plants,* 355.
12. Mechoulam, "Cannabis: The Israeli Perspective," 1.
13. Quoted in Littledale, *Commentary on the Song of Songs,* 339.
14. Paul of Aleppo, *Travels of Macarius,* 469.
15. Smith, *Jesus the Magician,* 86–87.
16. Pagels, *Adam, Eve, and the Serpent,* 27.
17. Irenaeus, *Against Heresies,* 3.28.8.
18. Hatsis, *Witches' Ointment,* 79.
19. Randolph, *Mandragora of the Ancients,* 503.

20. *Aponii Scriptoris Vetustissimi in Canticum Canticorum Libri Duodecim* (Romae, Apud Typographiam S. Congregationis de Propaganda Fifi, 1845), 210: *"Quae mandragora, ferocissimae et quae omnes actus suos terrae demersos habuerunt, gentes intelligi mihi videntur, quae per legem naturae rationabilibus hominibus similes sunt, caput vero fidei non habent, idest Christum; caput enim viri Christus."*

21. Hatsis, *Witches' Ointment*, 84.

22. von Langenfeld, *Cautio Criminalis*, 103.

23. *Joe Rogan Experience* #1035, "Paul Stamets episode," podcast, Nov. 7, 2017. www.youtube.com/watch?v=mPqWstVnRjQ.

24. Samuel Davies, "A Christmas-Day Sermon, 1758," in Bond, *Spreading the Gospel in Colonial Virginia*, 159.

25. Roberts and Donaldson, *Ante-Nicene Fathers*, 498.

26. Lucian, *Lucian*, 107.

27. Lucian, *Lucian*, 113.

28. Forbes, *Christmas*, 10.

29. Quoted in Forbes, *Christmas*, 12.

30. Rätsch and Müller-Ebeling, *Pagan Christmas*, 118.

31. Rätsch and Müller-Ebeling, *Pagan Christmas*, 120–21.

32. See Brown and Brown, *Psychedelic Gospels*.

33. See Rush, *Mushroom in Christian Art*.

34. Cooke, *Seven Sisters of Sleep*, 253; Letcher, *Shroom*, 121–23.

35. Wasson, *Soma: Divine Mushroom of Immortality*, 161.

36. Forbes, *Christmas*, 73–74.

37. Forbes, *Christmas*, 87.

38. Quoted in Forbes, *Christmas*, 74.

39. Sack and Niermann, *Curious World of Drugs*, 139.

40. Dugan, *Fungi, Folkways and Fairy Tales*, 54; Morgan "Who Put the Toad in Toadstool?"; Abel, *Intoxication in Mythology*, 122.

41. Kleijn, *Mushrooms and Other Fungi*, 37–41.

42. Hamilton and Henry, "Post Card Manufacturers," 7836.

43. Brown and Brown, *Psychedelic Gospels*, 118.

PART III. PSYCHEDELIC MYSTERY TRADITIONS IN RENAISSANCE WITCHCRAFT AND MAGIC

1. Kieckhefer, *Magic in the Middle Ages*, 151 *ff.*

9. WYLD AND WYRD

1. Ginzburg, *Ecstasies: Deciphering the Witches' Sabbath*, 91.
2. Russell, *Witchcraft in the Middle Ages*, 158–59.
3. Bailey, *Historical Dictionary of Witchcraft*, 26.
4. Hansen, *Quellen*, 38.
5. Quoted in Baroja, *World of the Witches*, 56.
6. Russell, *Witchcraft in the Middle Ages*, 49.
7. Ginzburg, *Ecstasies: Deciphering the Witches' Sabbath*, 92, 129 *ff.*
8. Russell, *Witchcraft in the Middle Ages*, 49. See also Rider, *Magic and Religion in Medieval England*, 74
9. See Ginzburg, *Ecstasies: Deciphering the Witches' Sabbath*, 99 *ff.*
10. Polyaenus, *Strategems*, 6.7.2.
11. Cohn, *Europe's Inner Demons*, 6–7.
12. Cohn, *Europe's Inner Demons*, 7–11.
13. Cohn, *Europe's Inner Demons*, 37.
14. Ginzburg, *Ecstasies: Deciphering the Witches' Sabbath*, 307.
15. Hansen, *Quellen*, 119: "*Item postquam seductus fecit homagium diabolo presidenti, dat sibi unam pixidem unquento plenam et baculum ceteraque omnia, cum quibus debet seductus ire ad synagogam, docetque cum, qumomodo et qualiter debet baculum inungere. Illud namque unguentum diabolice malignitatis mysterio conficitur ex pinguedine puerorum assatorum et elixatorum cum aliquibus allis, ut patebit.*"
16. Hansen, *Quellen*, 118.
17. Mormando, *Preacher's Demons*, 4.
18. Bernard Gui, *Practica inquisitions haereticae pravitatis des inquisitors*, in Hansen, *Quellen*, 48 : "*Item, de fatis mulieribus quas vocant 'bona res' que . . . vadunt de nocte*"; "*Collection herbarum flexis genibus versa facie ad orientem cum oration dominica.*"
19. Hatsis, *Witches' Ointment*, 31.
20. Hatsis, *Witches' Ointment*, 31.
21. Wenzel, *Fasciculus Morum*, 579–81.
22. Harms, *Book of Oberon*, 358.
23. Peters, *Magician, the Witch, and the Law*, 28.
24. Hansen, *Quellen*, 437: "Die ersten tund wider das gebot, die unholda sind, die vil unglucks tribent und salb machent und enweg farent. Als ainost aime, du sas in ain mult, du stund uff aim tisch, und wand ouch,

si wolt uber den Howberg faren und hottet nun fast in der mult und fiel in des tufels namen undern tisch, das du mult uff ir lag. Sie fiel ouch gewis nit in gotz namen. Wer solt sollichs volcks nit lachen, das also an deu wenden gant, es sind unholdan." (Gerhild Williams, trans.)

25. Nider, *Formicarius,* book 2, chap. 4 (unpaged): ". . . feminam quondam demantatem . . ."

26. See Hatsis, *Witches' Ointment,* 78 *ff.*

27. Hansen, *Quellen,* 109: "*Nam quaedam mixtiones sunt, quibus si ungantur, partes corpis, quae urendae vel secandae sunt, non erit sensus doloris. Scimus quoque, genus unctionis esse, quo tanta fit mentis alienatio et abstractio hominis a se ipso, ut per certum temporis spacium nulla sensatio inveniatur in eo*"; "*Sunt enim mulieres quaedam, quas maleficas vocamus, quae profitentur facta quandam unctione cum certis verborum observationibus ire, quando voluerint, ad diversa loca, viros et foeminas convenire, ubi omnium voluptatum generibus, tam in cibis quam in complexibus perfruantur.*"

28. Hansen, *Quellen,* 119: "*Et patet, quod iste sit sensus litterae, quia cum dicitur . . . et qui rectam fidem non habet . . . sed illius, in quem credit, id est diaboli. . . . Hoc autem est, quia credunt Dianam deam esse, et tamen Diana est diabolus;* "*Ideo negandum non est, mulieres maleficas et etiam viros, factis quibusdam nefandis cæremoniis et unctionibus a dæmonibus assume et per diversa loca portari, et multos huius generis in unum locum convenire, et daemonibus honorem quondam exhibere ac libidini et omni turpitudini vacare.*"

29. Kramer and Sprenger, *Malleus Maleficarum,* 107.

30. Kramer and Sprenger, *Malleus Maleficarum;* references to Nider appear: 66, 82, 90, 94, 99, 100.

31. Jean Vincent in Hansen *Quellen,* 230: "*Venenis igitur utuntur venefici pariter et poculis quibusdam atque unguentis, quibus humanas mentes perturbant, corpora alterant et plerumque homines interficiunt. Horam eciam venenorum virtute per noctes se dicunt ad sabbata longe remota demonum portari. Que tanem singular recte iudicanti naturali non sunt virtuti alicui talium venenorum attribuenda, sed magis fallaci astucie demonis, qui huismodi unguentorum linitionibus aut poculorum exhaustionibus ex pacto cum primis huius damnatu artis inventoribus expresse inito assistit et illa, que virtute predictorum fieri creduntur, ipse demon applicando active passivis operator, qui causa principalis est et effective, huismodi vero venena per maleficis adhibita causa sunt, sine qua non fierent ista.*"

32. Hatsis, *Witches' Ointment,* 134.

33. Shaw, "Otherworld Gnosis," 47.

34. Hatsis, *Witches' Ointment,* 35.

35. Augustine Thompson, trans., "A Trial for Witchcraft at Todi (1428)," in Jansen, Drell, and Andrews, *Medieval Italy,* 210.

36. Hatsis, *Witches' Ointment,* 21.

37. Jansen, Drell, and Andrews, *Medieval Italy,* 203.

38. Jansen, Drell, and Andrews, *Medieval Italy,* 210–11.

39. Jansen, Drell, and Andrews, *Medieval Italy,* 211.

40. Harms, "On Hatsis' *The Witches' Ointment* and Abramelin."

41. Von Worms, *The Book of Abramelin,* 20–21.

42. Quoted in Shaw, "Otherworld Gnosis," 42.

43. Quoted in Shaw, "Otherworld Gnosis," 44.

44. Bever, *Realities of Witchcraft,* 133–34.

45. Letcher, *Shroom,* 27–28.

46. Ginzburg, *Ecstasies: Deciphering the Witches' Sabbath,* 97.

10. ONE CONSTANT STORY

Epigraph. Quoted in Ruck and Hoffman, *Effluents of Deity,* 6.

1. Quoted in Russo, "Pharmacological History of Cannabis," 18.

2. Maxwell-Stuart, *Chemical Choir,* 4.

3. Cooper, *Chinese Alchemy,* 13.

4. Maxwell-Stuart, *Chemical Choir,* 7

5. Maxwell-Stuart, *Chemical Choir,* 8.

6. Holmyard, *Alchemy,* 79.

7. Holmyard, *Alchemy,* 68 *ff.*

8. Quoted in Bennett, *Cannabis and the Soma Solution,* 517.

9. Russo, "Pharmacological History of Cannabis," 24.

10. See Aldridge, "Cannabis and Its Derivatives."

11. Holmyard, *Alchemy,* 93.

12. Quoted in Idel, *Studies in Ecstatic Kabbalah,* 112.

13. Al-Hakim, *Picatrix,* 147.

14. Al-Hakim, *Picatrix,* 257.

15. Maxwell-Stuart, *Chemical Choir,* 55.

16. Holmyard, *Alchemy,* 87.

17. Maxwell-Stuart, *Chemical Choir,* 60.

18. Quoted in Maxwell-Stuart, *Chemical Choir,* 70–71.

19. Heinrich, *Magic Mushroom in Religion and Alchemy,* 165 *ff.*

20. White, *Isaac Newton,* 123–24.

21. Ball, *Devil's Doctor,* 182.

22. Quoted in Ball, *Devil's Doctor,* 198.

23. Ruck and Hoffman, *Effluents of Deity,* 8.

24. Butler, *Ritual Magic,* 57.

25. Kieckhefer, *Magic in the Middle Ages,* 9.

26. Cohn, *Europe's Inner Demons,* 108.

27. Quoted in Ogden, *Magic, Witchcraft, and Ghosts,* 275.

28. Quoted in Ogden, *Magic, Witchcraft, and Ghosts,* 277.

29. Kieckhefer, *Magic in the Middle Ages,* 20.

30. Quoted in Ogden, *Magic, Witchcraft, and Ghosts,* 280.

31. Quoted in Ogden, *Magic, Witchcraft, and Ghosts,* 284.

32. Origen, *Contra Celsum,* 1.68.

33. Maxwell-Stuart, *Chemical Choir,* 32.

34. Kieckhefer, *Magic in the Middle Ages,* 40.

35. Quoted in Ogden, *Magic, Witchcraft, and Ghosts,* 335.

36. Quoted in Ogden, *Magic, Witchcraft, and Ghosts,* 336.

37. Tavennar, *Studies in Magic from Latin Literature,* 14.

38. Kieckhefer, *Magic in the Middle Ages,* 11.

39. Peters, *Magician, the Witch, and the Law,* 64–65.

40. Bennett, *Liber 420,* 489.

41. Mora, *Witches, Devils, and Doctors,* 227.

42. Butler, *Ritual Magic,* 57.

43. Quoted in Bennett, *Liber 420,* 380.

44. Agrippa, *Three Books of Occult Philosophy,* 133.

45. Ogden, *Magic, Witchcraft, and Ghosts,* 141–42.

46. Albertus Magnus, *De vegetabiblius,* 527: "*Qui autem in nigromanticis student, tradunt characterem iusquiami pictum debere esse in homine, quando faciunt daemonum invocationes.*"

47. Leland, *Etruscan Magic and Occult Remedies,* 319.

48. Mora, *Witches, Devils, and Doctors,* 230.

49. Kieckhefer, *Forbidden Rites,* 187.

50. Bever, *Realities of Witchcraft,* 171.

51. Bever, *Realities of Witchcraft,* 171–72.

52. Nauert, *Agrippa and the Crisis of Renaissance Thought,* 286.

53. Hatsis, *Witches' Ointment,* 177.

54. Mora, *Witches, Devils, and Doctors,* 230–31.

55. Mora, *Witches, Devils, and Doctors,* 408–9.

56. Mora, *Witches, Devils, and Doctors,* 269.

57. Mora, *Witches, Devils, and Doctors,* 248–49.

58. Mora, *Witches, Devils, and Doctors,* 268–69.

59. Quoted in Davenport-Hines, *Pursuit of Oblivion,* 92–93.

60. Deveney, *Paschal Beverly Randolph,* 2–3.

61. Randolph, *Sexual Magic,* xxiii.

62. Deveney, *Paschal Beverly Randolph,* 10.

63. Deveney, *Paschal Beverly Randolph,* 55.

64. Randolph, *Sexual Magic,* xxiv.

65. Lee, *Smoke Signals,* 34.

66. Deveney, *Paschal Beverly Randolph,* 71.

67. Quoted in Deveney, *Paschal Beverly Randolph,* 70.

68. Nettesheim, *On the Vanities,* 203.

69. Deveney, *Paschal Beverly Randolph,* 312–14.

70. Randolph, "Ansairetic Mystery," 314.

71. Regardie, *Eye in the Triangle,* 117.

72. Crowley, *Psychology of Hashish,* 4.

73. Crowley, *Psychology of Hashish,* 4–5.

BIBLIOGRAPHY

Abel, Ernest L. *Intoxication in Mythology, A Worldwide Dictionary of Gods, Rites, Intoxicants, and Plants.* Jefferson, N.C.: McFarland, 2006.

Agrippa, Henry Cornelius, of Nettesheim. *Three Books of Occult Philosophy.* Edited and annotated by Donald Tyson. Translated by James Freake. Woodbury, Minn.: Llewellyn, 1992.

———. *Of the Vanitie and Uncertaintie of Artes and Sciences.* Edited by Catherine M. Dunn. Northridge: California State University Foundation, 1974.

———. *On the Vanities and Uncertainties of the Arts and Sciences.* London: Forgotten Books, 2017.

Albertus Magnus. *De Vegetabilibus,* vol. VII, edited by Carolus Jessen. Berlin: Georgh Reimeri, 1867.

Aldridge, Michael. "Cannabis and Its Derivatives." In *High Times Encyclopedia of Recreational Drugs,* edited by Andrew Kowl et al. New York: Stonehill, 1978.

Al-Hakim, Ghayat. *Picatrix: The Goal of the Wise.* Translated by Hashem Atallah. Seattle, Wash.: Ouroboros Press, 2008.

Allegro, John Marco. *The Sacred Mushroom and the Cross.* N.p., 1970.

Ankarloo, Bengt, and Stuart Clark. *Witchcraft and Magic in Europe.* Vol. 2. Philadelphia: University of Pennsylvania Press, 1999.

Apollodorus. *Biblotheca.* Accessed via www.perseus.tufts.edu.

Apuleius. *Apology.* Accessed via http://classics.mit.edu.

Aquilecchia, Giovanni. "La favola Mandragola si chiama." In *Collected Essays on Italian Language and Literature Presented to Kathleen Speight,* edited by Giovanni Aquilecchia et al. Manchester, UK: Manchester University Press, 1971.

Aristophanes. *Wasps*. Accessed via http://classics.mit.edu/Aristophanes.

Astour, Michael C. *Hellenosemitica: An Ethnic and Cultural Study in West Semitic Impact on Mycenaean Greece*. Leiden, Netherlands: Brill, 1967.

Attrell, Dan. *Shamanism and the Mysteries: A Brief History of the Cult of Ecstasy*. North Charleston, S.C.: CreateSpace, 2017.

Augustine of Hippo. *Enchiridion*. Accessed via newadvent.org.

Baigent, Michael, and Richard Leigh. *The Dead Sea Scrolls Deception*. New York: Summit Books, 1991.

Bailey, Michael. *Historical Dictionary of Witchcraft*. Lanham, Md.: Scarecrow Press, 2003.

Ball, Philip. *The Devil's Doctor*. New York: Farrar, Straus and Giroux, 2006.

Baroja, Julio Carlo. *The World of the Witches*. London: Phoenix Press, 2001.

Baudelaire, Charles. *Artificial Paradise: Baudelaire's Classic Work on Opium and Wine*. Edited and translated by Stacy Diamond. New York: Citadel Press, 1996.

Bennett, Chris. *Cannabis and the Soma Solution*. Walterville, Ore.: TrineDay, 2010.

———. *Liber 420*. Walterville, Ore.: TrineDay, 2018.

———. "The Scythians Ancient Ritual Use of Cannabis." In *One Toke to God*, edited by Mark Estren. Malibu, Calif.: Cannabis Spiritual Center, 2017.

Betz, Hans Dieter. *The Greek Magical Papyri in Translation*. Vol. 1. Chicago: University of Chicago Press, 1992.

Bever, Edward. *The Realities of Witchcraft and Popular Magic in Early Modern Europe*. New York: Palgrave MacMillan, 2008.

Boethius. *Consolatio philosophiae*. Accessed via faculty.georgetown.edu.

Bond, Edward L., ed. *Spreading the Gospel in Colonial Virginia: Preaching Religion and Community*. Lanham, Md.: Lexington Books, 2005.

Broad, William J. *The Oracle: Ancient Delphi and the Science Behind Its Lost Secrets*. New York: Penguin Books, 2006.

Brown, Jerry, and Julie Brown. *The Psychedelic Gospels*. Rochester, Vt.: Park Street Press, 2016.

Burkert, Walter. *Greek Religion*. Translated by John Raffan. Cambridge, Mass.: Harvard University Press, 1985.

Butler, Elizabeth. *Ritual Magic*. Philadelphia: University of Pennsylvania Press, 2002.

Campbell, Joseph, ed. *The Mysteries: Papers from the Eranos Yearbooks*. Vol. 2. Bollingen Series 30. Princeton, N.J.: Princeton University Press, 1978.

Campion, Nicholas. *The Dawn of Astrology: A Cultural History of Western Astrology.* New York: Continuum Books, 2008.

Clement of Alexandria. *Exhortation to the Greeks.* Accessed via newadvent.org.

Cohn, Norman. *Europe's Inner Demons: The Demonization of Christians in Medieval Christendom.* Chicago: University of Chicago Press, 2000.

Colavito, Jason, trans. *Argonautica Orphic: An English Translation.* Albany, N.Y.: JasonColavito.com Books, 2011.

Collins, Siobhán. *Bodies, Politics, and Transformations: John Donne's Metempsychosis.* New York: Routledge, 2016.

Cooke, Mordecai. *The Seven Sisters of Sleep.* Rochester, Vt.: Park Street Press, 1997. Originally published in 1860.

Cooper, Jean. *Chinese Alchemy: Taoism, the Power of Gold, and the Quest for Immortality.* Newburyport, Mass.: Weiser Books, 2016.

Crowley, Aleister. *The Psychology of Hashish.* Edited by Adrian Axworthy. Lynnwood, Wash.: Holms Publishing, 2005.

D. Lit, Angus. *The Mystery Religions and Christanity.* New York: Charles Scribner's Sons, 1928.

Davenport-Hines, Richard. *The Pursuit of Oblivion: A Global History of Narcotics.* New York: W. W. Norton, 2002.

Davis, Erik. "Terence McKenna's Last Trip." *Wired,* May 2000. Accessed via erowid.org.

della Porta, Giambattista. *Natural Magic in XX Books.* London: Thomas Young and Samuel Speed, 1558. Facsimile of original English edition, Kesinger, 2010.

Del Rio, Martin. *Investigations into Magic.* Edited and translated by P. G. Maxwell-Stuart. Manchester, UK: Manchester University Press, 2000.

Demosthenes. *Against Aristogiton.* Accessed via www.perseus.tufts.edu.

Deveney, John Patrick. *Paschal Beverly Randolph: A Nineteenth-Century Black American Spiritualist, Rosicrucian, and Sex Magician.* New York: State University of New York Press, 1996.

Diodorus of Sicily. *Library of History.* In *The Historical Library of Diodorus the Sicilian: In Fifteen Books.* 2 vols. Translated by G. Booth. London: W. McDowall, Pemberton Row, 1814.

Dioscorides. *De materia medica.* Edited and translated by Tess Anne Osbaldeston. Johannesburg, South Africa: Ibidis Press, 2000.

———. *Pharmacorum simplicium* (1529) accessed via http://reader.digitale -sammlungen.de.

Dugan, Frank M. "Fungi, Folkways and Fairy Tales: Mushrooms and Mildews in Stories, Remedies and Rituals, from Oberon to the Internet." *North American Fungi* 3, no. 7 (August 29, 2008).

Ehrman, Bart. *Jesus: Apocalyptic Prophet of the New Millennium*. Oxford, UK: Oxford University Press, 2001.

Eisler, Riane. *The Chalice and the Blade: Our History, Our Future*. San Francisco: Harper and Row, 1987.

Electronic Text Corpus of Sumerian Literature. "Inanna's Descent into the Underworld." Accessed via http://etcsl.orinst.ox.ac.uk.

Eliade, Mirea, chief editor. *Hidden Truths: Magic, Alchemy, and the Occult*. New York: Macmillan Publishing Company, 1989.

"Ellis: No-Hitter While on LSD." *Register Guard* (Eugene, Ore.), April 18, 1984, 6E.

Epiphanius. *Panarion*. Accessed via archive.org.

Estren, Mark J., ed. *One Toke to God: The Entheogenic Spirituality of Cannabis*. Malibu, Calif.: Cannabis Spiritual Center, 2017.

Eusebius, *Ecclesiastical History*. Accessed via newadvent.org.

Finkelstein, Honora M. "Inanna and the God of Wisdom." Accessed via www.new-wisdom.org/cultural_history1/04-mesopotamia/2_wisdom.htm.

Forbes, Bruce David. *Christmas: A Candid History*. Berkeley: University of California Press, 2007.

Fox, Irving P., ed. *The Spatula: An Illustrated Monthly Publication for Druggists* 20, no. 1 (October 1913).

Ginzburg, Carlo. *Ecstasies: Deciphering the Witches' Sabbath*. Translated by Raymond Rosenthal. New York: Pantheon Books, 1991.

Goodart, Stephanie. "The Lesser Mysteries of Eleusis." *Rosicrucian Digest* no. 2 (2009).

Goodrich, Norma Lorre, ed. *Priestesses*. New York: Harper Perennial, 1990.

Griffiths, John Gwyn. *The Origins of Osiris and His Cult*. Leiden, Netherlands: Brill, 1980.

Hamilton, Francis E., and Louis Henry. "The Post Card Manufacturers and Allied Trades' Association Advocate a Duty of 100 Per Cent on Post Cards." *Tariff Hearings before the Committee on Ways and Means of the House of Representatives, Sixtieth Congress, Second Session; House*. Washington, D.C.: Government Printing Office, Jan. 1909.

Hansen, Joseph. *Quellen*. Bonn, Germany: Carl Georgi, 1901. Facsimile edition available through Nabu Public Domain Reprints, www.publicdomainreprints.org.

Harms, Daniel. "On Hatsis' *The Witches' Ointment* and Abramelin." Accessed via https://danharms.wordpress.com/2016/01/04/on-hatsis-the-witches -ointment-and-abramelin.

Harms, Daniel, et. al. *The Book of Oberon.* Woodbury, Minn.: Llewellyn Publications, 2015.

Hatsis, Thomas. "The Dogmatists' Debacle." *Psychedelic Press U.K.* 1 (2014).

———. *The Witches' Ointment: The Secret History of Psychedelic Magic.* Rochester, Vt.: Park Street Press, 2015.

Heinrich, Clark. *Magic Mushroom in Religion and Alchemy.* Rochester, Vt.: Park Street Press, 2002.

Herodotus. *The Histories.* Edited and translated by John M. Marincola. New York: Penguin Classics, 1996.

Hillman, David. *The Chemical Muse: Drug Use and the Roots of Western Civilization.* New York: Thomas Dunne Books, 2008.

Hippolytus. *Refutation of All Heresies.* Accessed via newadvent.org.

Hislop, Alexander, Rev. *Two Babylons: Or the Papal Worship Proved to Be the Worship of Nimrod.* London: A & C Black, 1959.

Holmyard, E. J. *Alchemy.* New York: Dover, 1990.

Homer, *Hymn to Demeter.* Accessed via ancient-literature.com.

———. *Odyssey.* Accessed via ancient-literature.com.

Idel, Moshe. *Studies in Ecstatic Kabbalah.* Albany: State University of New York Press, 1988.

Irenaeus. *Against Heresies.* Accessed via newadvent.org.

———. *Refutation of Gnosis Falsely So-Called.* Accessed via newadvent.org.

Jackson, Blomfield, trans. "St. Basil of Caesarea." In *The Nicene and Post-Nicene Fathers of the Christian Church,* series 2, vol. 7, edited by Philip Schaff and Henry Wace. Buffalo, N.Y.: The Christian Literature Company, 1895.

Jansen, Katherine L., Joanna Drell, and Frances Andrews, eds. *Medieval Italy: Texts in Translation.* Philadelphia: University of Pennsylvania Press, 2009.

John Chrysostom. "Eighth Homily on Colossians." Accessed via newadvent.org.

———. *The Fathers of the Church: John Chrysostom Homilies on Genesis.* Translated by Robert C. Hill. Washington, D.C.: Catholic University of America Press, 1986.

Josephus. *Antiquities of the Jews.* Accessed via sacred-texts.com.

———. *The Jewish Wars.* Accessed via Chicago.edu.

Justin Martyr. *Dialogue with Trypho.* Accessed via newadvent.org.

———. *First Apology.* Accessed via newadvent.org.

———. "Urbicus Condemns the Christians to Death." In *Second Apology.* Accessed via newadvent.org.

Key, Howard Clark. *Medicine, Miracle, and Magic in New Testament Times.* Cambridge, UK: Cambridge University Press, 1988.

Kieckhefer, Richard. *Forbidden Rites: A Necromancer's Manual of the Fifteenth Century.* Philadelphia: University of Pennsylvania Press, 2006.

———. *Magic in the Middle Ages.* Cambridge, UK: Cambridge University Press, 2005.

Kirton, J. W. *The Temperance Handbook.* London: Smart and Allan, London-House Yard, 1874.

Kleijn, H. *Mushrooms and Other Fungi: Their Form and Colour.* New York: Doubleday, 1962.

Kleps, Arthur. *Millbrook: The Story of the Early Years of the Psychedelic Revolution.* Oakland, Calif.: Bench Press, 1975.

Kramer, Heinrich, and James Sprenger. *Malleus Maleficarum.* Translated by Montague Summers. New York: Dover, 1971.

Lee, Martin A. *Smoke Signals.* New York: Scribner, 2012.

Leland, Charles Godfrey. *Etruscan Magic and Occult Remedies.* New York: University Books, 1963.

Letcher, Andy. *Shroom: A Cultural History of the Magic Mushroom.* New York: HarperCollins, 2007.

Lewin, Louis. *Phantastica: A Classic Survey on the Use and Abuse of Mind-Altering Plants.* Rochester, Vt.: Park Street Press, 1998.

Liberalis, Antoninus. *The Metamorphoses of Antoninus Liberalis: A Translation with Commentary.* Translated by Francis Celoria. New York: Routledge, 1992.

Littledale, Richard Frederick. *A Commentary on the Song of Songs: From Ancient and Medieval Sources.* London: Joseph Masters and Son, 1869.

Lucan, *Pharsalia.* Accessed via archive.org.

Lucian. *Lucian.* Vol. 6. Translated by K. Kilburn. Reprint. N.p.: Forgotten Books, 2018.

Lucian of Samosata. *Timon the Misanthrope.* Accessed via http://aristologos.net.

Luck, Georg. *Arcana Mundi: Magic and the Occult in the Greek and Roman Worlds.* Baltimore, Md.: Johns Hopkins University Press, 2006.

Maccoby, Hyam. *The Mythmaker: Paul and the Invention of Christianity.* New York: HarperCollins, 1987.

Macmullen, Ramsay. *Paganism and Christanity: 100–425 CE.* Minneapolis, Minn.: Fortress Press, 1992.

Macrobius. *Saturnalia.* Accessed via penelope.uchicago.edu.

Maxwell-Stuart, P. G. *The Chemical Choir: The History of Alchemy.* Reprint. London: Continuum International, 2012.

McCabe, Elizabeth A. *An Examination of the Cult of Isis with Preliminary Exploration into New Testament Studies.* Lanham, Md.: University Press of America, 2008.

Mead, G. R. S. "Ode to Sophia." In *Fragments of a Faith Forgotten: The Gnostics, a Contribution to the Study of the Origins of Christianity,* edited by G. R. S. Mead. N.p.: A Mystical World Reprints, 2012. Originally published by the Theosophical Publishing Society, London, 1900.

———. *Simon Magus: Essays on the Founder of Simonism Based on Ancient Sources.* Leipzig, Germany: edidit G. Dindorfius, 1859.

Mechoulam, Raphael. "Cannabis: The Israeli Perspective." *Journal of Basic and Clinical Physiolology and Pharmacology* 27, no. 3 (2015): 181–87.

Merkur, Dan. *Psychedelic Sacraments: Manna, Meditation, and Mystical Experiences.* Rochester, Vt.: Park Street Press, 2001.

Merlin, Mark D. "Archaeological Evidence for Cannabis Use." In *One Toke to God,* edited by Mark J. Estren, 33–40.

Mirecki, Paul Allan, and Marvin W. Meyer, eds. *Magic and Ritual in the Ancient World.* Leiden, Netherlands: Brill, 2002.

Moore, Clement Clarke. "A Visit from Saint Nicholas." Originally published in 1823. Accessed via www.poetryfoundation.org/poems/43171/a-visit-from-st-nicholas.

Mora, George, ed. *Witches, Devils, and Doctors in the Renaissance: Johann Weyer, De praestigiis daemonum.* (1583 ed.) Translated by John Shea. Binghamton, N.Y.: Medieval and Renaissance Texts and Studies, 1991.

Morgan, Adrian. "Who Put the Toad in Toadstool?" *New Scientist,* nos. 1540/1541 (December 25, 1986–January 1, 1987).

Mormando, Franco, *The Preacher's Demons: Bernardino of Siena and the Social Underworld of Early Renaissance Italy.* Chicago: University of Chicago Press, 1999.

Myers, Jacob M. *I & II Esdras: A New Translation with Introduction and Commentary.* New York: Doubleday, 1982.

Nauert, Charles G., *Agrippa and the Crisis of Renaissance Thought.* Champaign: University of Illinois Press, 1965.

Newberg, Andrew, Eugene D'Aquili, and Vince Rause. *Why God Won't Go Away: Brain Science and the Biology of Belief.* New York: Ballantine Books, 2002.

Newman, P. D. *Alchemically Stoned: The Psychedelic Secret of Free Masonry.* N.p.: The Laudable Pursuit Press, 2017.

Nigg, Walter. *The Heretics.* Translated by Richard Winston and Clara Winston. New York: Dorset Press, 1962.

———. *The Heretics: Heresy through the Ages.* New York: Dorset Press, 1990.

Nigro, Johannes Dominicus de. *Liber de venenis* (opera Bernardini Ricij de Nouaria, 1492). Accessed via https://digitalis-dsp.uc.pt.

Noconi, Amanda. "Entheogens and the Eucharist: Altered States and the Origin of Sacrament." Paper presented at "Exploring Psychedelics," Ashland, Oregon, May 25, 2017.

Nynauld, Jean de. *De la lycanthropie transformation et extase des sorciers.* Paris: Chez Jean Millot, 1615. Reprint of the original edition. Paris: Editions Frenesie, 1990.

Ogden, Daniel. *Greek and Roman Necromancy.* Princeton, N.J.: Princeton University Press, 2001.

———. *Magic, Witchcraft, and Ghosts in the Greeks and Roman Worlds.* Oxford, UK: Oxford University Press, 2009.

O'Reilly, James, and Larry Habegger, eds. *Travelers' Tales, Thailand: True Stories.* Palo Alto, Calif.: Travelers' Tales, 2002.

Oisteanu, Andrei. *Narcotice în cultura român: Istorie, religie și literatură.* Iași, Romania: Polirom, 2010.

Origen. *Contra celsum.* Accessed via www.newadvent.org/fathers/0416.htm.

Osmond, Humphrey. "A Review of the Clinical Effects of Psychotomimetic Agents." *Annals of the New York Academy of Sciences* 66 (1957): 418–34.

Otto, Walter F. "The Meaning of the Eleusinian Mysteries." In *The Mysteries: Papers from the Eranos Yearbooks,* edited by Joseph Campbell.

Ovid. *Metamorphosis.* Accessed via sacred-texts.com.

Pagels, Elaine. *The Gnostic Gospels.* New York: Vintage Books, 1989.

Paul of Aleppo. *The Travels of Macarius, Patriarch of Antioch.* Vol. 2. Translated by F. C. Belfour. London: The Oriental Translation Fund of Great-Britain and Ireland, 1836.

Pausanias, *Geography of Greece*. Accessed via archive.org.

Peters, Edward. *The Magician, the Witch, and the Law*. Philadelphia: University of Pennsylvania Press, 1982.

Philostratus. *Life of Apollonius of Tyana*. Accessed via earlychristianwritings.org.

Pindar. *Pythian*. Accessed via perseus.tufts.edu.

Plato. *Symposium*. Translated by Benjamin Jowett. Accessed via lulu.com. Online publisher, Demosthenes Koptsis, 2016. Originally published by Pearson, 1956.

Pliny the Elder. *Natural History*. London: Penguin, 1991.

Plutarch. *Alexander*. Accessed via perseus.tufts.edu.

———. *Conjugalia praecepta*. Accessed via perseus.tufts.edu.

———. *De defectu oraculorum*. Accessed via perseus.tufts.edu.

———. *Life of Phocion*. Accessed via perseus.tufts.edu.

———. *Moralia*. Accessed via perseus.tufts.edu.

———. *Roman Questions*. Accessed via perseus.tufts.edu.

Polyaenus. *Stratagem*. Accessed via attalus.org.

Pseudo-Plutarch. *De fluviis*. Accessed via perseus.tufts.edu.

Rahner, Karl. *Schriften zur Theologie*. 16 volumes. Eisiedeln, Switzerland: Benziger Verlag, 1954–1984.

Raine, Kathleen. *Blake and Tradition*. Abingdon, UK: Routledge, 2002.

Randolph, Charles Brewster. "The Mandragora of the Ancients in Folk-lore and Medicine." *Proceedings of the American Academy of Arts and Sciences* XL, no. 12 (January 1905).

Randolph, Paschal Beverly. "The Ansairetic Mystery: A New Revelation Concerning SEX." In Deveney, *Paschal Beverly Randolph*.

———. *Sexual Magic*. Edited and translated by Robert North. New York: Magickal Childe, 1988.

Rätsch, Christian. *Encyclopedia of Psychoactive Plants*. Rochester, Vt.: Park Street Press, 2005.

Rätsch, Christian, and Claudia Müller-Ebeling. *Pagan Christmas: The Plants, Spirits, and Rituals at the Origins of Yuletide*. Rochester, Vt.: Inner Traditions, 2006.

Regardie, Israel. *The Eye in the Triangle: An Interpretation of Aleister Crowley*. Tempe, Ariz.: Falcon Press, 1989.

Riddle, John M. *Goddesses, Elixirs, and Witches*. New York: Palgrave Macmillan, 2010.

Rider, Catherine. *Magic and Religion in Medieval England.* Islington, UK: Reaktion Books, 2012.

Rinella, Michael A. *Pharmakon: Plato, Drug Culture, and Identity in Ancient Athens.* Lanham, Md.: Lexington Books, 2010.

Roberts, Alexander, and James Donaldson, eds. *Ante-Nicene Fathers.* Vol. 7 of *Ante-Nicene Fathers: The Writings of the Fathers down to A.D. 325.* Peabody, Mass.: Hendrickson Publishers, 2004. Originally published 1885.

Robinson, James M., ed. *The Nag Hammadi Library: The Definitive Translation of the Gnostic Scriptures Complete in One Volume.* San Francisco: HarperSanFrancisco, 1990.

Rubin, Vera D., ed. *Cannabis and Culture.* The Hague, Netherlands: Mouton & Co., 1975.)

Ruck, Carl, ed. *Dionysus in Thrace.* Berkeley, Calif.: Regent Press, 2017.

Ruck, Carl, and Mark Hoffman, eds. *Effluents of Deity: Alchemy and Psychoactive Sacraments in Medieval and Renaissance Art.* Durham, N.C.: Carolina Academic Press, 2012.

Ruck, Carl, Blaise Daniel Staples, and Clark Heinrich. *The Apples of Apollo: Pagan and Christian Mysteries of the Eucharist.* Durham, N.C.: Carolina Academic Press, 2001.

Rudgley, Richard. *The Alchemy of Culture: Intoxicants in Society.* London: British Museum Press, 1998.

Ruether, Rosemary, and Eleanor McLaughlin. *Women of Spirit: Female Leadership in the Jewish and Christian Traditions.* New York: Simon and Schuster, 1979.

Rush, John. *The Mushroom in Christian Art.* Berkeley, Calif.: North Atlantic Books, 2011.

Russell, Jeffery Burton. *Witchcraft in the Middle Ages.* New York: Cornell University Press, 1984.

Russo, Ethan B. "The Pharmacological History of Cannabis." In *Handbook of Cannabis,* edited by Roger Pertwee. Oxford, UK: Oxford University Press, 2014.

Rutilius Claudius Namatianus. *On My Return.* Accessed via uchicago.edu.

Sack, Adriano, and Ingo Niermann. *The Curious World of Drugs and Their Friends.* New York: Penguin, 2008.

Schmitt, Paul. "The Ancient Mysteries in the Society of Their Time, Their Transformation, and Most Recent Echoes." In *The Mysteries: Papers from the Eranos Yearbooks,* edited by Joseph Campbell.

Shaw, Norman, Dr. "Otherworld Gnosis: Fairy Ointments and the Nuts of Knowledge." *Psychedelic Press* 17 (2016).

Smith, Morton. *Jesus the Magician*. San Francisco: Hampton Roads, 2014.

Spence, Lewis. *Ancient Egyptian Myths and Legends*. New York: Dover, 1990.

St. Ambrose. "Splendor paternae gloriae." Accessed via www.preces-latinae.org /thesaurus/Hymni/Splendor.html.

St. Basil of Caesarea. *Letters*. Accessed via newadvent.org.

Strabo. *Geography*. Accessed via perseus.tufts.edu.

Tavennar, Eugene. *Studies in Magic from Latin Literature*. New York: Columbia University Press, 1916.

Tertullian. *The Remedy for Heresy* (*De praescriptione haereticorum*). Accessed via newadvent.org.

Theocritus. "The Spell." In *Idyll*. Accessed via theoi.com.

Theodoret of Cyrus. "On Divine Providence." Translated and annotated by Thomas Halton. In *Ancient Christian Writers: The Works of the Fathers in Translation,* vol. 49, edited by Walter J. Burghardt and Thomas Comerford Lawler. Mahwah, N.J.: Paulist Press, 1988.

Theodoretus. "Hæreticarum fabularum compendium." Accessed via st-takla.org.

Theophrastus. *Enquiry into Plants and Minor Works on Odours and Weather Signs*. 2 vols. Translated by Sir Arthur Holt. New York: P. G. Putnam, 1916.

Thorwald, Jurgen. *Science and Secrets of Early Medicine: Egypt, Babylonia, India, China, Mexico, and Peru*. Translated by Richard Winston and Clara Winston. London: Thames and Hudson, 1962.

Titus Livius. *History of Rome*. Accessed via perseus.tufts.edu.

Torjesen, Karen Jo. *When Women Were Priests*. San Francisco: HarperCollins, 1995.

Uvarov, Sergeï Semenovich. *Essay on the Eleusinian Mysteries of Eleusis*. Translated by J. D. Price. London: New Bond Street, 1817.

Valeriano, Pierio. *Hieroglyphica, sive, De sacris Aegyptiorvm aliarvmqve gentivm literis commentary*. Basel: Per Thomam Guarinum, 1567.

Van Arsdall, Anne, Helmut W. Klug, and Paul Blanz. "The Mandrake Plant and Its Legend: A New Perspective." In *Old Names—New Growth: Proceedings of the 2nd ASPNS Conference, University of Graz, Austria, 6–10 June 2007 and Related Essays,* translated by H. Klug, 316. Frankfurt, Germany: Peter Lang, 2009.

Virgil. *Eclogues*. Accessed via ancient-literature.com.

von Langenfeld, Freidrich Spee. *Cautio criminalis*. Translated by Marcus Hellyer. Charlottesville: University of Virginia Press, 2003.

Von Worms, Abraham. *The Book of Abramelin*. Edited by Georg Dehn. Translated by Steven Guth. Lake Worth, Fla.: Ibis Press, 2006.

Wasson, R. Gordon. *Soma: Divine Mushroom of Immortality*. Ethno-mycological Studies, book 1. New York: Harcourt Brace Jovanovich, 1968.

Wasson, R. Gordon, Albert Hofmann, and Carl A. P. Ruck. *The Road to Eleusis: Unveiling the Secret of the Mysteries*. Berkeley, Calif.: North Atlantic Books, 2008.

Wasson, R. Gordon, Stella Kramrisch, Jonathon Ott, and Carl A. P. Ruck. *Persephone's Quest: Entheogens and the Origins of Religion*. New Haven, Conn.: Yale University Press, 1986.

Webster, Peter. "Mixing the Kykeon." *ELEUSIS: Journal of Psychoactive Plants and Compounds*, new series 4 (2000).

"We Drank the Soma, We Became Immortal." *Science: First Hand* 3, no. 9 (2015). Accessed via https://scfh.ru/en/news/we-drank-soma-we-became -immortal-/.

Wenzel, Siegfried, ed. and trans. *Fasciculus morum: A Fourteenth-Century Preacher's Handbook*. University Park: Pennsylvania State University Press, 1989.

West, M. L. *The Hymns of Zoroaster: A New Translation of the Most Ancient Sacred Texts of Iran*. New York : I. B. Tauris, 2010.

White, Michael. *Isaac Newton: The Last Sorcerer*. New York: Basic Books, 1997.

Wilson, Colin. *The Occult: A History*. New York: Vintage Books, 1973.

Wooster, David, et al., *Pacific Medical Journal*. Vol. 42 (1849).

Wright, Robert. *The Evolution of God*. New York: Little, Brown, 2009.

Yasna. Accessed via http://avesta.org/yasna/yasna.htm.

Zosimos of Panopolitanus. *De zythorum confectione fragmentum nunc primum Graece ac Latine editum*. Solisbaci, Moravia: Soidelianis, 1814.

INDEX

Abraham of Worms, 197

Abulafia, Abraham, 211

aconite, 80, 81, 87, 91, 205

Adam, 13, 114–18, 120–21, 127, 151,
  188–89

Africa, 16, 24, 76, 203, 232

Agrippa von Nettesheim, Heinrich
  Cornelius, 217, 228

alchemy, 204–6, 208, 214, 217, 235

Allegro, John Marco, 108, 113, 158,
  167, 223

Amanita muscaria, 11, 113, 115,
  157–63, 165–170, 180, 209,
  234

  or fly agaric, 165

Ambrose, 146–47

Anatolia, 30, 49, 79

ancestor, 9, 12, 18, 21, 24, 27–29,
  31–32, 35, 38, 45, 49, 57–58,
  63–64, 67, 76, 133, 154, 232

angel, 10, 28, 110, 153, 165–66, 202,
  214, 217

apocalypticism, 110, 118, 125

Apollonius of Tyana, 124

Apponius, 151–52

Apuleius, Lucian, 34–35

Artemis, 91–92, 97–98, 177

Asclepius, 32

Assyrian, 23, 87

Astarte, 89

Augustine, Emperor, 148, 213

Avicenna, 206–7, 210–11

Bacchus, 70–72, 154

barley, 38, 40, 43–44, 56–58, 65–66,
  86, 91

Basil, St., 34, 84, 146, 149, 153, 160

Bennett, Chris, 23–24, 26, 49

bicameral, 11–12, 37, 75

Boethius, 147

Book of Poisons, The, 223–25

Camma, 97–98

cannabis, 23–24, 30, 35, 49, 139, 207,
  216–18. *See also* hash; kaneh bosm
  Aleister Crowley and, 230–32
  connection to asterion, 88–90
  familiarity to early Christians,
    148–49
  as "strongest frankincense," 93

under Saturn's rule, 220
zythi and, 65–66
canon Episcopi, 177–78, 183–84
Carpocrates, 136–137, 140, 143
Cathars, 182
Ceres, 48, 80
Christianity, 107, 156, 158
Christmas, ix, 154–55, 157, 159,
    161–62, 164–67, 169, 170
Chrysame, 96–97
Chrysostom, John, 84, 102
Circe, 80–83, 86–87, 123–24
Clement of Alexandria, 136, 148
Corinth, 128–129
Cosmic Christ, 121, 138, 141–42
Cosmic Graell, 37–38, 58, 135
cosmos, 45, 118, 131, 227
Crowley, Aleister, 229–31

daemon, ix, 15, 28, 100–101, 198, 214,
    217
daemonic magic, 15
Deianeira, 84
Demeter, 38–41, 43, 45–47, 49, 55–57,
    60, 63, 76–77, 80, 94
Demeter-Kore, 54–55
demon, 10, 15, 28, 84, 111, 124–25,
    177, 183–85, 190, 193, 196,
    212–13, 215, 219, 222
Didache, 154–55
Dionysus. *See* god
Dioscorides, 56, 69, 83, 88, 93
discipuli Allegrae, 108, 113, 159,
    161–62, 166
divination, 61, 70, 88, 92–93, 103, 117,
    120, 136, 198, 212, 217–19

drugs, xi, 1, 6–7, 32, 56, 59, 62, 80, 84, 98,
    102, 120, 124, 176, 193, 203, 218, 231
War on, 173
Dumuzi, 50, 52–53, 63, 67, 76

Ebionite, 133
Eden
    Garden of, 13, 54, 84, 114–15, 189
    she who has my heart, xv
Egypt, 30, 34, 59, 63, 65, 101, 125,
    202, 225
Egyptian, 28, 31–34, 65, 68, 76, 79, 89,
    102, 137, 208, 213, 232
"Egyptian, the," 111
Eleusis. *See* mystery
el–Hayyan, Jabir Ibn, 205–6
Ellis, Dock, 1–2
elves, 162, 166–67, 183–84, 198
entheogens
    added to wine, 68–70
    defined, 7
    described in rituals, 60–62, 94–96,
        141–43
    in early Christianity, 106–8, 234
    new vocabulary for, 8–11
    used by witches, 80, 87–88, 91–92,
        103, 175–76
enthousiasmos, 66, 68–70
ergot, 43–44, 58, 76
ergotism, 44
erôs magic, 83–85
Errores Gazariorum, 181
Esdras, 116–22, 234
esoteric, 80
Eucharist, ix, 126–29, 140–42, 143,
    154, 172, 179–82

Eusebius, 135–36, 143
Eve, 13, 114
extheogen, 10, 217, 218
extheogenic, 10–11, 185, 217, 221, 231

fairy, 198
    ointment, 174, 192, 199, 205, 222
    queen, 186
    realm, 116, 198
    women, 182–83, 186, 200
Fertile Crescent, 76
Fireside Goddess, 27, 29, 31, 175
fly agaric. *See Amanita muscaria*
flying ointment, 80, 176, 182, 192

Gaia, 8, 31, 38, 60, 88, 232
gnostic, xi, 28, 107–8, 121, 130–34,
    136–43, 147, 150–51, 170, 180,
    206, 214, 234
gnosticism, 106–7, 130, 135, 138, 155
goddess, x, 15, 22, 26, 29–33, 37, 39,
    45, 48, 52, 56–57, 79, 88, 90, 92,
    99–100, 139, 175, 184, 186, 196,
    233
    Diana, 177–78, 184, 186, 190–91
    Earth, 60
    fertility, 3, 27, 173, 178, 181,
        183–84, 186–88, 191–94, 197,
        199
    Grace, 60
    Hecate, 80–81, 86, 88, 91–92, 96
    Hera, 66, 88–90, 94, 96
    Holda, 178, 183, 186–87
    poppy, 67, 72, 77
    Syrian, 89
God, 13, 22–23, 100–101, 109–10,

    112, 115–16, 118–19, 121,
    124–26, 131–32, 136, 145, 147,
    155, 181, 188–89, 212, 220, 228
god, ix, xiii, 10–11, 13–15, 21–23,
    27, 20–30, 33, 40, 47, 52, 60, 61,
    63–64, 66, 79, 86, 88–89, 97, 103,
    112, 127, 129, 139, 157, 177, 202,
    234
    Apollo, 60–63, 67, 94, 141
    Dionysus, 10, 63–68, 70, 72–76, 80,
        89, 128, 141, 151
    Ra, 33
    Sabazios, 73
    Trophonius, 96
    of vegetation, 76, 155
gospel, 124–25, 148–49, 216
    of John, 107, 124, 147
    of Luke, 111, 115, 125, 215
    of Mark, 111, 125
    of Matthew, 115–16, 125, 189–90, 195,
    of Peter, 28
    of Thomas, 129–30
grain, 29, 37, 40, 44, 50, 54–55, 93, 174
    and poppies, 50–51, 53–54, 57, 218
    goddess, 48–49, 58, 73, 76
    mother, 37–38, 45, 47, 58
Greek Magical Papyri, 85

Hades, 38–40, 46, 99, 177
Hafez, 206
hallucinogen, 6, 44, 62
haoma, 3, 23, 53, 72–73
hash, ix, 206, 218, 225–28, 230
Hathor, 33–34, 65, 68, 75, 106
Hebrew, 13, 69, 74, 85, 100, 110,
    118–19, 132, 151

Helen of Troy, 83, 95
  Simon Magus and, 135
hemlock, 34, 146, 148–49, 206
heresy, 107, 111, 131, 182
heretic, 134, 143, 181–82
Herodotus, 70, 148
Heuberg, 186–87, 192, 195, 199
Hieropolis, 89
Hildegard of Bingen, 152
Hippolytus, 46, 134, 143
hippomanes, 79, 87
Hofmann, Albert, 1, 43–44
Homer, 59, 82–83
Hosea, 74, 100
Hugh of St. Victor, 216

Ialdabaoth, 131–33, 138
Inanna, 50–53, 55–56, 67, 76, 100
interpretatio heretica, 176, 181,
    183–85, 188–89, 191–92, 196
interpretatio romana, 176–78, 181–85,
    187–89, 191
Irenaeus, 107, 131, 133, 139–40, 143,
    150–51
Isis, 31–32. 34, 56, 86, 95–96, 189
Islam, 202–3, 206, 235

Jason, 91–92, 103
  Argonauts and, 91, 99
Jeremiah, 100
Jesus, 12, 106–7, 109, 111–15,
    117–19, 121–22, 124–30, 133–34,
    136, 140, 142, 147–52, 154–55,
    158, 162, 170, 189–90, 215–16,
    223, 229–30, 234
Julbeer, 157, 161–62, 170

Justin Martyr, 100–101

kaneh bosm, 90, 149
Key of Solomon, 212
Kingdom of Heaven, 107, 109, 111–13,
    118, 121, 190
Kirk, Robert, 198
Kore, 38–41, 47, 54–55, 77, 206
kykeon, 38–39, 41–44, 47–49, 53,
    55–57, 76, 77

laurel, 61, 81, 87
Letcher, Andy, 199
Liber de venenis (The Book of Poisons),
    223–25
love potion, 82, 84, 86, 136, 193
LSD, 1, 2, 5, 43–44, 51
Lucian of Samosata, 89, 145, 156

Macarius, 149
magic
  Abulafia and, 211–12
  alchemy and, 204–6
  Apollo and, 60–64
  Avicenna and, 207
  in *The Book of Abramelin,* 197–98
  Carpocrates and, 136
  in Christian Europe, 172–73
  in Christian psychedelic traditions,
    106–8, 170
  Circe and, 81–82
  daemonic and natural categories of,
    15, 212
  evolved from intuition, 21
  Jesus's miracles and, 124–25
  law and, 213–215

love, 15, 62, 82–84, 124, 152, 193,
    195, 217, 228–30
mercenary, 96–99
mirror, 218
mushroom, 24–25, 34, 83, 108, 158,
    209, 224
new vocabulary for, 8–11
psychedelics and, 3
psychedelic witches and, 80
Ra and, 33–34
religion contrasted, 14–15
sacred fertility and, 24–26, 36
survived in texts, 235
treasure hunting and, 219
used to cause harm, 220–23
magical ointment, 175, 185, 190,
    195–197
magical plants, 79, 80–82, 87, 103,
    120, 123, 145, 151, 156, 175,
    193–94, 200, 216, 218, 220
magician, 11, 15, 85–86, 98, 100,
    124–25, 134, 151, 173, 181, 197,
    201–2, 211–13, 216–20, 226,
    228–29, 231
magick, 230–31
Maimonides, 149
Maiden's Well, 39, 48
Malleus Maleficarum, 192
mandrake, ix, 7, 33–35, 65, 68, 75, 79,
    81, 83, 87, 91, 98, 116, 120–21,
    123–25, 129, 145–52, 156, 170,
    185, 188–89, 200, 206–7,
    216–17, 228, 232
Marcellina, 137, 141, 143, 151, 214
Marcus, 140–41, 151, 214
Marcus Lucanus, 79

Mary, 106, 220–21, 229
Matteuccia di Francesco, 193–96
McKenna, Terrence, 43, 146
Medea, 80–81, 86–87, 91–92, 98–99,
    103
Mediterranean, 3, 54, 67, 72, 79, 101,
    134, 202
Metaneira, Queen, 39–40
Moreau de Tours, Jacques-Joseph,
    226–27
mushroom, 3, 5, 7, 10, 24–26, 34, 43,
    58, 65, 68–71, 83, 95–96, 108,
    113–14, 129, 144, 146, 154, 157,
    158–59, 161–62, 164–67, 169–70,
    180, 199, 209, 211, 216, 233–25,
    232, 234
mystery, xiii, 10–14, 37–38, 41, 46–49,
    53–54, 56, 60, 62–63, 65, 76–77,
    91, 102, 106, 108, 113–14, 116,
    118, 126–28, 134, 138–39, 141,
    145, 147, 148, 150–52, 157, 170,
    172, 236
    Ansairetic, 225, 228
    of the Bridal Chamber, 138–42
    of Eleusis, 7, 15, 41–43, 46–47,
        52–53, 55, 76, 106, 230
    of the Light Maiden, 138
    of the Lord's Supper, 126–28,
        234
Mycenaean, 31, 42, 45, 47, 56, 76
mystes, 38, 42, 46
mystheogen, 31, 42, 45, 47, 56, 76
mystheogenic, 11, 49, 62, 90–92, 97,
    101, 108, 133, 139, 142

Nag Hammadi, 131, 139

Nazarenes, 107, 109–10, 113–14, 116–17, 121–22, 125, 130–32, 136, 151, 170, 229
Neolithic, 24–25, 30, 32, 75
Neoplatonist, 107, 150, 206, 208
Nepenthes, 83, 95
Nider, Johannes, 185–88, 191–92, 194
Noah, 75, 82, 116
Noconi, Amanda, 42

occult
    Aleister Crowley and, 230
    forces in the natural world, 21
    Hecate as "mother of the," 80, 92
    properties of opium, 32, 207
opium, 23–24, 26
    Ceres and, 48–49
    Hecate and, 80–81
    illustration in *Liber de venenas,* 224
    love potions and, 84–85
    mixed with wine, 67–68, 129
    Theodorat and, 146
    shamanism and, 31
    Uruk vase depictions, 50–52
oracle, 60, 96
    of Colophon, 93–94
    of Delphi, ix, 54, 60–63, 93, 233
    of Dionysus, 70
    of Trophanius, 94–95
Origen, 145–46, 148
Osmond, Humphry, 5–6, 8

pagan, 7, 14, 74, 82, 84, 100–103, 106–11, 118, 121, 126–29, 133, 139–40, 142–45, 147, 150–53, 155–57, 166, 170, 177–81, 183–84, 192, 213–14, 234

paganism, 113, 127, 151, 172
Paleolithic, 24, 26
Paracelsus, 210–11
Paul of Tarsus, 112, 114, 127–28, 137, 154
Pausanias, 49, 88–90, 94–95
Persephone, 40, 42, 47, 54, 56–57, 60, 63, 76, 156
pharmakon
    accidental discovery of, 23–24
    agency ascribed to, 16
    as anesthesia, 35, 188
    "centralized" by a culture, 199–200
    church fathers and, 145–47
    defined, xi, 7
    Dionysus and, 65
    East meets West and, 202–4, 232
    Medea and, 91–96, 99
    mixed with wine, 68–73, 128–29, 155
    oracle and, 62
    Simon and, 135–36
    used to elicit confessions, 153
philia magic, 83–84, 86, 98
philosopher's stone, 210–11
Physiologus, 150–51
Pleroma, 131–33, 136, 138–39, 142
Pliny, 69, 81, 93
Plutarch, 56, 61, 68–70, 84
pocula amatoria, 81, 84, 193, 228
poetigen, 9, 11, 25, 226
poetigenic, 62, 75, 83, 207, 210, 223–24, 231
poison
    added to Eucharist, 143, 180
    alchemy and, 205, 208–9

blamed for Eve's actions, 84
in *The Book of Poisons,* 223
outlawed, 213
transformed by Christ, 152
used by witches, 193
used to cause harm, 221–24
pomegranate, 54–56
priest, 31, 34, 37, 47, 60–61, 72–74,
    89–90, 95, 149, 172
priestess, 15, 31, 34, 44, 46–47, 60,
    78–80, 87–92, 94, 96–97, 101,
    103, 233
Pseudo-Plutarch, 48–49
psychedelic renaissance, ix, x, xv, 8,
    158, 232, 235
psychenaut, xv, 5–7, 9–10, 25, 42, 51,
    148, 199, 235
    vs. psychonaut, 5
psychotomimetic, 1, 5–7
pythiagen, 11, 103, 108, 121, 137, 141,
    143, 181, 211
pythiangenic, 61–62, 80, 85, 93,
    96–99, 101, 121, 137, 141, 193,
    211–12, 218, 231, 234

Queen of Heaven, 50, 100

Ra, 33
Randolph, Paschal Beverly, 225–28
reindeer, xi, 97, 159–61, 165
    herders, 159, 166
Ripley, George, 208–9
Rome, ix, 16, 32, 34, 80, 110–12, 114,
    119, 125, 137, 155, 172, 178–79,
    203, 213–14, 235
Ruck, Carl A. P., 6–8

Sabbat, 175, 181–82, 193
Sacred Marriage, 46, 50, 52, 60, 62, 65,
    67, 71–72, 74, 75–76, 131, 138,
    228, 233
sacrifice, 40, 45, 52, 64, 72, 94, 97,
    135, 179
sacrificed, 13, 30, 46, 75, 118
Santa Claus, xi, 12, 158–62, 165–69
Saturnalia, 155–157, 170
Scythian, 73–74, 148
    drugs, 218
shaman, x, 13, 23, 25, 30–31, 42, 120,
    160–61, 167, 174, 222
shamanism, 30, 161, 165
Simon Magus, 134, 142
Simeon Seth, 202–03
Skyles, 73–74
Solanaceae, 9, 34–35, 116, 123, 208,
    217, 227
somnitheogen, 9, 30–31, 45, 57, 108,
    176, 185
somnitheogenic, 9, 32–34, 49, 65, 103,
    145, 148, 175–76, 192, 197, 218
Song of Songs, 116, 147
Sophia, 131–32, 135, 138–39
    and Cosmic Christ, 141, 140
    Ode to, 140
soporific, 9, 29, 35, 102, 108, 146
spirit flight, 185–87, 190, 193
Stamets, Paul, 153–54
Sumer, 49, 63
Sumerian, 50, 55, 76

Tassili, 25–26, 70, 75
Tatian, 93, 150–51
Telesterion, 42, 46, 56, 58

Theodorat of Syria, 146–49
Theodosius, 214
theogen, ix, xiii, 5, 8–9, 113, 137,
    140, 145–47, 149, 152, 156, 160,
    166–67, 173
theogenic, 106, 128, 146–47, 160, 167,
    170, 172, 233
Theophrastus, 83
Theôris, 101–3
Thessaly, 78, 80, 99
Thomas of Perseigne, 148
Thrace, 101–3
Thracian, 48–49, 70–73, 154
Tostado, Alonso, 188–92, 194–95,
    200
Tree of Knowledge, 84, 113–14, 150
Tylor, Edward, 9–10, 232

Uruk Vase, 50–53, 55, 70
unholden, 187, 191–92

Valentinus, 131, 140
Vedic, 23, 26, 53
Venus, 154
Venusberg, 187
Vincent, Jean, 192

von Langenfeld, Friedrich Spee, 153

Wei Po-Yang, 204–5
Weyer, Johannes, 210, 222
wheat, 21, 28–29, 38, 50–57, 174
wine, 141, 143, 147, 154–57, 170,
    179–80, 203, 207, 209, 21, 222,
    229, 233
wise woman, 94, 98, 103, 193–94
witch, 80, 87, 92, 99, 101, 103, 124,
    153, 157, 179, 182, 198
witchcraft, 172–73, 179, 183, 213
witches, ix, 80, 157, 173, 179, 182–83,
    186, 188–89, 192, 196, 222
witches' ointment, 175–76, 179, 182,
    189, 191, 192
Wotan, 161–62, 165

Yahweh, 14, 100, 114, 118–19, 121,
    126, 128, 131
Yule, 156–57, 161

Zalmoxis, 74
Zoroaster, 32, 118, 120
Zeus, 14, 39–40, 66, 89–90, 94
zythi (Egyptian beer), 65

BOOKS OF RELATED INTEREST

The Witches' Ointment
The Secret History of Psychedelic Magic
by Thomas Hatsis

DMT: The Spirit Molecule
A Doctor's Revolutionary Research into the Biology
of Near-Death and Mystical Experiences
by Rick Strassman, M.D.

The Psychedelic Explorer's Guide
Safe, Therapeutic, and Sacred Journeys
by James Fadiman, Ph.D.

The Psychedelic Gospels
The Secret History of Hallucinogens in Christianity
by Jerry B. Brown, Ph.D., and Julie M. Brown, M.A.

Psychedelic Medicine
The Healing Powers of LSD, MDMA, Psilocybin, and Ayahuasca
by Dr. Richard Louis Miller

Dreaming Wide Awake
Lucid Dreaming, Shamanic Healing, and Psychedelics
by David Jay Brown

The Encyclopedia of Psychoactive Plants
Ethnopharmacology and Its Applications
by Christian Rätsch
Foreword by Albert Hofmann

Witchcraft Medicine
Healing Arts, Shamanic Practices, and Forbidden Plants
by Claudia Müller-Ebeling, Christian Rätsch, and Wolf-Dieter Storl, Ph.D.

INNER TRADITIONS • BEAR & COMPANY
P.O. Box 388
Rochester, VT 05767
1-800-246-8648
www.InnerTraditions.com

Or contact your local bookseller